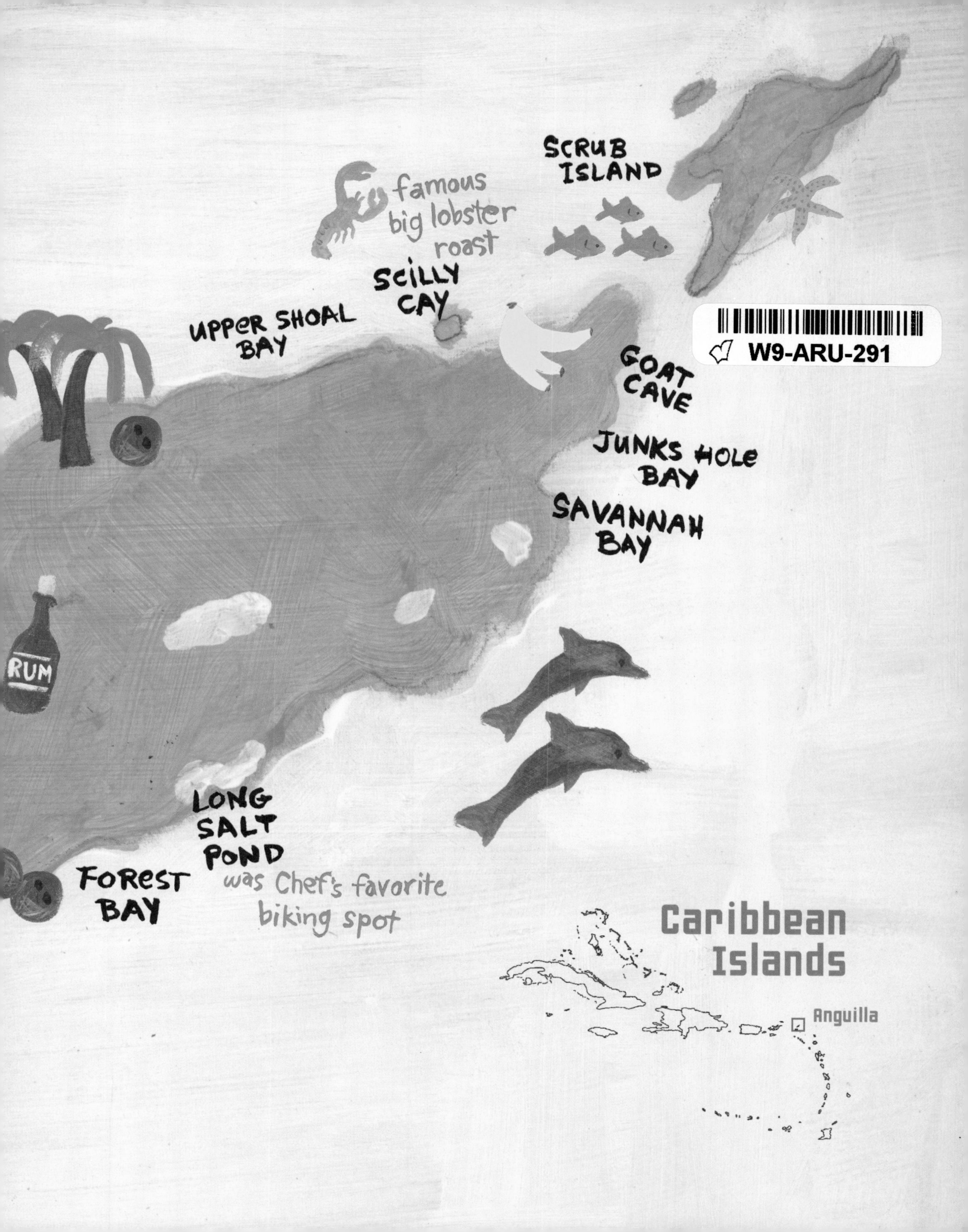

famous
big lobster
roast

SCRUB
ISLAND

SCILLY
CAY

UPPER SHOAL
BAY

GOAT
CAVE

JUNKS HOLE
BAY

SAVANNAH
BAY

RUM

LONG
SALT
POND
was Chef's favorite
biking spot

FOREST
BAY

Caribbean
Islands

Anguilla

PARADISE KITCHEN

#

CARIBBEAN COOKING WITH CHEF DANIEL ORR

Daniel Orr

Indiana University Press
Bloomington and Indianapolis

This book is a publication of

Indiana University Press
601 North Morton Street
Bloomington, Indiana 47404-3797 USA

iupress.indiana.edu

Telephone orders   800-842-6796
Fax orders   812-855-7931
Orders by e-mail   iuporder@indiana.edu

This book is printed on acid-free paper.

Manufactured in China

Library of Congress Cataloging-in-Publication Data

Orr, Daniel, [date]
 Paradise kitchen : Caribbean cooking with Chef Daniel Orr / Daniel Orr.
   p. cm.
 Includes index.
 ISBN 978-0-253-35608-6 (cloth : alk. paper) 1. Cooking, Caribbean. 2. Cookbooks. I. Title.

TX716.A1O72 2011
641.59729--dc22

                                                        2010035366

1 2 3 4 5 16 15 14 13 12 11

Contents

Acknowledgments   vii
Introduction: Finding Paradise   xi
Caribbean Food Glossary   xix

1. Breakfast at the Beach   1
2. Sunrise Shakes and Smoothies   21
3. Soups and Salads to Beat the Heat   25
4. Energize Your Afternoons: Anytime Energizing Vegetable Juices   63
5. Tango with Tapas   67
6. Caribbean Cocktails   79
7. Homemade Flavored Rums   95
8. Island Starters   101
9. Liming It Up under Pressure: Making Your Gramma's Pressure Cooker Your Friend   121
10. Fish: Brain Food   133
11. Grilled Lobster 101   157
12. Cooking for Carnivores: Getting to the Meat of It   163
13. Sides and Accompaniments   183
14. Caribbean Condiments: Making Every Day Extraordinary   199
15. Bush Teas   217
16. Sunny Sweets   221
17. Recipes for the Body   243

Appendix 1: The Perfect Storm: How to Prepare for a Hurricane   247
Appendix 2: From One Island to Another: Daniel Orr's Article from the *Anguillian*   253
Index   255

Acknowledgments

"Paradise Kitchen" is best summarized as a state of mind . . . a feeling one gets when surrounded by an incredible array of aromatic, succulent, pungent, and piquant foods, not to mention oceans, sunsets, dusty island roads, and unforgettable island folk. Behind the culinary ingredients available on an island come a long history and a deep recipe file of traditional family and folk dishes to work with. I've updated and recreated these recipes for a new, healthier recipe file, but I'll never forget their past. History is to be thanked and remembered.

It was a "chef's dream," enjoying all this, with sand between my toes and the straw in my tall cool rum drink waving back and forth in fragrant, salty, ocean breezes. I describe this as a chef's paradise. Paradise Kitchen. Those years in the Caribbean will always put fire into my sauté pan. And the thought of my chef friends back in New York freezing their tushes off all winter long . . . That was priceless. Now I'm back home in Indiana and the memories of those warm island days and the warmer island people get me through the toughest of winters and the dreariest of "life issues." Thanks for the memories, Anguilla.

I've traveled throughout the Caribbean from time to time throughout my life. When I was a youngster, scuba diving with my family took us to the islands for holiday vacations. As an adult, I escaped the crazy life of being a New York chef to Caribbean oasis destinations as a source of energy, revitalization, and inspiration. I've also visited vicariously through the cuisines of my culinary compadres in the island-inspired restaurants and books of Latin American chefs and others (Douglas Rodriguez, Norman Van Aken, et tous). These and others all excited and intrigued me to try a new way of cooking, and my 2 years in paradise gave me the opportunity. Thank you, kitchen people, for your sweat and toil.

All my thanks and admiration go to my friend Christopher Heath, whom I refer to as "my partner in culinary crime." Christopher worked alongside me for 10 years making the things I dream up come true, as well as inspiring me with his own dreams, skill, vision, and perspective. I miss him daily, but new cooks have come into my life and stolen my heart. Sorry, Christopher! None of this would have happened without Christopher's "better two-thirds," his wife, Jessica, and their precious little Isabella. I miss you guys! Hope to meet the new one soon.

My thanks go out to Lee Rizzuto and family, and Bob Dixon and the entire staff at CuisinArt Resort and Spa for welcoming me to Anguilla, especially those who shared their recipes, family histories, and personal experiences so whole-heartedly. Special thanks go to the Arts Department at CuisinArt and to Nik Douglas for use of his archeological photos.

Thanks to Dr. Paul and Darlene, whom I met in a bar in Anguilla and who have supported me in many ways both in the islands and back here in Indiana. I love you guys. Come back to Bloomington soon!

Mari, I'm still waiting on you here in southern Indiana. You owe me a visit!

Lindsey Schechter was my muse during her visit with me. Her interest and writing skill was an encouragement and aid in completing this project. Thank you, thank you, and thank you!

To my "Hoosier momma" Claire Burke for her editing assistance.

To Linda Oblack, Peter Froehlich, Miki Bird, Chandra Mevis, Sarah Brown, June Silay, Bernie Zoss, and Dan Pyle at Indiana University Press for all their help, and to Anne Richmond Boston for the fabulous design of the book and jacket.

To Mom and Dad, and my brother Dave and his family who have always been there for me, even more so when I lived in beautiful, warm Anguilla!! I *NEVER* saw so much of them.

To my friends back in New York who stuck with me during my adventures: You are the best! Lula, Regina and Peter, Helio, George, Rodrigo, Tommy, Debbie, and oh so many others. You are in my heart even though you aren't next to me right now.

I also want to show appreciation to past kitchen and dining room staff members who have crossed my path over my last 30 years of professional cooking. Even though they're no longer cooking at my elbow or comforting my clients at restaurants like La Grenouille, Guastavino's, or CuisinArt, I think of them often. Their old family recipes and personal anecdotes, often given to me spelled out on tattered, sauce-soaked recipe cards, continue to inspire me. It is so fun to Facebook with you all and catch up from time to time. These memories and those of Anguilla remind me to let the islands speak and tell me "what's missing" in both my recipes and my life.

And finally, to all of Anguilla, I've fallen madly in love with your island, your people, and your cuisine. The following is the tale, told through your recipes and firsthand experiences, of my year in paradise.

Introduction

Finding Paradise

I've had therapists; remember, I'm a former Manhattan chef and my father was a shrink! Those therapists I ended up with told me to close my eyes and go to that "special place" where I feel safe and peaceful. For years I'd been picturing myself on a Caribbean island whenever stress levels got too high or a personal crisis hit me hard. My vision has been talcum-powder-white sands underfoot, relaxing on a beach chair with the cool salty water licking my toes, warm sun shining, and an icy Carib beer tucked in an empty coconut shell packed with ice keeping it refreshingly cold.

After nearly 15 years swimming upstream in Manhattan's culinary East River, I was stressed, tired, and a bit overwhelmed. 9/11 and the emotionally charged aftermath made running Guastavino's, one of the country's largest high-end restaurants, no longer a wonderful challenge but a major psychological burden. I needed to find my "special place"—and live there. Pronto!

As luck would have it, paradise arrived at my doorstep, in the form of an invite to discuss the culinary program of the resort run by one of my Guastavino's "habitués" in the Caribbean. My chef at the time, Christopher Heath, and I were whisked off to Anguilla to take a look and report back on what could be done to revitalize the property after their last chef took flight. What came from that trip was the chance to live out my culinary fantasies, and—get this—do it in sandals! Christopher and I found Paradise Kitchen.

Anguilla is a chef's paradise. All the Caribbean clichés fit: seven shades of blue, turquoise dream, etc., etc., etc. But the difference at CuisinArt Resort and Spa is the culinary angle: lines of coconut palms dripping with water-filled fruit like tropical canteens, lush herb gardens, "bush tea" gardens inspired by the folklore and traditional medicinal practices of the island, and orchards of key limes, soursops, grapefruits, star apples, sugar apples, avocados, and more. CuisinArt's hydroponic farm is on the cutting edge of luxurious healthy living and produces all the lettuce, herbs, chilies, bell peppers, bok choy, tomatoes,

and cucumbers that the kitchens use. All picked that morning and served fresh for lunch!

Although this paradise owes greatly to the natural surroundings, the people are really what make it. Anguilla and Anguillians are unique. Each new encounter is memorable, from sharing hearty laughs with the fishermen dropping off their colorful morning catch of slippery potfish and fluttering spiny lobsters, to the gentle smile one gets from a local girl dressed in her school colors, waiting under the shade of a flamboyant tree. This place is unique and less spoiled.

I've heard locals say that Anguilla isn't a physically beautiful island. They admire the more dramatic volcanic peaks of St. Barts, St. Martin, and Saba. Anguilla forces you to look deeper than showy mountains for beauty. It is a much older island, an ancient reef formation shaped like an eel (hence the French-inspired name). Its beauty lies in its salt ponds full of birds, old dirt roads leading to "undiscovered" beaches, frangipani trees, and turban cacti sticking up riotously through tangles of rock. And one must not, cannot, forget the beaches. They are the least trampled and most pristine in the Caribbean. Believe me, all those other islands envy Anguilla. Think of all those clichés again—they are true.

The culinary beauty of this place also lies low. The old ways of the island are still practiced by a few, and the kitchen history, lore, and techniques are rich subjects. If you are lucky enough to speak to the right people, you can learn about fire rock cooking, conky dumplings, homemade charcoal, fish and goat waters (island stews), reef fish, guinea corn porridge, johnnycakes, coal keel ovens, cornmeal fungi, sea moss, "bush fruit," and wild herbs. They were all part of everyday life as little as 20 years ago. Iva the Dive-a, the conch diver from Sandy Ground, and others still live this traditional island lifestyle. This is what interested me and this is what I wanted to cook. I decided that this history would bring the kitchen at CuisinArt to the forefront of the culinary spectrum. After all, every nation is fueled by its stomach, and island nations are justly proud of their vital legacy built around the vittles shared at their dinner tables.

Christopher and I were eager to put a star on the culinary map of the West Indies. We had a 2-year contract that inspired us to work quickly. Then it would be on to new adventures. With our newfound love of Caribbean ingredients and Anguillian traditional recipes, we got into our kitchens and never looked back. We also wanted to teach other "foodies" about this new passion for the island table and how to create these gourmet delights back home. We used our daily demonstrations, hands-on classes, elegant demonstration dinners, and master classes to test the recipes that follow. That experience also allowed us to work directly with home cooks and answer their questions as we progressed. I

have adapted the more difficult restaurant dishes to the home kitchen, answering many of the questions that came up during these cooking classes. The recipes, writings, and photos that follow are my way of sharing these adventures with you. I think you will enjoy them and, if you haven't been down to experience the Caribbean firsthand, go there and find your own "special place" soon. But remember, this is our little secret paradise, so only tell your best of friends!

A Bit of "Brain Food" about the Caribbean's Culinary History

Gather around chefs and chefettes for a bit of Caribbean culinary history . . .

Once upon a time, there were two Amerindian tribes occupying the islands—the Arawaks and Caribs. Culinary sleuths have uncovered clues that point to the Caribs being the ones to start the intense flavoring of dishes with chilies, herbs, and spices, which they brought with them from the mainland, most likely Brazil. They only beat Columbus to the islands by several hundred years. Misinformed historians from the past told us Caribs enjoyed munching on human flesh. I guess they named the region after them to keep them happy. My friend Nik Douglas and other archeologists and sociologists have uncovered new data from sifting

through the clues left in long-forgotten table scraps and have learned more than ever before about the ancient tribes of the Caribbean, especially their culinary habits. The Caribs are no longer thought of as cannibals eating human flesh as their protein source, but as aggressive fighters who, in quest of strength, may have eaten the hearts of their bravest defenders in post-battle religious ceremonies. They honored their chiefs, warriors, and beloved family members with ritual displays of bones and prayer. The Caribs partied in a pretty hardcore way, making a drug from the sap of a tree that when ingested gave them a high that was much like crack cocaine. It made them antisocial and gave them grimacing fits and ultimately violent behavior. Although they may have been bad neighbors because of their drug use, much of their poor reputation was created by Europeans looking for scapegoats to justify their mass execution of indigenous peoples. Ponce de León II, governor of Puerto Rico, can be credited for developing the story of cannibals. It was easier to kill them than convert them. Today, sadly, the only island where Caribs are still found is Dominica.

The Arawaks, on the other hand, put the B in BBQ with their technique of cooking on *barbacoa*, grills made of moist green branches. Their #1 delicacy was conch, which was barbequed or stewed. They also caught all kinds of fish—from reef fish to the big tuna, swordfish, mahimahi and so forth, as evidenced from their trash heaps. For meat they ate hutia (a kind of small rat-like creature, now extinct in Anguilla)—lots of their bones in the middens—and of course turtle, tortoise, and all kinds of birds. Their staple fruits were genip, West Indian cherry, pineapple, pomsurrete, hog-plums, sea grapes, and so on. They favored a pound of veggies over a pound of flesh and were savvy to plant hybridization, creating varieties of many of the crops still used today such as pineapple, squash, corn, and cassava. They made cassava flesh into a "bread" (and pancakes!) and fermented its juice for use in spicy sauces and an island brew. In fact, their supreme god, Jocahu (a.k.a. Yocahu), was actually the embodiment of the cassava root. Arawaks were also the first hippies to use a drug called yopo, a sort of LSD/Ecstasy-type hallucinogen, as their "love drug." Although gentle, Arawaks were also good hunters and gatherers both on water and in the bush. On the sea they caught reef fish (potfish) in traps whose design is still used today. Sea turtles, conch, crabs, and lobster were all in their diets. On land they hunted for teas, West Indian cherries, pope's head and prickly pear cactus fruit, mauby bark, stinkweed for coffee, tortoise, and the now-extinct hutia rice rat. Fish was baked in salt-crusts with salt harvested from the still-existing salt ponds. Annatto, now used for coloring cheese and butter, was used as body paint and had a secondary benefit as a mosquito repellent. These peaceful, mystic people and their Arawakan predecessors, the archaic Ciboney "Stone Age" people and the Taino "golden age Greater Antilles" people, inhabited all the Caribbean island chain for several thousand years. The Arawaks arrived in Anguilla circa 1500 BC (the Archaic, pre-ceramic period) and stayed until about AD 1500—when they gradually died out from disease, slavery, and general malaise. One of their main outposts and religious temples still stands in Anguilla and may be visited with a guide. These guys created the hammock and named the hurricane. They were lovers, not fighters. My kind of people.

There are more than five thousand landmasses bobbing pleasantly in the crystal clear blue waters that make up the paradise we now call the Caribbean. They form a massive arc stretching from northern South America to the Everglades. In 1493, Christopher Columbus made his way into the neighborhood, and following him closely were sugarcane and disease. Chris did some stuff that really rocked the world, but he kinda screwed things up at the Arawak's and Carib's parties. We almost lost paradise! By bringing in sugarcane to fulfill the demanding European sweet tooth, Columbus and those who followed him also brought on the exploitation of human beings. It was later discovered that rum could be made from fermented molasses or cane juice, and an industry was built on the backs of the slaves. The history of oppression, persecution, and slavery with its evil cultural double standard really screwed up paradise for a long time. This bitterness and imbalance still resonates throughout the islands at times and will take many more years of hard work to successfully eradicate completely.

The influx of cultures did have one positive note, and it is one that soothes and delights. Food and drink! Beginning with the slave trade in the early 1600s, foods from West Africa came to the Caribbean islands, including okra, pigeon peas, plantains, callaloo, taro, breadfruit, and ackee. Following the abolition of the slave trade in 1838, laborers from India and China came to work in the fields and plantations, adding two very different culinary influences to the already long list. Spaniards introduced other foods, notably coconut, chickpeas, cilantro, eggplant, onions, and garlic. Widespread nautical travel and domination of the seas by the Europeans also brought a bounty of ingredients from like climates around the world. Colonial culinary trademarks appeared, such as coffee, oranges, limes, mangoes, and the mainstay, rice. Other ingredients are now so tied to the local cuisine that we think they've always been here. Though now commonplace in the backyards and on dinner tables throughout the region, potatoes and passion fruit originally came from Peru and Brazil, and papaya, avocado, chayote, and cocoa were Mexican contributions.

Pineapples, bananas, melons, figs, pomegranates, breadfruit, Ugli, naseberry, tamarind, sapodilla, soursop, plantains, cherimoya, monstera, loquat, carambola, guava, and mamey sapote also thrived in the lush vegetation. And garden plots provided yams, pumpkin, yucca, calabaza, chayote, sweet peppers, tomatoes, zucchini, cucumbers, and numerous legumes such as cow, red, and black beans and black-eyed and pigeon peas. Local and transplanted herbs were highly prized

and cultivated or gathered wild in "the bush." They provided flavor and aroma to dishes and were made into teas with folkloric and medicinal values.

With all the fruits and veggies around, you could easily become a vegan, but there is a tradition of keeping livestock as well. Most Caribbeans, except the Rastas and a few others, are lusty carnivores. You'll find recipes for meat, poultry, and game of all sorts in almost every family kitchen. A meal without meat for most islanders is no meal at all.

Let's not forget our omega-3s; being surrounded by the ocean you also have more saline sources of protein as well. Anguillians love their fish with abandon. Reef fish, deep-sea fish, crustaceans, and mollusks are all enjoyed at the island table. Seafood is enjoyed in stews, chowders, soups, or simply on the BBQ.

The cuisine of Anguilla and her fellow islands is based on this palate of cultural influences and the culinary bounty that naturally thrives there. The people who call Anguilla home took whatever good they could gather from the European interlopers and blended it with their own history and heritage to form a cuisine and a way of life. Now, we "up north" desire to escape our own hectic schedules and share the local culture and seasonal warmth, often without a second thought of its less sunny side. When you prepare these recipes, you're sharing in Caribbean history and culture at your dinner table.

These Are Not Gramma's Caribbean Recipes

The recipes that follow are my interpretation of Caribbean culture through food. Food as a way of life is what I do for a living. This project is a natural extension of my fascination with people and shows that, by using food as my sleuth's magnifying glass, I can really discover and enjoy a new culture. Food becomes a metaphor for the way an outsider sees a group of people. I have had a great time watching, listening, eating, reading, and experimenting in the kitchen to come up with what I feel is a fun representation of the deeply complex and sociological history of the Caribbean people. These are recipes/dishes from a way of life that I can thoroughly enjoy, yet never truly understand.

I've focused on Anguilla, but none of the dishes is wholly Anguillian. In Anguilla you have the belongers and non-belongers. The belongers are legally native to the soil or have gone through a long immigration process. "Anguillian born" is a moniker that has bragging rights. There are large subcultures of non-belongers on all the islands, each adding their own flavor to the mix. In Anguilla there are expats from St. Martin, St. Kitts, Jamaica, Santa Domingo, and Dominica, and the East Indian influences of Guiana, Trinidad, and Tobago . . . not to mention North Americans and Europeans. All have given their flavors to the Paradise Kitchen stew

as well. Tourist trade, with large resorts and demanding guests, has brought a new level of sophistication (some would say "putrefaction") to the islands, with restaurants of infinite variety from lowly sub shops to haute cuisine temples. I guess I can say this because I'm a part of it. The Caribbean is also becoming a major player in many industries, so this international commerce has also widened the palate and allowed it to become more varied.

I have not documented exact family recipes but used them as a starting point. I employed my American and European culinary background and blended it with what I was learning in the Caribbean to create a hybrid that adapts well to any kitchen where people love to cook and eat. I hope friends from the Caribbean will approve. I know the flavors will excite you and give you a celebratory feeling, making every minute you spend playing in the kitchen memorable, fulfilling, and, I hope, transporting. Ahh . . . paradise found!

Defining "Healthy" in Paradise Kitchen

Good culinary choices, like most choices, are all about balance. Most of my dishes combine proteins with veggies and leave most of the "white" carbs out. Complex carbs like whole grains and legumes that contain fiber are used, but I try to stay away from white sugars, flours, and white potatoes unless the dish really demands it. When I do use carbs like pasta and rice, I usually combine them with great veggies.

Breakfasts with starchy side dishes and dessert recipes are for special occasions. Those you'll have to try at your own risk to your waistline! Please don't hold me responsible. If you eat a balanced diet and exercise I believe you can eat almost anything as long as you do it in moderation. If you are being healthy you'll have to balance out those days you eat "high on the hog" with plenty of good old-fashioned exercise or hard work.

I believe that being a great chef is 90 percent knowing how to shop and 10 percent knowing enough not to screw up the good things you've bought. I based these dishes, as I do most of my cooking, on regional and seasonal products. Because they are grown in their optimal season and don't have to be shipped to you from across the country or the world, these ingredients are the best source of vitamins and minerals as well as all those great enzymes that keep you regular and glowing! In a chef's paradise, all you have to do is step out the back door and into the garden to do your shopping. There are healthy ways to coax out flavors with herbs, spices, and citrus so you don't have to be too heavy handed with a salt shaker.

I think you'll find the recipes that follow will be helpful in putting a balance in your kitchen. I know I feel more energetic eating this way and my hope is that you will too. And THAT feeling beats the deprived angst every time.

I use some recipes for sauces, spice blends, or sides and accompaniments in numerous places. These are marked with "see recipe" and are listed by name in the index to help you hop around. All of my Kitchen D'Orr spice blend recipes used in the book are given in full on pp. 213–215. Or you can just go online and order them ready to go at www.farm-bloomington.com.

Caribbean Food Glossary

I have chosen some of the more esoteric ingredients to describe. Many may not be available in most markets but are of cultural and historical interest and make for fun reading. I have given substitutes whenever possible.

Agave: Although best known for the fact that Mexicans make tequila from it, agave has been used for years for its fibrous leaves. Anguillians made rope out of these fibers for their fish traps. Agave nectar is also used as a sweetener.

Aloe: Fresh aloe is used by many once a month as a cleansing potion. The slimy sticky gelatinous juice is mixed with that of oranges to cover the bitter taste. It is said to ease intestinal and bowel disorders. Aruba is one of the Caribbean's largest producers. Aloe is known for its high content of vitamins, amino acids, and essential minerals. Aloe juice may be bought already prepared in health food stores. It is usually kept refrigerated to maintain quality. Aloe is easily grown in most of the United States.

Amaranth: Known as callaloo on isles in the British West Indies, amaranth is thought of as a bothersome weed by many gardeners. It has been foraged for years and used as a wild spinach. Full of protein, vitamins, and minerals, the complete plant may be eaten. The seeds may even be dried and ground into a flour to be used in baking. Wild amaranth may be harvested in many areas of the United States. Spinach and other greens may be used in its place or combined with it. Lamb's-quarters, another wild weed available in the summer in much of the United States, is a great local substitute. Amaranth comes in many colors and is an easy plant to grow. Give it a shot.

Annatto: An orange-colored seed that grows well in Anguilla. Most important for Arawaks, the natives colored their bodies with it by grinding the seeds and coloring oil. It has the added bonus of keeping away mosquitoes. Nature's first OFF! It was also used in cooking for coloring and flavoring. Today, annatto is used commercially to color butter and cheeses. Annatto seeds can be found in the spice area of Latino markets, where it is a favorite seasoning for rice and poultry dishes.

Bananas: Bananas are large herbaceous plants that are originally from the Middle East. The word *banan* means finger in Arabic. Each banana plant produces one "rack" of bananas and then falls down and is replaced by new

growth from below. The huge grass-like plants send a flower bud, called the heart, from the center of the plant. The heart then blossoms in a series of orchid-like blooms that yield the "hands" of banana. The banana can be eaten throughout this process from flower to ripe bananas. There are many different types of fruit in all colors and sizes, each with a distinctive flavor and texture. Homegrown bananas have nothing to do with the supermarket varieties grown for their shelf life. They are as different as heirloom tomatoes are from the pink cardboardy ones sold out of season. Originally bananas were full of inedible seeds, but these are all but nonexistent these days due to centuries of hybridization. When I lived in Anguilla I loved planting and caring for my banana trees. I had five varieties to choose from and used the leaves and flowers in the kitchen as well. What great memories.

Bitters: As their name suggests, bitters are bitter or bittersweet. Originally used for their medicinal value, bitters were a prized commodity in days gone by. This product is a type of spirit made from different herbs, roots, and plants. Now they are mostly used to flavor and add a dry zest to cocktails and cooking. Because of their function as a digestive aid and appetite stimulant, bitters are often used in aperitifs and digestifs. They are also used to balance out the sweet flavors of many island cocktails and punches. Be cautious when using

bitters, as a little too much can ruin the cocktail or dish. Most bitters also have high alcohol content and shouldn't be used in non-alcoholic drinks.

Breadfruit: These are the imported trees that got Captain Bligh into hot water. Breadfruit was "cheap eats" for the slaves, but now it is a beloved visitor to the Caribbean table. It has the texture and starchiness of a potato but also many subtle differences. I love it as homefries for breakfast, sautéed with garlic as a side dish, or pureed and made into fried croquettes, as Chef George does over at Cap Juluca. Breadfruit is simple to cook. Just put the whole fruit in the coals or over a gas flame and cook, turning as needed, until well charred on all sides and easy to pierce with a skewer. Remove the skin and the center core and use as desired.

Callaloo: This is a generic term used throughout the islands for wild spinach. In Anguilla, amaranth (see above) is the callaloo of choice, but in Dominica their callaloo is what we would call vine-spinach or New Zealand spinach. Some islands even call dachine leaves and sweet potato leaves callaloo. One of Jamaca's national dishes is Run Down, made with callaloo, crabmeat, and coconut. Callaloo may be sautéed, boiled, stewed, or steamed.

Cassava: A root vegetable that the Arawaks learned to grow and use. It was the staff of life for the early islanders. Cassava was used to make breads and pancakes as well as a spicy sauce, and also beer! Bitter cassava is poisonous if not prepared properly. To make flour from the root, it is grated and squeezed (the juice is used for the brew and sauces). Then it is dried over heat or in the sun. Cassava is used to make tapioca. I love to peel, cut, and par-cook the cassava for French fries and homefries.

Christophene: Christophene, also called chayote or mirliton, is a member of the squash family that is about the size and shape of a pear. The skin is pale green, waxy, and smooth. The flesh is white and there is one soft seed in the middle. Chayote is grown in several states including California, Florida, and Louisiana, but it is native to Latin America. The squash was one of the primary foods of the Aztecs and Mayas.

Coal Keel: An old wood-burning, rustic stone oven used for baking and roasting in the old days.

Coconut: A member of the palm family, coconuts are used for food and drink throughout the Caribbean. Coconut milk or coconut cream adds a wonderful richness to many dishes and is a great addition to your pantry, especially if you are vegetarian or vegan.

Cocoplums: A fruiting bush growing near the ocean in many of the same areas as sea grape trees. These fruits resemble persimmons in both flavor and texture and can leave the mouth feeling cottony if not perfectly ripe. They may be eaten out of hand or made into marmalades and preserves.

Conch: Anguilla became "special" for the Amerindians because of its conch. Every beach used to have MOUNTAINS of conch residue (the pierced shells), up to 10–20 feet high! Acres of the stuff. The Arawaks had a "conch purification" diet—eating only conch—and at one point may have come here just for that, as part of their visionary quest. An exclusively conch-based diet is invigorating. Iva the Dive-a, a fisherman who dives for conch off the waters of Sandy Ground, is a great guy to meet. He still does things the old-fashioned way, and if you get up early enough in the morning, you'll find him cleaning conch at the north end of the beach. Just look for his mountains of shells.

Crabs:

Land Crabs: Great big crabs with a single large claw, found especially in the Cinnamon Reef area around the pond. The French used to come over with lights and harvest these incredible-tasting critters. At one stage the Amerindian culture here was a "crab" culture—meaning that crab was their main source of protein. MASSES of crab residue have been found in their middens.

Sand Crabs: These are not what North Americans think of as sand crabs. These are caught in the ocean in sandy areas. They are light in color and are about the same size as blue crabs. They make great crab soup, stuffed crabs, and crab curry.

Sea Hermit Crabs: In past days these were standard food, gutted and roasted. The indigenous people just pulled them from the shells the crabs were inhabiting, cleaned them, dusted them with spice, and roasted them right on the coals. They may also be steamed, removed from the shells, and the internal white meat and claw meat eaten.

Dried Salt Beef (*tasajo* in Latin American markets): Dried and salted beef used to be a Caribbean household staple back in the days when a cow was slaughtered and drying and salting was a strategy to preserve the meat. It was brined and crusted with sea salt, then tied to a rope and thrown on the roof to dry in the sun. If it looked like rain, the beef was pulled down until the sun came back out. Dried salt beef must be soaked overnight and boiled in a couple of changes of water before use. It has a unique flavor and texture; nothing replaces it. Go to your nearest ethnic food store or Latin bodega to buy it, or check it out on the internet.

Ginips: In July and early August you see kids along the road with small bundles of ginips for sale. Ginips remind me a bit of lychee nuts in that they have a large central seed surrounded by the fruit, which is encased in a non-edible peel. Although not as sweet as lychees, ginips are good if perfectly ripe. They are a local delicacy but seem like a lot of work for a little pleasure. They ripen and become available right around Anguilla's carnival time. They can be made into a tasty drink as well. Lychees may be used in their place.

Guavaberry: Used to infuse rum or as a separately made unique liqueur. There is a guavaberry native to St. Martin. In fact, the guavaberry and its namesake liqueur are synonymous with St. Maarten/Martin. Growing wild on the island's rolling hills, the berries were originally only enjoyed by the birds until about 300 years ago, when people began preserving the fruit with rum and sugar. Today it is still aged in oak barrels, which lend a woody flavor to the sweet, fruity, and spicy flavor of the guavaberry. Guavaberry products can be found on both the French and Dutch sides of the island. Fresh guavaberries are not available in North America, but the liqueurs can be found.

Hardbacks: Also known as chiton, these little crustaceans are some of the oddest things I ate on Anguilla. They are delicious, but they look like prehistoric trilobite fossils. They are basically flat, oval-shaped, gray to brown segmented shellfish that apply themselves to the rocks right around where waves break. They are 1–4 inches long. To harvest the hardbacks, you need a strong thin-bladed knife and you must pry them off the rocks. You must surprise them or they will tenaciously adhere. With your knife, remove the center yellowish-orange (think smoked salmon) colored muscle and rinse well. I like them simply dipped in sea water and eaten raw, but they are good marinated like ceviche or breaded and quickly fried. Clams are a good substitute.

Mangoes: Mango season is a celebration in the islands. You see neatly stacked fruit at markets and on tables set up alongside the road. No one "owns" a mango tree; everyone in the neighborhood seems to know where they are and when they ripen, so if you have a tree on your property, expect visitors. Mangoes may be eaten shredded green in salads or out of hand when ripe. Imported mangoes are available all year long, but when picked ripe from the tree, mangoes are a wonder and never have that "soapy peach" flavor that supermarket imports sometime have.

Mauby Tree: Makes an important Arawak and West Indian drink, plus it can be used in cooking. Anguilla has the best mauby in the region. Anguilla even exported the bark to St. Kitts and other nearby islands. Mauby is a root beer–like drink with a bitter aftertaste. Locals spice it with cloves, cinnamon, ginger, and star anise. In the old days, mauby bark was also used as a soap replacement because of its natural bubble-forming quality. Root beer would be our closest cousin but is much sweeter than Caribbean mauby.

Okra: Okra is a member of the hibiscus family that originated in Africa and was brought west to the Caribbean and the Americas by African slaves. It is the base for many stews but also makes wonderful pickles. Okra is easy to grow as far north as Indiana.

Old Wife (a.k.a. triggerfish): This fish has a firm white texture and a mild flavor, somewhat like Dover sole or John Dory. It is difficult to scale so it must be skinned. Its island nickname may have come from the fact that the "old wife" was the only one who could skin it, or because the old wife knew how to make use of the skin as a pot scrubber or as a sort of sandpaper. It is delicious braised whole in a sauce, grilled, or panfried.

Passion Fruit: Passion fruit is a round, yellow or dark purple fruit packed with seeds and juice. It grows on a vine and has a wonderfully ornate flower. To eat right out of the skin, allow to wrinkle for a few days to raise the sugar levels and enhance the flavor or just cut in half and sprinkle with a teaspoon of sugar. Makes a great flavored rum or syrup for fresh fruit.

Pawpaw (papaya): This fruit is a survivor. It will grow just about anywhere, whether the soil is good or not. All it seems to need is steady water. The papaya can be used green in salads, soups, and stews or ripe in smoothies and desserts, or it can simply be eaten with a bit of lime juice. The seeds, which are usually discarded, have a peppery flavor and may be ground as a pepper replacement. Papaya is often eaten first thing in the morning as a digestive aid to help with constipation. Green papaya is available in Asian markets. Now that I'm back in Indiana, we get local pawpaws, a seedy fruit that

tastes a lot like the papaya. It is available about 2 weeks out of the year in September.

Plantains: Not just green bananas, plantains are a member of the banana family, generally much larger than the sweeter varieties. Plantain has a higher starch content and may be used either green, when it is almost potato-like, or when it ripens and the skin turns brown. Then it has a much sweeter flavor and a softer, creamier texture. See recipe for Soft Mofungo.

Popes: These small, fabulous, fuchsia-colored fruits of the pope's head (turk's head cactus) are good for garnishing both sweets and savories. I love the sweet-and-sour contrast and the crunch of the tiny, kiwi-like seeds. The flavor is somewhere between a tomatillo, a kiwi, and a grape. I cut them in half or into little rounds and scatter them over ceviches or use them to decorate fruit tarts. You really have to live in cactus land to get these, and I miss them a lot.

Potfish: Potfish are what Anguillians call "the daily catch" from the reef. There are many varieties one may eat. They are stewed, grilled or roasted.

Prickly Pears: In old times this was traditional dessert food. My friend "Granny" from Old Ta told me that children, especially young girls, loved the fruit for a

different reason. She said that they made your lips "red like lipstick" and "made you feel all growed up." They are great in sauces, drinks, desserts, or eaten out of hand (after you remove the hair-like cactus nettles, that is).

Purslane and Sea Purslane: Purslane is a succulent that grows wild all over the Americas, including the Caribbean. It is said to have the highest omega-3 content of any vegetable. I love its citrusy, cressy crunch. Sea purslane grows along the ocean in the oddest and most inhospitable places. It, too, can be eaten, though it is usually quite salty. I like using it as a salt replacement over steamed seafood or fish wrapped in foil destined for the grill. It is also good with raw fish preparations. Purslane is also known as pig weed in the islands. This former "weed" is now being sold for top dollar in many greenmarkets. I pull it out of my bean rows all summer long.

Raw Sugar (also called *piloncillo* in Mexico): Sold in Latin markets like truncated cones. In Central and South America they are called *panela* or *tapa dulce*. Raw sugar is grated and used like traditional brown sugar but has a deeper, richer flavor. It is worth the extra effort of grating. It stores well in an airtight container. If you want to make it easier to grate, put it in a plastic bag with half an apple for a day or two. The moisture of the apple will soften the sugar cake.

Sea Cat (a.k.a. octopus): Anguillian waters have very good octopus. I like to steam it lightly just until it firms up, then chill it and serve it as sashimi with an Asian dipping sauce or marinade. More typically it is stewed a long time until tender. It is also great cooked tender and then tossed on the grill with garlic and chili oil.

Sea Eggs, Sea Urchins, Poor Man's Caviar: Urchins were another prime food of the Amerindians and are best harvested just before the full moon when they are full. I fished for these with a fella appropriately known as Nature Boy. We snorkeled off the East End for lobsters, whelk, and urchins (old English for hedgehog). Back onboard we cut them in half and I scooped them out of the shell with a sun-warmed crust of bread from Le Bon Pain Bakery. Lubricated with a bit of salted butter, they slid down great! Each urchin has five yellow fleshy tongues—actually the animal's gonads. You can also use a spoon to remove them. For me they taste of the sea and are wholly delicious. Some folks aren't as enamored. West Indians often mix the urchin with polenta and put it back into the shells to serve. If you don't live by the ocean, you can try them at fine sushi places under the name "uni" as well.

Sea Grapes: The round, plate-like leaves of the sea grape tree are seen all over the island all year round. But the grapes start forming in June and July and ripen in

the end of August and September. Sea grapes may be eaten as is when ripe or made into wine, jelly, vinegars, and chutneys. In Belize the fresh fruit is dipped in salt and eaten as a snack with beer.

Sea Louse/Lice (a.k.a. slipper lobster): A strange-looking crustacean often brought up in the traps with the local spiny lobsters. It is a much rarer catch and tends to be sweeter than its more familiar cousin. They really look like lice that you see greatly enlarged in encyclopedia photos. You can use them like lobster. Their meat is good in fish cakes as well.

Sea Salt: Island Amerindians ate fish baked under a thick layer of sea salt from the salt ponds. This was a common method of cooking by the local indigenous tribes who didn't have metal pots and pans. The salt was also used as a major source of revenue for the islands for many years. The Europeans often traded hand-raked sea salt for salted cod from northern Europe. Salt was later harvested mechanically and used in oil refining.

Seaweeds and Sea Moss: Anguillians used to harvest and use a lot of seaweed; some of it is very tasty and tremendously nutritious. My friend Guy Gumbs and his mother harvest and make sea moss into a "vigorating" drink—an old West Indian treat. I make a breakfast smoothie called Reef-Freshing with it. Good for man,

good for woman. Other seaweeds are made into soups, stews, and salads.

Sherry (a.k.a. West Indian cherry): Makes an intense sorbet; very high source of vitamin C. Anguilla has a lot of it, but it is rarely used these days.

Soursop: A native tree from the tropical Americas, soursop fruits are widely prized throughout the Caribbean. On Spanish islands the fruit is known as *guanabana*. Most soursop is served as smoothies and ice cream. It has a creamy, rich, milky look to it and its aroma is of pineapple, citrus, and condensed milk. Soursop may also be eaten as a vegetable when it is young. Pregnant women in the Caribbean often crave the fruit. One of my favorite ways to take soursop is in bush tea. It is a wonderful after-dinner beverage made with the leaves. It works even better than chamomile. I often served it when I was ready for my guests to leave. Ten minutes later they were yawning and looking for their car keys!

Spiny Lobster: Spiny lobsters, also known as langouste or rock lobsters, are found in the warmer waters of the Caribbean. They are different from their cold water relatives such as Maine lobsters because they don't have claws. In their place they have long spiny antennas that they use to catch prey and as protection. If you can't get

spiny lobsters, use their northern cousins. Frozen spiny lobster tails are often found in the frozen fish section of your gourmet grocers.

Stinkweed Coffee (an Anguillian favorite and an Arawak thing): This is a wild weed on the island that one often smells and thinks there is a skunk around. Actually, it isn't quite that bad, but more of a mix of dark roasted coffee and skunk. It is dried and boiled for a hot beverage. It was widely used in the old days but has fallen out of favor with the availability of store-bought coffee and tea.

Sugarcane: Much of the reason for slave labor in the Caribbean was based around the planting and harvesting of this large member of the grass family. For many years the economies of the islands, and the wars to control them, were literally rooted in cane production. Europe's sweet tooth had to be satisfied, and cane ruled. Today, sugar beets are used to produce granulated sugar and they can be grown as far north as Canada. The beets are easier to grow and refining sugar from them is less costly. Sugarcane is no longer a viable crop on most islands, although St. Kitts still grows many acres and even has a "Sugarcane Train," a restored old train for tourists to ride around the island. I like to cut the stalks into drink stirrers and BBQ brochettes. One of my friends, a farmer named Franklyn Brooks, told me he

"remembers being little and beating the fibrous cane until tender, then wringing out the sweet juice into a small glass, flavoring it with lime, and going to school quite contented."

Tamarind: A tree from the Far East, tamarind is now grown in many Caribbean backyards both for its lovely shade and its sweet-and-sour fruit. I often took my guests on tours of the gardens and asked them if they knew what type of tree it was. Its fruit looks like small brown dried sausages hanging on strings from the branches; "sausage tree" became my comedic answer. Tamarind must be shelled, boiled, strained, and reduced to a syrup for cooking. Prepared tamarind pastes, sauces, and condiments are available in Asian and other specialty markets. Tamarind is used in both savory and sweet dishes. In the Caribbean it is most often made into candies, soft drinks, and desserts but is also found in curries.

Taro (a.k.a. dasheen): This plant has three major uses. Usually, the corms and tubers are prepared much as one would potatoes in chips, soups, stews, and mashes. Young, tender leaves are eaten as greens but must be boiled 15 minutes in water with a pinch of baking soda, drained, and then rinsed with boiling water to remove their poisoning effect. The blanched young shoots may also be eaten. These are obtained by forcing plants in

the dark. A tender, earthy, mushroomy flavored dish can be made from these. A stew dish called callaloo (see above) is prepared from dasheen leaves. Poi is made from fermented taro starch. Taro root can be found in Caribbean and Latino markets and some supermarkets. Potatoes are a good substitute. The greens may be replaced with spinach or chard in recipes.

Whelks: In the British Caribbean these are called whelks, but on other English-speaking islands they are called turbans for their namesake shape. They are black-and-white sea snails with a mother-of-pearl-like interior and are a local favorite cooked many different ways. Often they are simply thrown in the coals of a seaside fire and roasted for 30–45 minutes. Once cooked you take them to the sea and rinse them with salt water and remove

the sandy bits and the operculum and eat them. I like to simmer them in a court bouillon until tender. Take them out of the shell and clean them, then braise them in a coconut curry sauce. Whelks can be purchased frozen, often under the Italian name *scongili,* and may be replaced in recipes with clams or canned snails.

Yabbi Pot: The earthenware or clay pot used by Rastafarians for their cooking. Yabbi pots are commonly used over "fire rocks" heated by locally gathered wood for their vegetarian dishes. Wooden spoons are preferred over aluminum or other metal when preparing *Ital* foods. *Ital* comes from the word "vital" and refers to the support of a healthy diet free from chemical additives, most meats (except small fish), excess fat, and salt. Some "herbs" are allowed, of course.

PARADISE KITCHEN

BReAK-fAST at the BeACH

Remember when your mother told you, "Breakfast is the most important meal of the day"? When it comes to Caribbean cookery, most people forget what old Mom said. I fell for the island breakfast years ago at the Cuban eateries on Miami's South Beach. Sautéed plantains and fried eggs sprinkled with garlicky mojo, hearty plates of stick-to-your-ribs foods that fire the engine to drive you back to the sea, earth, or office for another day of toil. When you have an extremely hot midday, as you do in the South, your morning and evening meals are the ones you want to linger over. The island-style breakfast is a case in point. Many of us may be too busy to cook breakfast with Caribbean flare ... there's more to it than two boiled eggs and toast. But my idea of a perfect weekend is getting up late, putting on some reggae from my MP3 player, and banging a few pots and pans together.

Many of the ingredients may seem scary if you haven't eaten them before. Saltfish (salt cod), green bananas and plantains, cornmeal mush, and ackee might not be what you are usually grabbing when you are first awake. Talk about an eye-opener! When you think of where these recipes come from, though, it makes perfect sense: the islands! Surrounded by water, fish naturally became a part of every Caribbean meal, even breakfast.

Most Anguillians are real salt-of-the-earth types (or should I say salt-of-the-sea). Their personal histories are peppered with memories of fishing—pulling the seine with their neighbors, spearing jacks, and trapping lobsters. Everything they caught, raised, or harvested was used and shared. In the mornings, there would be raisin-spiked buns, johnnycakes, and sweet rolls fresh from the village hearth, which may have been a stone "keel" or simply a re-fashioned oil barrel. Mothers and grandmothers would make a sweet porridge with milk, sweet spices, honey, or cane from a brother's homegrown guinea corn. Your auntie would add her ripe bananas, fried until the natural sugars caramelized, to a dish of roasted fresh fish. Last night's repast, whether garlicky pork stew or braised fish, would appear with fungee, the local polenta, and wild calalloo. Comforting and filling, that breakfast set a wonderful tone for the new day. These are the

types of foods that I have learned to crave while living in this paradise. Whenever I'm lonely for my island, I get in the kitchen and cook one of these dishes and all seems right again.

I have included some "resort-y" dishes as well. Showstoppers such as Lobster Benedict with Key Lime Hollandaise and Shaved Nori, Jerked Steak and Eggs with Lime and Chili Pepper Hollandaise, and Banana Waffles with Passion Fruit Rum Syrup and Mango Butter will put a smile on the face of even your least adventurous table companions. I hope you'll try these recipes at home with family and friends. Each time you experiment with a recipe, new or old, consider it a voyage. Whether it be down memory lane or on an exotic adventure, exploration is what spending time in the kitchen and around the table is all about.

Coconut and Sesame Cereal

FOR 8–10 FRIENDS

¼ c.	honey
¼ c.	butter
½ c.	light brown sugar
½ tsp	salt, heaping
3 c.	raw rolled oats
½ c.	pecan halves
½ c.	walnut halves
⅔ c.	shredded coconut
2 T	white sesame seeds
2 T	black sesame seeds
⅔ c.	wheat germ
⅔ c.	shelled sunflower seeds
¼ c.	flax seeds
½ c.	dried apricots, diced
½ c.	dark brown raisins
½ c.	golden raisins

Note: Other nuts, seeds, or grains may be substituted

A fiber-rich combination that you can eat with milk or soy milk; however, it's also great in a parfait with yogurt, honey, and berries. I eat it as a snack by the handful when I need an energy boost during the day. Cool well and store in an airtight container and it will last a couple of weeks in a cool dark place. Ball jars of the stuff tied with raffia make wonderful healthy gifts during the holidays or any time of the year.

Melt in a large pan the butter, honey, and sugar. Add the rolled oats, pecans, and walnuts over medium heat, stirring constantly so they don't burn, until they begin to brown, about 15 minutes.

Add coconut, sesame seeds, wheat germ, and sunflower and flax seeds to the pan. Lower the heat and toast for an additional 7–8 minutes, stirring constantly.

Sprinkle salt evenly over the cereal and cook, still stirring, for another 3–5 minutes until sugar has dissolved and lightly coats each morsel. Add the dried fruit and cook for a few more minutes. The cereal should be nicely caramelized when ready.

Cool on a sheet pan and add the apricots and raisins.

Surreal Tropical Cereal Parfait

FOR 6 FRIENDS

2 c.	vanilla or lemon yogurt
¼ c.	honey
1 pint	assorted fruit and berries
2 c.	Coconut and Sesame Cereal (see recipe) or use your favorite granola
mint sprigs for garnish	
6	wine glasses

Use the coconut cereal recipe above to make this satisfying breakfast dish that can be served in an elegant wine glass for special occasions or simply presented in a cereal bowl if you're running late for work. You can also replace the yogurt with ice cream or frozen yogurt for a healthy dessert treat boasting contrasting colors, flavors, and textures.

Being careful to keep the rim and sides of the glasses neat and tidy, layer the ingredients in the glasses. Garnish with mint sprigs.

I like to drizzle the honey between layers of cereal because it forms a protective seal, keeping the cereal from becoming "yogurt soggy."

Tropical Muffins

FOR 12 LARGE MUFFINS

2 c.	unbleached all-purpose flour
1 c.	granulated sugar
¼ c.	brown sugar
2 tsp	baking powder
½ tsp	baking soda
1 tsp	salt
1 c.	dried fruit (raisins, papaya, mango, pineapple, or currants)
¾ c.	nuts, chopped (macadamia nuts work well)
2	eggs
1 c.	sour cream
6 tsp	oil
1 tsp	vanilla

This recipe is very adaptable. You can make these muffins with what you have on hand and to fit any occasion. Great for using little bits of this and that are left over and lonely in your pantry. The sour cream is the "secret" ingredient.

Mix together flour, sugars, baking powder, soda, and salt.

Stir in fruit and nuts.

Whisk together eggs, sour cream, oil, and vanilla.

Make a well in the dry ingredients; pour in liquid mixture and stir just to combine.

Spoon into 12 large muffin cups and bake in preheated 400° oven for 20–25 minutes or until they test done with a toothpick.

FOR 6 FRIENDS (6 JUMBO OR
12 MEDIUM MUFFINS)

1½ c.	bran cereal
¾ c.	milk
2	medium ripe bananas, mashed
½ c.	butter, melted
¼ c.	honey
¼ c.	molasses or sorghum
½ T	fresh ginger, minced
1	large egg, slightly beaten
¼ c.	all-purpose flour
1	baking powder
½ tsp	salt
½ tsp	Kitchen D'Orr Sweet Seasons Spice Blend
6–12	thick, chunky slices of banana for putting on top
1 T	decorative white sugar crystals

Kitchen D'Orr
Banana Bran Muffins

Fresh, warm, sweet breakfast muffins are mini-celebrations of life. You rarely get a good one off the streets, but nothing is better than getting a bit of sweet muffin at home. They are easy to make once you know how, and they are something that you can be creative with throughout your life. Toss in your favorite flavors and make this recipe your own. Keep it healthy by adding your favorite nuts and seeds. They are good for your libido too.

Heat oven to 375°. Stir together bran cereal and milk in large bowl. Let stand 5 minutes. Stir in banana, butter, honey, molasses, ginger, and egg. Stir in flour, baking powder, spices, and salt just until moistened. Do not over-mix.

Spoon batter evenly into 6 paper-lined or greased giant muffin cups. Top each with a thick chunk of banana and sprinkle with sugar crystals. Bake for 28–32 minutes or until lightly browned.

Lobster Benedict with Key Lime Hollandaise and Shaved Nori

There is nothing sexier than a great breakfast on a long weekend. This dish has several steps and does take some good technique, but if that "someone special" has earned it, this is a great payback. You can use this hollandaise on tons of dishes. It is good on everything from asparagus to Astroturf. The shaved nori is achieved by cutting the seaweed paper in very thin strips that can be sprinkled over the eggs or over a Caesar salad or fried rice. If you want to simplify things use some poached, peeled, deveined shrimp instead of the lobster.

TO PREPARE HOLLANDAISE

In a food processor or blender, combine egg yolks, lime juice, orange juice, lime zest, salt, and mustard. Process for 10–15 seconds or until thoroughly combined. In a small saucepan (or in microwave) melt butter until bubbling but not browned. With the food processor running, add hot butter in a thin, steady stream to egg mixture. Transfer mixture to a small bowl, thin as needed with warm water, and season to taste. Cover with plastic wrap and keep hollandaise warm.

TO PREPARE LOBSTER BENEDICT

In a small skillet, melt butter. Over medium-low heat, gently sauté shallot and garlic until tender, about 3 minutes. Add white wine and reduce until almost dry, add the heavy cream and lobster meat, and heat through. Add spinach, stirring and cooking just until spinach begins to wilt, about 1 minute. Keep warm until needed.

Poach eggs in a pot of simmering salted water. Split, butter, and season the muffins and toast until nicely browned. To serve, place two muffin halves on each warmed plate and spoon lobster mixture onto them. Top each muffin half with a poached egg. Spoon on Key Lime Hollandaise. Sprinkle eggs with nori. Garnish with roasted tomatoes, watercress, and herbs.

Note: Poached eggs may be made in advance, held in cold water, and then warmed in simmering water when ready to serve.

FOR 4 FRIENDS

FOR THE HOLLANDAISE
(MAKES 1 CUP)

3	egg yolks
1 T	key lime juice
1 T	orange juice
2 tsp	lime zest
¼ tsp	kosher salt
½ tsp	dry mustard powder
½ c.	butter

FOR THE LOBSTER MIXTURE

1 tsp	butter
1	shallot, minced
1	garlic clove, minced
1 c.	cooked lobster meat
2 c.	calalloo or spinach
¼ c.	dry white wine
¼ c.	heavy cream
¼ c.	herbs (tarragon, parsley, chervil, or a mixture)

OTHER ITEMS NEEDED

8	poached eggs
4	English muffins, split
1 sheet	nori (Japanese dried seaweed paper, cut into very thin strips with scissors)

8 pieces Roasted Tomatoes with Garlic and Fresh Herbs (see recipe)

watercress and herbs for garnishing

Chef D's Famous French Bread French Toast Casserole

FOR 6 FRIENDS

1 loaf	French bread, day old is fine, cut into 1" cubes
4	bananas, ripe, roughly chopped
½ c.	raisins
2 tsp	Kitchen D'Orr Sweet Seasons Spice Blend (or Chinese 5-spice powder)
½ c.	brown sugar
1 tsp	vanilla extract
½ c.	dark rum or banana liqueur
1 c.	heavy cream
2 c.	milk
6	eggs
1 pinch	salt
1 pinch	ground pepper
1 c.	slivered almonds

powdered sugar as needed for garnish

syrup or custard sauce as needed

What a way to use up leftover baguettes. This is a great Sunday brunch recipe because normally the French toast always gets cold. Baked in a dish, it stays nice and warm for at least 30 minutes. If you want to make an easy custard sauce for this, simply melt some vanilla ice cream and you have instant crème anglaise, a fancy way of saying custard. A water bath is when you bake a custard-style dish like this placed in a larger pan with water to protect it from direct heat. It helps to keep the dish from curdling.

Combine the milk and eggs and flavor with the sugar, vanilla, rum, salt, and pepper. Fold in the bread, bananas, and raisins. Allow to soak and absorb the custard. Pour into a baking dish and top with slivered almonds, lightly patted into the surface.

Bake in a water bath at 350° until set, approximately 45 minutes, covering with foil if it starts to darken.

Sprinkle with powdered sugar.

Serve warm with syrup or custard sauce.

Island Cornmeal Breakfast Porridge

FOR 4 FRIENDS

4 c.	water
½ tsp	salt
1 c.	fine ground cornmeal
1 T	flour
1 c.	milk
1 tsp	vanilla extract
½ tsp	Kitchen D'Orr Sweet Seasons Spice Blend (or cinnamon)
¼ c.	condensed milk

This is what Caribbean folk hunger for on those cold (70° is a chilly morning!), windy, rainy days of February and March. It reminds me of the breakfast rice my Grampa used to make for me when he was taking care of us. This porridge offers you warm and comforting memories of a simpler time.

Boil water with salt.

Combine dry ingredients, mix, and stir in milk, vanilla, and spices.

Whisk milk and cornmeal mixture into the boiling water and stir to prevent lumps. Reduce heat to a simmer and cook, stirring, for 15 minutes. Add the condensed milk to taste, then return to stove and cook an additional 10–15 minutes or until done. Serve hot.

Saltfish and Yam Cakes

These salty, sweet cakes are great for breakfast with scrambled eggs or at lunch with a lightly dressed salad. I even use them as hors d'oeuvres with spicy chutney or sour cream and caviar or as an accompaniment for a fish main course. Whenever you eat them, remember the hot sauce! As the name states, saltfish is salty, so I leave the salt out until I've cooked a test batch. You can make the batter ahead of time, but place it in a container and drizzle with oil and press down a piece of plastic wrap on top to keep it from oxidizing and discoloring. Keep in the refrigerator until needed (up to 2–3 hours).

Preheat oven to 300°.

Grate yam and quickly mix with remaining ingredients before it discolors.

Form a test cake to taste for seasoning.

Heat oil over high heat. When hot, fry test cake until brown and crispy on both sides.

Taste, adjust seasoning, and add water if too dry.

Form and cook remaining cakes until crispy on both sides. Keep warm in oven until ready to serve.

FOR 4–6 FRIENDS (10–15 CAKES DEPENDING ON SIZE)

1 c.	prepared saltfish, well flaked (see recipe note p. 71)
1½ c.	yam (sweet potato or baking potato can be used as a substitute)
1	egg
½ tsp	cracked black pepper
2 T	flour
olive oil, for sautéing	
assorted chopped herbs and chilies for garnish	
salt to taste if required	

1 lb.	boneless saltfish
¼ c.	olive oil
4	garlic cloves, minced
2	medium white onions, thinly sliced
1 branch	thyme
1	small red pepper, thinly sliced
1	small yellow pepper, thinly sliced
1	small green pepper, thinly sliced
3 stalks	celery, finely chopped
5	medium tomatoes, seeded and chopped
2 cans	prepared ackee
½	Scotch Bonnet pepper, seeded
salt and pepper as needed	

Note: When ackee is prepared, it resembles scrambled eggs with a hint of nuttiness. It's not commonly shipped to other parts of the world, as the fruit must be eaten when it turns ripe. Under-ripe ackee is poisonous. Canned ackee is available in Caribbean markets. If you are unable to find it, use scrambled eggs.

Anieta's Ackee and Saltfish: Jamaica's National Breakfast Dish

Ackee is the fruit of a tree that grows throughout Jamaica. The fresh fruit is wonderful and very unique. It has a hard, flower-like shell that pops open when the fruit is ripe, exposing little fillets of custardy flesh. I would describe it as vegetarian uni or vegan scrambled eggs. Although the fresh fruit is better than canned, most of us will never see it. I was lucky that some Jamaican girls brought fresh ackee to me after they smuggled it into Anguilla. This was Anieta's recipe for her national dish, which is eaten for breakfast or lunch. Anieta was always there with a laugh, a smile, and some great Jamaican recipes for me to try. A bowl of her ackee, some reggae, and a Red Stripe and you'll know that "Ja" is good.

Cut the saltfish into 1" cubes and soak overnight in a pot of cold water in the refrigerator. Rinse and cover with fresh water. Let sit in fresh water for another hour or 2.

Prepare all the vegetables and set aside.

Heat oil in large saucepan and add garlic, onions, thyme, peppers, celery, and tomatoes. Stew until tender and add saltfish. Cook until fish falls into flakes, about 20–25 minutes. A pressure cooker will speed this up if needed.

Remove from heat and add ackee and chilies to taste. Lightly toss, but leave ackee in as large of pieces as possible. Season with salt and pepper (remember that saltfish is already salted, so be careful not to over-season). Serve.

FOR 4 FRIENDS

FOR THE HOLLANDAISE

3	egg yolks
1 T	key lime juice
2 tsp	lime zest
¼ tsp	kosher salt
½ tsp	dry mustard powder
½ c.	butter
½ T	Holland red flame or your favorite chili, sliced as thinly as possible

FOR THE STEAK AND EGGS

1 T	vegetable oil
1 lb.	beef tenderloin (cut into 4 steaks)
1	large onion, peeled and cut into thick rings
4 T	Paradise Kitchen Jerk Spice Blend (see recipe) or your favorite jerk seasoning
1 tsp	cracked black peppercorns
2 T	unsalted butter
8	large eggs
kosher salt as needed	

SUGGESTED ACCOMPANIMENTS

Roasted Tomatoes with Garlic and Fresh Herbs (see recipe)

Paradise Kitchen "Homies" (see recipe, facing page)

watercress or fresh herbs for garnish

crispy bacon

Jerked Steak and Eggs with Lime and Chili Pepper Hollandaise

This is the perfect dish for splurging a bit on the weekends. There is nothing more decadent than having steak before noon! This one will take you "back to the beach" whenever you need that little culinary escapism. If you have a gentle stomach in the morning, leave out the chili from the hollandaise and replace it with diced sweet red pepper.

TO PREPARE HOLLANDAISE

In a food processor or blender, combine egg yolks, lime juice and zest, salt, and mustard. Process 10–15 seconds or until thoroughly combined. In a small saucepan, melt butter until bubbling but not browned. With the food processor running, add hot butter in a thin, steady stream to egg mixture until thickened. Transfer mixture to a small bowl, fold in chilies, cover with plastic wrap, and keep hollandaise warm over simmering water, being careful not to overheat.

TO PREPARE STEAK AND EGGS

Preheat a large cast-iron skillet over medium heat until hot, about 5 minutes. Season the steaks and onions generously with jerk seasoning and cracked pepper. Raise the heat to high and add the oil. Place the steak in the skillet and cook, turning once, until well browned, about 2–3 minutes per side or until cooked to desired doneness. Transfer the steaks to a plate and cover with aluminum foil to keep warm.

While the steaks are resting, cook the eggs. Return the skillet to a medium-low stove. Melt the butter and break the eggs into the skillet. Season the eggs lightly with salt and pepper, and cook until the whites are just set, about 3½ minutes. (If you want the yolks to be cooked through, cover and continue cooking for 1–2 minutes more.) Divide the eggs among 4 warmed plates.

On warm plates, spoon the homefries and grilled tomatoes. Carefully arrange the eggs and steaks on the plates. Top with Lime and Chili Pepper Hollandaise and garnish with watercress or herbs.

Paradise Kitchen "Homies"

FOR 4–6 FRIENDS

These are a wonderful way to start the day. I love to use bacon or sausage drippings if I have them around, but plain old salad oil will work as well. You can substitute shredded Romano or Asiago for the Parmesan. For the potatoes, I use up leftovers whenever I have them on hand. You can add some chopped fresh chilies if you want to spice up your life a bit! Make these for your "homies" and they'll love you for it.

Note: If you don't have leftover potatoes, make them! Cook off a batch the night before and chill them in your fridge. When doing this cook them a little less than you would normally; that way they won't get too mushy in the pan. You can almost make these in your sleep.

Heat oil or bacon grease in a large non-stick skillet over medium heat. Add garlic and rosemary and cook until it just starts to lightly brown. Quickly add onion and bell peppers and cook without coloring until tender, about 2–3 minutes. Stir in potatoes, season with salt and pepper, and cook another 4–6 minutes, stirring occasionally, until the potatoes start to get brown and crispy around the edges and are heated through. Toss in the cheese and herbs, taste and adjust seasoning, and serve at once.

¼ c.	oil of choice (salad, light olive, or bacon or sausage drippings)
3	garlic cloves, finely chopped
2 tsp	fresh rosemary leaves removed from stems but left whole
1	small red bell pepper, coarsely chopped
1	small green bell pepper, coarsely chopped
1	small Spanish onion, coarsely chopped
6–8	red skin potatoes, boiled, or 3–4 baked potatoes cut into ½" chunks, skin on
salt and pepper to taste	
⅓ c.	shredded Parmesan cheese
½ c.	fresh herbs, chopped (I use a mixture of scallions, parsley, and cilantro and add a little mint, tarragon, or any others I have on hand)

½ c.	all-purpose flour
½ c.	whole wheat flour
¼ c.	instant oatmeal
3 T	brown sugar
2 tsp	baking powder
½ tsp	baking soda
2	eggs
1¼ c.	buttermilk
2	bananas (1 very ripe, 1 medium-ripe), diced
1 T	vegetable oil
2 T	butter, melted

additional butter as needed for cooking

| 2 | fresh passion fruits, seeds and pulp |

syrup of your choice

1 lb.	butter (room temperature)
1 c.	mango pulp
2 T	sugar
1 pinch	salt

juice of one lemon

Banana Waffles with Passion Fruit Rum Syrup and Mango Butter

Eating well is the best defense for Mother Nature's bone-chilling gusts. I make these great waffles for overnight guests if they haven't snored and kept me awake all night. They are a great escape from a cold snowy day when eaten in front of a fireplace. These will give you enough energy to face the cold and get to the gym or at least take the dog for a walk!

In blender, combine flours, sugar, and baking powder. Add egg, milk, ripe banana, oil, and butter; process until mixed. Fold in remaining banana.

Heat waffle iron until hot; add butter to lightly grease. Spoon batter evenly into waffle iron and cook until golden brown. Keep on a platter in the oven covered lightly with aluminum foil until all waffles are ready.

Serve with Mango Butter (see recipe below) and your favorite syrup. I like warm maple syrup with a little rum, butter, and fresh passion fruit stirred in.

Mango Butter

Puree mango, lemon juice, sugar, and salt in a blender. Add butter and pulse to combine. With a piping bag, pipe butter in curls on parchment paper and freeze until hard. Remove to container and seal. Store in freezer or refrigerator until needed.

⅓   cooked breadfruit, diced into ¼" cubes (see Breadfruit Salad recipe)

¼ c.   olive oil

½ lb.   button mushrooms

1   small white onion

3   garlic cloves

¼ tsp   freshly cracked black pepper

salt to taste

¼ c.   parsley or green onion, chopped

1T   butter

Breadfruit Homefries with Mushrooms and Garlic

This dish is great any time of the day, but it is an especially great eye-opener on the weekend with some scrambled eggs and sausage. Prepare the breadfruit in advance; it cuts best when chilled. Cook a whole fruit for an hour on an open burner and you will get several meals out of it. You can do just about anything with a breadfruit that you can do with a potato, but the flavor and texture are quite different.

Heat oil on medium heat in a large sauté pan and add the breadfruit.

Cook, stirring for 2–3 minutes.

Mix in mushrooms and onions.

Allow to cook without moving for 2 minutes so the mushrooms and onions begin to caramelize.

Stir and repeat until mushrooms and onions are cooked through and beginning to brown. Add garlic, cracked pepper, and salt and toss.

Cook for an additional minute or 2 and remove from the fire.

Stir in herbs and butter and serve immediately.

Caribbean "Pain Perdu" with West Indian Spiced Caramel Syrup

Pain perdu is French and literally translates to "lost bread," but it is really just French toast to you and me. As Steve Martin says, "It's like those French have a different word for EVERYTHING." The recipe is excellent with all sorts of tropical fruits such as pineapple, banana, or mango. Add a drizzle of syrup and some good yogurt and you've got one decadent and guilty pleasure. Sprinkle with toasted macadamia nuts or almonds and someone will need a spanking!

Cut French bread into 1½" slices. If you have time, place slices on a wire rack and let stand overnight to stale.

In a large bowl, whip together the orange juice, whipping cream, eggs, Sweet Seasons Spice Blend, ginger, and sugar. Whisk until very well blended and frothy. Pour into a 9 × 13" pan. Lay bread on top of egg mixture for 1 minute. Turn and let stand for 5–10 minutes.

In a large heavy skillet, melt half the butter over medium-high heat. Place half the soaked bread into the hot pan and cook until golden brown, about 3–4 minutes. Turn and brown the other side. Remove and set aside. Repeat with the remaining butter and soaked bread slices. Serve hot with sliced fruit, powdered sugar, and the Spiced Caramel Syrup.

Note: The syrup may be made up to 3 days in advance and reheated gently in a water bath. Great on almost any dessert, pudding, or ice cream.

FOR 6–8 FRIENDS

1 loaf	French bread
1 c.	orange juice
½ c.	heavy cream
2	eggs, whisked
½ T	Kitchen D'Orr Sweet Seasons Spice Blend (or Chinese 5-spice powder)
½ tsp	ground ginger
¼ c.	sugar
4–5 T	butter, for cooking
	powdered sugar for dusting
	fresh fruit for garnish
1½ c.	Spiced Caramel Syrup (see recipe below)

FOR THE WEST INDIAN SPICED CARAMEL SYRUP (MAKES 3 CUPS)

3 c.	sugar
1 T	vinegar
1 c.	heavy cream
1	vanilla bean
1 pinch	Kitchen D'Orr New Regime Spice Blend
1 pinch	sea salt
2 T	ginger, minced
1 T	lemon zest
	juice of 2 lemons
1 lb.	butter, room temperature

Caramelize sugar to a dark amber color. Break the caramel with the vinegar. Whisk in heavy cream and blend. Add remaining ingredients except butter and return to a boil. Cook stirring until sugar crystals have all melted. Whisk in the butter. Strain through a fine strainer and keep warm until needed.

SuNRiSe SHAKeS aND SMoO-THiES

Start your day the healthy way! Shakes and smoothies are filling and supply nutrients and lots of energy. As with all my recipes, choose ingredients that are seasonal and fully ripe. Buy local or regional products whenever possible. Picked ripe, they are thus more flavorful and richer in enzymes. I make my mornings easier by preparing the ingredients the evening before and storing them in the fridge. They will be ready in the morning without a lot of cleanup when my eyes and brain are a bit blurry with my dreams from the night before.

Citrus Trio Master Recipe

Citrus trio is one of the bases in many of my smoothie and juice drinks. It is simply equal amounts of orange, lemon, and lime juices. You can make a bottle of this and keep it in the refrigerator to use for all types of vinaigrettes, marinades, and sauces, as well as for the juices on pages 63–65.

Silky Strawberry

A vegan shake of frozen strawberries, silken tofu, and orange juice.

MAKES 1 FRUITY DRINK

½ c.	strawberries (frozen work great)
2 oz.	silken tofu
1 c.	orange juice
1 scoop	ice

Combine ingredients and blend until smooth and silky. Pour into chilled glass. Serve with a straw and garnish with a strawberry and a slice of orange.

Rasta Frappé

It's all about "herb" in this minty island cooler.

MAKES 1 FRUITY DRINK

¼ c.	pineapple chunks
splash of citrus trio	
½ scoop	crushed ice
¼ c.	fresh mint leaves
1 c.	orange juice
¼ c.	pineapple juice

Combine ingredients and blend until smooth and silky. Pour into chilled glasses. Serve with a straw and garnish with pineapple and mint.

Scoopy Dew

A comical concoction of honeydew melon, citrus trio, and scoops of frozen yogurt.

Shaggy says, "Great with scoopy snacks!"

MAKES 1 FRUITY DRINK

2 scoops	yogurt
2 scoops	ice
1½ c.	melon
splash of citrus trio	
1 c.	orange juice

Combine ingredients and blend until smooth and silky. Pour into chilled glass. Serve with a straw and garnish with a skewer of melon balls.

Georgia on My Mind

Peaches & Herb could have come up with this one. Frozen peaches and fresh herb tea blended into a cool, dairy-free, frozen tea. This one's for you, Ray!

MAKES 1 FRUITY DRINK

½ c.	peaches (frozen work great)
splash of citrus trio	
1 c.	West Indian Spice (see recipe in the "Bush Teas" section)
1 scoop	ice

Combine ingredients and blend until smooth and silky. Pour into chilled glass. Serve with a straw and garnish with fresh peaches and herbs.

Reef-Freshing

Hand-picked local sea moss (good for man, good for woman!) blended with low-fat milk, orange juice, frozen yogurt, vanilla, and honey. The Irish and Japanese also use a lot of sea vegetables. They are a great source of vitamins and minerals.

MAKES 1 FRUITY DRINK

2 large scoops	vanilla frozen yogurt
½ c.	orange juice
½ scoop	ice
1 tsp	honey
¼ c.	sea moss, soaked until soft, rinsed well
¼ c.	1 percent milk

Combine ingredients and blend until smooth and silky. Pour into chilled glass. Serve with a straw and garnish with an orange slice.

Sun, Sea, and Soy

Great source of vegetable protein, silken tofu blended with banana, frozen yogurt, and vitamin C–packed citrus juices.

Note: When I have over-ripe bananas in the house I peel them and put them in a Ziploc bag in the freezer. They make great smoothies and shakes.

MAKES 1 SHAKE

1	whole banana
1 c.	orange juice
1½ T	silken tofu
2 scoops	frozen yogurt
honey	
citrus juices	

Combine ingredients and blend until smooth and silky. Pour into chilled glass. Serve with a straw and garnish with a wedge of banana or tie a strip of banana peel around the stem of the glass.

SoUPS and SaLADS to BEAT the HEAT

Lunching in paradise has its challenges. I mean, you have to get up off your beach towel and walk across the burning sand. The sun is beating down and you're hot, but you've still gotta eat, right? Jump in the ocean and then head for the shade of a lobster shack or upscale eatery. Or try one of my noontime classics. If you are going to do the cooking, I say, "If you can't stand the heat, get IN the kitchen." Good, clean, simple foods are perfect midday fodder any time of the year. They allow your palate to relax and appreciate the quality of ingredients you've so carefully selected. Keep it simple, colorful, and sunny, and even if it's snowing outside you'll feel a bit warmer.

For a chef cooking at a Caribbean resort, lunch can be the busiest time. Compared to the more leisurely pace at dinner, the short lunchtime rush can be made hectic by the crush of people eager to get back to the beach or off to another exotic adventure, or simply to get started on the latest "hot read." Even if you're out to grab a simple bite "on the fly," lunch doesn't have to be boring, unhealthy, or without celebration. This is true whether at home or away. The following recipes are cool, many require no cooking, and they are are easy enough to become workweek classics. The Rasta Rap is a perfect example: a quick-to-make and quick-to-eat vegetable wrap with sun-dried tomato pesto, red bean butter, and veggies from the garden.

Salads are another great midday choice, as they offer unlimited opportunity for creativity. I suggest you develop a couple of "house salads" at your home that will accommodate whatever you find at the market. A crispy island slaw (hold the mayo!) is equally good made with green papaya, mango, christophene, or jicama, and it gladly welcomes a topping of grilled fish, chicken, or tofu. A simple mesclun salad picked up at the grocery store becomes yours when you toss in mint leaves, purslane, and small fillets of sweetly acid key lime. For simple entertaining, add to the plate some local goat's cheese, grilled eggplant, or fresh-picked tomatoes. Or make the noontime nosh a real celebration with some grilled Caribbean lobster or Anguillian crayfish. You'll be getting culinary kudos from all of those lucky enough to be around your table.

Caribbean soups are plentiful. Buy a good heavy-duty stainless steel pot and brush up on your soup recipes. Whether you call it potage, bisque, velouté, or just plain old soup, it is "good food" and will keep you feeling great during times of feast or famine.

¼ c.	olive oil
2	Spanish onions
4	shallots
4	garlic cloves
1 T	fresh ginger, minced
4 c.	cooking pumpkin (butternut squash or other hard squash will also work)
1	banana, ripe
1	green apple, peeled, cored, and roughly chopped
1	chili pepper, fresh (use your favorite depending on your tastes; leave whole so you can remove it when it gets to your desired spiciness)
4 c.	water (or light vegetable or chicken stock)
1 T	kosher salt
1 T	Paradise Kitchen Jerk Spice Blend (see recipe) or your favorite dry jerk or chili rub

juice of 1 lime

salt and pepper to taste

West Indian Pumpkin and Banana Bisque

This soup is wonderful using any hard squash like butternut, acorn, or sweet dumpling. Up north we think of pumpkin as a winter thing, but it is used all year long throughout the Caribbean and in Brazil. If you want a simpler soup, leave it rustic and don't puree it. You can make a dish out of it by adding chunks of tofu, chicken, or sausage. As always with chilies, it is a matter of taste. Many folks in the Caribbean like flavorful foods but not spicy ones. To remove some of the heat from a chili, take out the seeds and white membrane. You can always add more but you can't take away once it's in there.

Heat a heavy-bottomed stainless steel pan over medium-high heat. Drizzle in the olive oil and follow with the onions, shallots, garlic, and ginger. Reduce heat, covering the pan, and sweat (cooking until tender but without coloring). Peel the pumpkin or squash and discard the seeds and peels to the compost. Add the pumpkin and the remaining ingredients except the lime and salt and pepper. Return heat to high and bring to a boil, stirring often. Reduce heat to a simmer and cook until squash is tender.

Remove chili pepper (unless you like it spicier) and puree until very smooth in a blender.

Season to taste with the lime, salt, and pepper.

Chilled Curried Carrot Soup with Orange

Chilled soups are loved by vacationers but "belongers" turn their noses up at them. They say that both hot soups and chilies cool you down. You get a little bit of sweat on your brow, add a little island breeze, and BAM, you're chillin'. Good thing this soup is delicious hot or cold! Garnish it with seafood, yogurt, or even crispy fried carrot tops to add a creative twist. This soup freezes well; thaw slowly in the refrigerator; bring to a boil and blend to ensure a nice smooth consistency.

Note: This soup is also a wonderful low-fat sauce for grilled or poached chicken or fish.

FOR 8–10 FRIENDS

1	onion, peeled and roughly chopped
1	fennel, tough outer leaves removed, roughly chopped
4	garlic cloves, roughly chopped
2 oz.	olive oil
8	large carrots, peeled and roughly chopped
1 sprig	thyme
1	bay leaf
1	orange plus zest of half an orange
1 T	curry
½ T	turmeric
2 T	sea salt
3 T	honey
2 qt.	water (or light vegetable or chicken stock)

salt and pepper to taste

1 c.	cream or soy milk (optional)

Place onions, fennel, garlic, and olive oil in large pot and cook for 4 minutes. Add the rest of the ingredients and cook until carrots are soft. Puree in blender until smooth. Pass through fine strainer. Add heavy cream to soup and return to a boil. Season to taste, then chill the soup in an ice bath.

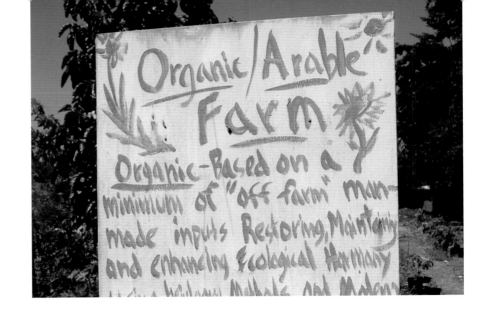

6	cucumbers
2	garlic cloves
1 T	ginger
5	scallions
1 c.	assorted herbs (basil, dill, chives, mint, parsley, etc.)
½ c.	olive oil
½ c.	yogurt

salt and pepper to taste

Don't Let Your Man-Go Hot Sauce (see recipe) to taste

OPTIONAL GARNISHES

½ c.	cucumbers, diced
½ c.	herbs, roughly chopped
½ c.	sweet peppers, diced (assorted colors)
½ c.	scallions, chopped
1 T	green chilies, minced
1 c.	shellfish

Green Gazpacho

Everyone loves my classic Spanish gazpacho, but this is a version using mostly green ingredients, giving it a wonderful herbaceous flavor. You can finish it as you wish with a splash of sherry vinegar, some shellfish, or simply with a spoon of thick yogurt.

Combine the cucumber, garlic, ginger, scallions, herbs, olive oil, and yogurt in a blender and puree until smooth. Season to taste with salt, pepper, and hot sauce. Chill well. Fold in remaining ingredients just before serving and adjust seasoning.

Garnish bowls with cucumbers, yogurt, herbs, and other condiments of your choice.

Serve the gazpacho at the table from a large decorative tureen.

Red Hot Gazpacho with Lobster Meat and Frozen Bloody Mary Ice

My gazpacho is one of the top-requested recipes but I'm sometimes embarrassed by how easy it is to make. Caribbean lobster, frozen Bloody Mary Granité, fresh herbs, and crisp fried tortilla chips dusted with my signature Paradise Kitchen Jerk Spice Blend are wonderful garnishes if you have time, but it is great plain as well. This is a smooth version of this classic soup; if you like it chunky, dice some of the vegetables and fold them in after blending.

Wash all vegetables well and trim away any bruised or brown areas. Puree all ingredients in powerful blender or food processor in batches until smooth. Adjust seasoning and spice as necessary.

Chill soup well and serve with condiments of choice.

Note: If you need to thin soup down, add more tomato juice.

FOR 8–10 FRIENDS

1 qt.	tomato juice
6	medium tomatoes, roughly chopped
½	large Spanish onion
1	bell pepper
1 stalk	celery (white part only, save leaves for garnish)
¼ c.	fresh basil, chopped
¼ c.	cilantro
½ tsp	jalapeños (seeds and veins removed if you are a wuss)
2	garlic cloves
¼ c.	sherry wine vinegar
½ c.	extra-virgin olive oil
1 c.	stale bread, crusts removed, diced in medium-large pieces
1 tsp	cayenne pepper
1 T	kosher salt (or to taste)
black pepper to taste	

OPTIONAL GARNISHES

Bloody Mary Granité (see recipe note p. 87 and recipe p. 105)

diced lobster meat

diced tomato, bell peppers, cucumbers, and herbs

tortilla chips or croutons

FOR 8–10 FRIENDS

1 lb.	yellow or red lentils
¼ c.	extra-virgin olive oil
1 T	garlic
8	plum tomatoes, diced
1	carrot, peeled and diced
1	Spanish onion, peeled and diced
2 T	Kitchen D'Orr New Regime Spice Blend
4 T	curry powder
2 qt.	water (or light vegetable stock)

salt, pepper, and Tabasco to taste

GARNISHES

¼ c.	labne or thick drained yogurt
cilantro	
pita chips (optional)	

Rastafarian West Indian Yellow Lentil Bisque

This is a filling bowl of vegetarian love. You can make it rustic by leaving unblended and unstrained or make a more elegant bisque by whizzing it in a blender for a couple of minutes. Either way it is hearty and delicious. I like to serve this with crispy pita chips or croutons. It is another soup that can replace a sauce when you are serving fish.

Labne is the thick, yogurt-like cheese found in Middle Eastern markets. It can easily be replaced with plain yogurt drained in a coffee filter overnight in the fridge. Save the remaining whey for healthy shakes.

Rinse the lentils in cold water. Sauté the vegetables and spices in olive oil. Add the lentils, cover with water, and bring to a simmer.

When all the vegetables and lentils are cooked and tender, puree the mixture with a stationary or handheld blender and pass through a fine chinoise or strainer.

Adjust thickness with additional water or vegetable stock as needed.

Season to taste with salt, pepper, and hot sauce.

Serve in warm bowls topped with cilantro and bowls of labne and pita chips.

Caribbean Chicken Soup with Pigeon Peas and Coconut Dumplings

Guy Gumbs, the chef at CuisinArt back in the day, created this recipe for the "cold and flu season" when all the northerners came down with colds and got the rest of us sick! It was so good we had to put it on the menu. Like all chicken soup, it is comfort food. Be it Jewish penicillin, Mexican tortilla soup, or Greek lemon and rice soup, it all calls us back to Momma's kitchen. If it doesn't make us well, at least it will make us feel better.

Note: Most good soups and sauces start from good stocks or broths. If you don't have time to make one you can doctor-up some store-bought by simply putting some canned broth in a pot with some leftover roasted chicken bones, fresh herbs, garlic, and vegetable scraps and simmer it for 30 minutes.

In a 2-quart saucepan, heat the olive oil and add the chicken, cook until slightly brown, then add the shallots and garlic.

Cook until garlic becomes lightly brown and has a toasty aroma. Add remaining vegetables and chicken broth and bring to a boil and add the dumplings. Cook until dumplings are done and vegetables are tender.

Adjust seasoning with salt and pepper and remove from heat. Add coconut milk and herbs and taste one last time.

Serve in a big soup terrine, accompanied by hot sauce.

FOR 6–8 FRIENDS

2 T	olive oil
1 lb.	chicken breast, diced
2	medium shallots, minced
2	garlic cloves, minced
1	small carrot, diced
1 stalk	celery, diced
½	sweet potato, diced
¼ lb.	pumpkin, diced
1 can	pigeon peas, drained and rinsed
½	red pepper, diced
½	yellow pepper, diced
1½ qt.	chicken broth
1 recipe	Guy's Coconut Dumplings with Cornmeal (see recipe below)
½ can	coconut milk
1 c.	fresh herbs (one or all: dill, parsley, basil, thyme, tarragon, cilantro, etc.)

accompany with hot sauce on the side

Guy's Coconut Dumplings with Cornmeal

Combine the flour, cornmeal, baking powder, salt, pepper, and butter and mix well to incorporate. Add enough coconut milk to bind into a dough. Roll out and cut into small dumplings. Chill for at least 30 minutes before cooking. Add to soup when required and simmer until done, about 7–10 minutes.

FOR THE DUMPLINGS

2 c.	flour
½ c.	cornmeal
¼ tsp	baking powder
½ tsp	salt
1 pinch	pepper
1 T	butter
1–1½ c.	coconut milk

Island Vegetable Pistou with Spiny Lobster and Herbs

This dish is based on a soup from Provence in the south of France. I've made it Caribbean with the addition of the lobster, chili pepper, and island vegetables. You can use whatever seafood is available or make it vegetarian by leaving out the seafood all together. Find the freshest vegetables and herbs you have around and make it your own by tossing these in. Small bowls of grated Parmesan cheese, crunchy croutons, and pesto put on the table as accents are traditional in France and make the dish interactive for your family and friends. This also allows everyone to truly "season to taste" so you'll only have happy customers around your table.

Note: One of the most important things about this soup is its freshness. Always make this soup at the last minute so all the ingredients retain their individuality and don't become muted by over-cooking.

Place the lobster carcass, bay leaf, garlic, tomato paste, chili, and vegetable stock in a saucepan and bring to a boil. Simmer for 30 minutes and strain. Adjust seasoning. Set aside until needed. May be made to this point several days in advance.

JUST BEFORE SERVING

In a saucepan large enough to hold all the ingredients, heat the olive oil until just below the smoking point.

Add the garlic and stir continuously until it is lightly brown and has a nutty aroma. Quickly add the stock to stop the garlic from over-cooking and becoming bitter. Return to a boil.

Add the callaloo, pasta, beans, vegetables, and basil and return to a boil.

Turn heat off and remove pan from the fire.

Add the remaining herbs and season to taste with salt and pepper.

TO SERVE

Heat lobster in a small amount of the broth. Place in warm soup bowls and ladle the soup on top. Serve quickly with small pots of cheese, pesto, and croutons.

Note to the home cook: If using canned stock, it is good to enhance the flavor by adding fresh vegetables, garlic, herbs, and spices and bring it to a boil. Simmer for 15 minutes and allow to cool slightly before straining.

FOR 8–10 FRIENDS

8 c.	vegetable stock (richly flavored and seasoned, not wimpy)
2	bay leaves
½ head	garlic, roughly chopped
1 T	tomato paste
1	chili pepper (leave whole so you can remove it when it gets to your desired spiciness)
¼ c.	olive oil
3	garlic cloves, minced
4 c.	callaloo, roughly chopped (may replace with regular spinach)
¼ lb.	capellini pasta or other spoon-sized pasta, cooked, rinsed, and tossed in olive oil (optional)
1 c.	rice beans or other small dried beans, cooked tender
1 c.	mixed vegetables, cut to fit on a spoon (fresh pumpkin, leeks, carrots, squash, scallions, etc.)
½ c.	basil leaves, cut chiffonade (thin ribbons)
½ c.	mixed herbs (tarragon, purple basil, chives, parsley, oregano, thyme, etc.)
salt and pepper to taste	
1	large lobster tail, poached and roughly chopped (I do this first and throw the body in my veggie stock)
accompaniments: grated cheese, pesto, croutons	

¼ c.	extra-virgin olive oil
3½ lb.	yellow tomatoes, roughly chopped
½ lb.	Vidalia onions
4 c.	vegetable or light chicken stock
1	yellow pepper, diced
½ c.	dried bread, diced and crusts removed
2 ears	white sweet corn, removed from cob and blanched
2	golden zucchini or yellow squash, diced fine
½ pt.	yellow "pear" tomatoes, cut in half
1 tsp	sea salt
½ tsp	hot sauce
¼ tsp	Kitchen D'Orr Mellow Yellow Spice Blend
1 tsp	lemon zest
2 T	chives, chopped
¼ c.	cilantro, roughly chopped
½ c.	beefsteak tomatoes, diced

Iced Golden Summer Bisque with Organic Herbs

This is another chilled soup that is a "can't be taken off the menu without a revolution in the dining room" kind of dish. I first created it one August with ingredients from the Union Square Market in Manhattan, thus the moniker "summer." In Anguilla, it is a refreshing break from the sun all year long.

Note: Uncooked corncobs may be reserved for your next vegetable stock. Corncobs give stocks a rich, dairy-like flavor that adds depth to all sorts of soups and sauces.

Note: In professional kitchens we use a lot of stocks. Chicken stock, beef stock, veal stock, fish stock, and vegetable stock are all widely used, but the most popular stock, and easiest to make, is affectionately known as "pipe stock": water.

In a large pot, heat the olive oil and toss in the garlic. Allow to lightly brown and quickly add the tomatoes, onions, chicken stock, half of the yellow pepper, and the bread. Bring to a boil and reduce heat to a simmer. Cook until tender, then puree, pass through a strainer, and chill. Thin as needed with a touch of water.

Once cold, add the corn, zucchini, tomatoes, herbs, and seasoning. Adjust seasoning to taste.

Note: Serve with bread crisps, aioli, or pesto.

Black Bean Soup

This potage has become a classic New World soup, and rightly so. Who doesn't love it? It's full of rich comfort without all the bad stuff so often associated with comfort food. Add some of your favorite salsa and chopped fresh avocado, and you've got a crowd pleaser.

Rinse the beans and soak overnight in 4 quarts of water. Drain and set aside.

Heat the olive oil in a large sauce pot. Add the onion, green pepper, chili, and garlic and sweat (cook without browning) over low heat for 10 minutes. Add soaked beans and ham hock and enough water to cover. Stir in tomato paste and seasonings (except for vinegar or sherry). Bring to a boil, cover, and simmer for 2 hours. (If using canned beans, decrease cooking time to 1 hour.)

Let cool slightly. Using a blender, remove half of the cooked beans and puree smooth. Return pureed beans to the pot. Add vinegar or sherry and stir well.

Serve soup with labne (drained yogurt) or sour cream, fresh minced onion, fresh cilantro, and a wedge of lime.

Note: I like to put some good aged dry sherry or a bottle of chili vinegar on the table to let friends and family drizzle it on the soup as they like. Crabmeat, lobster, or chorizo make nice added garnishes if you want to take it to another level.

1 lb.	dried black beans (or 4 c. canned beans, rinsed and drained)
4 T	olive oil
3	onions, chopped
1	green pepper, finely chopped
1	serrano chili
4	garlic cloves, minced
1	ham hock (unless you are using canned beans, in which case use ¼ lb. smoked ham)
2 T	tomato paste
2 tsp	cumin (toasted lightly in a dry pan)
2 tsp	dried oregano
1	bay leaf
1 T	salt
1 tsp	black pepper
1 T	homemade cherry pepper vinegar or some good dry sherry

2 oz.	salt pork or bacon, finely chopped
1 bunch	fresh callaloo or 1 lb. spinach, chopped
8 oz.	coconut milk
5 c.	water, fish stock, or vegetable stock
1	large onion, finely chopped
3	garlic cloves, minced
1	sweet red pepper, minced
8 oz.	okra, chopped
8 oz.	seafood (e.g., spiny lobster or crabmeat)

Callaloo and Crab Stew

Callaloo is the wild spinach used throughout the Caribbean. Although the actual green leafy vegetable may vary in Latin botanical background from place to place, the recipes are often similar. Some places use the young leaves of the taro root (dashin), which must be cooked thoroughly. Others use either New Zealand spinach, or what we would call wild spinach or lamb's-quarters in the Midwest, which needs little more than wilting. Good hearty spinach makes an easy substitute.

Place the salt pork or bacon in a large stew pot and cook until rendered and slightly crisp.

Add the callaloo, coconut milk, and water or stock and bring to a boil.

Reduce heat and simmer until the greens are tender.

Add the red pepper, okra, and seafood.

Simmer for an additional 5 minutes and season with salt and pepper.

Note: Great served with plain white or brown rice and some very thinly sliced kale tossed with olive oil and lime juice.

Anguillian Conch Chowder [a.k.a. Island Viagra]

Put a pot of conch on the fire and you'll soon have friends around. This is one of those dishes that everyone loves. If you want it in a hurry, you can use a pressure cooker and cut down the cooking time. You can add all sorts of stuff to this depending on your taste and what you have on hand. I throw in diced sweet potatoes or parsnips from time to time, or finish it with a float of seasoned savory whipped cream for a cappuccino effect. As the recipe's name suggests, many seafood dishes have a reputation, especially among the menfolk, of having that special power; conch is one of them. If conch isn't available, try sea scallops, abalone, or large chowder clams. Frozen conch often comes in 5-pound boxes, so once it is defrosted plan to make some conch salad, conch fritters, and conch stew as well.

1 lb.	fresh conch, trimmed and tenderized (beaten with the side of a cleaver or the bottom of a sauté pan). Frozen may be used as a substitute but may take longer to cook.
3 T	lime juice, strained
½ c.	tomato sauce
4 strips	bacon, chopped
3 T	oil
1	onion, finely chopped
3 ribs	celery, finely chopped
4	garlic cloves, minced
1	green bell pepper, seeded and finely chopped
1	chili pepper, seeded and finely chopped
4	tomatoes, seeded and chopped
¼ c.	rum
1 lb.	potatoes, peeled and diced
1	bay leaf
1 tsp	dried thyme
1 tsp	hot sauce
	salt and pepper to taste
¼ c.	fresh herbs, chopped (including cilantro) for garnish

Cut the conch into ½-inch pieces and place in a bowl. Add the lime juice and tomato sauce and mix well; set aside to marinate.

Meanwhile, in a large stew pot, cook the bacon until browned. Add the olive oil, onion, celery, garlic, green pepper, and chili. Cook over medium-low heat until very lightly browned. Add the tomatoes and cook for 1 minute. Add conch mixture, bay leaf, thyme, and 4 cups of water, cover with the top of a pressure cooker, and bring to a boil. You'll know it's boiling by the hissing sound. Reduce heat to a simmer and cook for about 1 hour.

Remove from fire and carefully take off the top of the pressure cooker. Add the potatoes, cover, and cook an additional 15–20 minutes until the potatoes are tender. Add the rum and simmer uncovered a final 5 minutes to allow the flavors to marry. Discard bay leaf. Stir in the hot sauce and season with salt and pepper to taste.

To serve, sprinkle with whatever fresh herbs you have but make sure there's some cilantro.

Note: I also love to finish the chowder with some fresh corn kernels or young okra at the last minute so they retain their crunch and color and add a layer of intrigue.

2 T	Annatto Oil (see recipe)
2	garlic cloves, minced
2	Spanish onions, thinly sliced
½ c.	Sofrito de Carlos (see recipe)
6	tomatoes, seeded, diced
8 oz.	favorite tomato sauce
2 lbs.	salt codfish, soaked, cooked, and shredded
1	green bell pepper, thinly sliced
1	chili pepper (use your favorite variety depending on your heat sensibility)
1 branch	fresh thyme
1	bay leaf
salt and pepper to taste	

Salt Codfish Stew

Saltfish or salt cod has long been a part of Caribbean culture. A long-lasting kitchen staple, it was also used for trade. Cod has since been endangered and is often substituted with other fish. In any case, saltfish has a special taste of its own and the distinct flavor can't be replicated. Although many feel the aroma of the uncooked fish is off putting, devotees can't get enough. So soak and rinse it well and add a completely new flavor to your cuisine.

Saltfish should be soaked in plenty of water for at least 12 hours before using. Change water frequently to get the most salt out of the fish.

Heat annatto oil with the garlic and onions in a large skillet and cook until tender, stirring often.

Add the sofrito and tomatoes and cook over medium heat for 10 minutes.

Stir in the tomato sauce. Add remaining ingredients and simmer for 15 minutes.

Season with salt and pepper to taste.

Serve with white rice or steamed potatoes or even over noodles or pasta. I also like to cook this down slowly and use it for a savory filling in pastries and hors d'oeuvres.

Grape and Grain Salad

Combine ingredients and season to taste. If made ahead, add herbs at the last minute. When ready to serve, toss with the vinaigrette. You can even drizzle the plates with Miso/Tahini Dressing (see recipe).

FOR THE VINAIGRETTE

Place ingredients in a clean jelly jar, put on the top, and shake. Store in refrigerator until needed.

Great with all grains and greens; just shake and serve!

½ c. ea.	rye berries, wheat berries, French lentils, and beluga lentils, cooked separately until tender, then rinsed and chilled
3 c.	carrots, thinly julienned
2 c.	assorted seedless grapes (large ones cut in half)
1 c.	Italian parsley, roughly chopped or torn (choose bunches with smaller, more tender leaves)
2 T	lemon zest
¼ c.	tarragon, roughly chopped
1½ c.	Verjus Vinaigrette (see recipe below)

VERJUS VINAIGRETTE

¼ c.	verjus (or your favorite vinegar such as cider or champagne)
2 T	lemon juice
¼ c.	extra-virgin olive oil
¼ tsp	minced garlic
salt and pepper to taste	

My Big Fat Greek Summer Salad

This is a salad of contradictions. Sweet, salty, spicy, and acidic ingredients tumble together to create a real carnival of flavors, colors, and textures. You can cut up all the ingredients ahead of time and dress it at the last minute or serve the vinaigrette on the side and pass it around the table. That way if you have any leftovers they will stay fresh and crunchy. Poached chicken or fish can be added to make this a wonderful main course salad. I love to serve this with an accompanying bowl of arugula. Its peppery bite adds another dimension to this already playful salad.

Note: You can put the ingredients for salad dressing in a glass jar with a lid and shake to combine; keep it in the refrigerator until needed.

Toss together the melon, tomatoes, fruit, feta, and olives. Just before serving, toss in the fresh herbs.

Whisk the vinegar, lime, brown sugar, olive oil, and spices together.

Just before serving, toss the fruit, vinaigrette, and herbs together.

Adjust seasoning.

FOR 4–6 FRIENDS

3 c.	assorted tomatoes, sliced
2 c.	seedless red and yellow watermelon, cut into ½" cubes
3 T	grapes, cut in half
3 T	mango, cut into ¼" cubes
½ c.	feta cheese, cubed
½ c.	kalamata olives
1 c.	snipped herbs (mint, coriander, basil, and chives)

FOR THE VINAIGRETTE

1 T	champagne vinegar or white balsamic vinegar
1	lime, juiced
1 tsp	brown sugar
2½ T	olive oil
½ tsp	Kitchen D'Orr Sweet Seasons Spice Blend (or Chinese 5-spice powder)
½ tsp	Kitchen D'Orr Aux Poivres Spice Blend (or cracked black pepper)

salt to taste

In Search of Greener Pastures

A Year of Caribbean Gardening

Being a farm boy from Indiana, I guess I was kinda born with a green thumb. My Grampa was an avid gardener into his late 80s. I remember him out there beating weeds with his cane when he was no longer able to bend down and pull them up. He took their presence personally.

One of the reasons I left Manhattan for Anguilla was to get back to my roots. Twelve years of nothing but concrete underfoot had me yearning for the "simple life" of my childhood. How quickly we forget that there is nothing simple about the simple life! A garden can teach us so much. It can be rewarding, heartbreaking, and spiritually uplifting. A garden can give us a reason to get up in the morning and then put food in our stomachs at dinnertime. You can't blame people who start talking to their plants! At least if you take good care of them they'll usually reciprocate; that's more than I can say about some people these days. Bitter? Not I!

I'd kept my gardening arm warm while in "The City" by growing rooftop herbs on my ninth-floor terrace in Hell's Kitchen on 42nd Street. I used them at both La Grenouille and Guastavino's and had become well known for them. During my time on the island I hit some agricultural homeruns, struck out more than once, and was even thrown a couple of beanballs, literally. It has been a real learning experience to see what grows well during what season. I've had fun talking with local gardeners, getting new tips and techniques, and trading seeds. I've even become a regular face at the Department of Agriculture and the garden center. But somehow I just couldn't get my beans to grow! Wax beans, pole beans, green peas, and asparagus beans have all rotted in the soil, presenting only a few weak rookies. I did have some luck with a Japanese lefthander called edamame.

One of the most compelling draws of CuisinArt Resort and Spa is its commitment to farming and gardening. You know it the minute you drive through the gates and see those canteen-like coconuts and then pass the huge hydroponic greenhouse where Dr. Howard Resh works his magic. But it goes much deeper than that, with orchards full of key limes, soursops, oranges, grapefruit, avocado, star and sugar apples, and tamarind. There is even a bountiful kitchen herb garden outside the back door. Truly paradise for a chef or guest!

And still there was more. A week after moving to Anguilla, I was introduced to Franklyn "Doc" Brooks, CuisinArt's organic/arable farmer. "Doc" Brooks, as we came to call him, had lovingly curated the outdoor-farming program since the resort's inception, but without much attention from the former culinary team. Most of his production was actually going to the "staff caf." What a shame to be stealing such wonderful culinary experiences from the guests! Franklyn's many charges include black-eyed peas, tender-sweet baby okra, wild calaloo,

purslane (pig's weed), Guinea corn, cow beans, local peppers, island pumpkin, and local cress. He also grows a chili pepper called the mini-wini that "makes a pot of rice sweet if you drop it in whole but is like a date with Lucifer if you chop it up." This is exactly what he does when he uses the same chili in the making of a "natural chase," a homemade natural pesticide that wards off soft-bodied pests with chilies, garlic, dish soap, and vegetable. Imagine a chef overlooking such bounty to import products from Europe and the States instead of cooking out of the backyard garden!

I decided to become allies with this garden guru. Cook local was my goal, and what could be more local than my own backyard? Throughout my first months in the Caribbean, I learned so much from Franklyn. He taught me how to shield tender, newly transplanted seedlings from the hot sun under "little umbrellas" made from sea grape leaves. He showed me how to "bathe" the seeds of over-ripe fruits such as peppers, tomatoes, and eggplant in garlic water to prevent fungus from ruining them. I learned how to properly prepare a pit (advance preparation is one of "Doc's" mantras) to hold moisture, give nutrition, and prevent root problems. Franklyn also taught me about crop rotation (so you don't "kill" your soil), mixed-farming to get the maximum out of a small plot of land, composting to enrich the soil, and about his "natural chases," which keep all the "little insurgents" out of your territory. This was the organic way: NO manufactured pesticides.

The more we worked together, the tighter the bond grew. I got him assistants, enlarging his staff to three, and in turn he tripled the size of the garden. I challenged him by bringing in new seeds, and he taught me about growing beans. I finally had a successful crop! All good farmers love to share their knowledge and every understudy should give back. Guests send Franklyn inspired e-mails, heirloom seeds, and books on organic gardening to thank him for the snippets of time he takes out of the field to walk them through his ward. When he shares his gift, you are filled with

warmth and hope—much like a good bowl of Anguillian peas and rice.

Mr. Brooks uses eggshells, Epsom salts, vinegar, coffee grounds, sulfur, fish bones, seaweed, ashes, discarded plastic cups and water jugs, cooking oil, neem plants, and marigolds to grow wonderful produce without manmade chemicals. I love to hear him talk about stopping at a field on the way home from church to pick up manure "cakes" while his girl sat in the car shaking her head. At the farm he rinsed and soaked them with other ingredients to make his "manure tea." I always tell him I'll go to his house for dinner but not for tea! His methods, both folkloric and scientific, have allowed him to take a sandy old duck yard and turn it into one of the top-producing outdoor farms on the island. He produced over 550 pounds of pumpkins alone last year and plans on topping his score this season.

The Caribbean farmer has so many obstacles to face: pests, poor soil quality, the sun, the wind, the dry season, the wet season, not to mention the plain old hard work of it all. Many people have altogether just given up the traditional way of island life. The freedom of jumping in the car and picking up whatever looks good at the supermarket is too tempting. In my midwestern hometown as well, the bountiful backyard vegetable plot is now only the domain of few folks with the farming "bug" and masochistic Martha wannabes. As my Grampa used to say, "If it's worth doing, it's usually not simple." Luckily, there is a new group of young farmers out there. Through opening my restaurant I've had the opportunity to meet other U.S. farmers who remind me of "Professor" Brooks. Truly "out-standing in their fields!"

Some Gardening Tips

- Make seaweed tea to water plants low in phosphorus and potassium: dry seaweed (fresh or saltwater varieties), rinse well, and soak in water. Also good for watering your compost. These can be made from either fresh or saltwater seaweed. Saltwater seaweeds must be washed well to remove excess salt.

- Use eggshells as deterrents for slugs and snails: break up eggshells and scatter heavily around melons and other produce that the little insurgents may bother.

- If you have poor soil, plant in prepared pits or pots: dig a hole or pick a container and do some pre-planting preparation. If digging a pit in sandy soil, place old newspaper in the bottom to "hold" the water, then top with a combination of soil and composted material. If digging in clay soil, make the bottom of the hole larger than the top to keep water from drowning your plants.

- When transplanting seedlings, use a grape leaf or other sturdy leaf as a shade for the first few days to keep your "young fella" out of the intense direct sunlight. For larger transplants, make a lean-to from an inverted V of cardboard or tin.

- Weed problems: in the midday sun, pour a bit of white vinegar on weeds. It takes them out without harming the beneficial elements in the soil.

- Natural "chase": create your own natural pesticide with chilies, garlic, neem leaves and berries, salad oil, and dish detergent. Spray today and eat tomorrow.

- Crop rotation: plant different items in different places and rotate them. All plants have different needs and will drain the soil of its richness if repetitively planted in the same spot. Some plants rebuild the soil's nitrogen (legumes, for example) and others naturally repel bothersome critters (marigolds), so experiment and have fun.

- Salt of the earth: Try Epsom salts as a natural plant food.

- When saving seeds for future planting, bathe them in garlic water, a natural fungicide.

- Small seeds: mix them with a bit of sand or dry soil before planting. This makes them easier to disperse evenly and prevents clumping of seedlings. Another tip: plant quick-to-germinate radishes with those lazy parsley seeds to indicate the row. Pull the radishes and the parsley will flourish.

- Manure tea: leave this recipe for the garden. Collect dry manure from cow and horse pastures. Rinse well and soak for a couple of days in water. Use tea to feed plants. You may also add other items such as eggshells and coffee grounds for added benefits.

- Plant lemon basil between sulfuric vegetables such as cabbages and broccoli to keep cabbage moths away.

- Encourage ladybugs and praying mantises to visit your plants and have their fill of pesky pests.

- Plant marigolds around the exterior of your garden to keep rodents and other critters away.

- Plant papayas at the eastern and western corners of your garden. Their umbrella-like shape will give your plants shade from the morning and afternoon sun.

- Compost your domestic waste: fruit and vegetable peelings, coffee grounds, eggshells, lawn and tree clippings. Even untreated paper products all make wonderfully rich soil.

  If you don't have a compost, these items may be placed in a black plastic bag and left in the sun until they break down into a dark rich material.

Grilled Tuna Niçoise with Paradise Kitchen Vinaigrette

We served this salad of Caribbean tuna, cherry tomatoes, lettuce, green beans, new potatoes, red onions (from the organic farm), and local hard-boiled eggs. That's about it for the ingredients. It is simple and simply wonderful. A champagne vinegar–based dressing, with overtones of Caribbean and Thai flavors, turns a tired classic into an exotic adventure. The tuna we used was Caribbean and caught by local fishermen who fish during the full moon when tuna come to the surface to feed. When using raw or lightly cooked seafood, you should try to buy the best quality available in your market. Shopping well is the key to cooking well.

In a small bowl, whisk together the vinegar, Thai fish sauce, mustard, chilies, and curry paste. Slowly whisk in olive oil. Mix in the tarragon, cilantro, and shallot and season with salt and pepper to taste.

Marinate tuna for 10–15 minutes in a little of the vinaigrette.

Blanch the green beans and chill in ice water. Dress with 1/8 cup vinaigrette.

Boil the potatoes until tender, about 12 minutes, chill, and dress with 1/4 cup vinaigrette.

Mix the greens and herbs in a bowl and arrange salad on one large serving platter, placing individual salad ingredients over the greens decoratively. This can be done ahead of time and placed in the refrigerator until needed. Remove 10–15 minutes before serving.

Just before you are ready to sit, preheat grill to high heat. Spray the grill with olive oil cooking spray. Grill tuna until cooked to desired doneness. I suggest rare to medium rare, approximately 2–3 minutes on each side depending on thickness and grill temperature. Let tuna rest for 2 minutes. Slice tuna into beautiful red ribbons.

Finish by arranging the tuna attractively over the salad and drizzle with remaining vinaigrette.

FOR 4–6 FRIENDS

PARADISE KITCHEN VINAIGRETTE

2 T	champagne vinegar
½ T	Thai fish sauce
1 tsp	Dijon mustard
¼ tsp	chilies, minced (use your favorite)
1 tsp	green curry paste
¾ c.	extra-virgin olive oil
1 T	fresh tarragon, chopped
2 T	fresh cilantro, chopped
1	small shallot, minced

sea salt and ground pepper to taste

TUNA

16 oz.	fresh tuna steak (sushi quality)

olive oil cooking spray

SALAD

½ lb.	green beans, trimmed, blanched
1½ lb.	small new potatoes
4 c.	assorted greens
1 c.	mixed herbs, such as chervil, parsley, and basil
½ c.	red onion, thinly sliced
½ c.	pitted Niçoise olives
1 c.	cherry tomatoes, halved
1	hard-boiled egg, peeled and quartered

1 T	simple syrup
1 tsp	salt
1	lime, juice and zest
4 oz.	pomelo or grapefruit segments
4 T	fresh water chestnut
1½ T	roasted peanut, chopped
1½ T	toasted grated coconut
1 T	shallots, sliced and deep-fried (canned fried onions will work if you're in a hurry)
1 T	garlic, sliced and deep-fried

Anguill-Asian Pomelo Salad

This recipe is based on a salad that Chef Christopher had when trekking through Thailand. He loved the markets there and came back with a pomelo addiction. Pomelos are a variety of citrus that is reminiscent of grapefruit, but their segments break into tiny, toothsome little packages of juicy sweetness. It is much like under-ripe grapefruit. If you can't find true pomelos, don't turn the page; just try the same ingredients tossed with grapefruit segments. Great as a side dish when served with grilled prawns or poached fish or chicken.

Mix simple syrup with salt and lime juice and zest. Add citrus, water chestnuts, peanuts, and coconut and mix well.

Finish with the fried shallots and garlic and serve.

4 oz.	Caribbean Sugarcane Vinaigrette (see recipe next page)
4 small heads	butter lettuce
½	small cucumber, sliced
12	cherry tomatoes, halved
16	oven-roasted tomato wedges (see Roasted Tomatoes with Garlic and Fresh Herbs recipe)
4 T	radish, shredded
½ c.	edible flowers (such as nasturtiums, marigolds, pansies, or violets)
8	basil leaves (we use a variety of basils such as Italian, Thai, lemon, purple, or cinnamon)

sea salt and freshly cracked pepper as needed

"Doc" Resh's* Butter Lettuce with Oven-Roasted Tomatoes and Four Basils

When I saw the perfect butter lettuce heads and tomatoes that Doc Resh was growing in his greenhouse in Anguilla, I knew I had to create a simple salad that really speaks of the freshness of his farm. The variety of basils make it sing in several languages, but it is wonderful with just one type if that is all you can find in your market. You can also use any other tender herbs you have on hand such as tarragon, cilantro, or Italian parsley.

Note: In restaurants, we put many of our vinaigrettes and cold sauces in plastic squeeze bottles so we can apply the dressing deep into the heads of lettuce or decoratively "paint" our plates. This is also fun to do at home and will allow you to get in touch with your inner Picasso or Jackson Pollock.

On 4 large plates, place a little dressing on the surface of the plates. Place 1 whole butter lettuce head in the middle of each plate. Creatively place all the remaining ingredients on the heads of lettuce, tucking them into the leaves of the lettuce. Spoon over a bit of the vinaigrette just before serving and sprinkle with a touch of sea salt and cracked pepper. Place a bowl of dressing on the table to accompany the salad.

*Dr. Howard Resh is one of the world's leading hydroponic farmers. Since he has several books on the subject, an interesting web site, and a tabletop hydroponic farm for the home kitchen, you can experience a bit of his magic in your own kitchen no matter where you live. If you can't go to the Caribbean to meet him, go to www.howardresh.com.

1 can	hearts of palm
½ lb.	new potatoes, quartered and cooked tender
½ pt.	cherry tomatoes, halved
¼ c.	herbs (your favorite), roughly chopped
2 T	capers, rinsed
½ c.	Caribbean Sugarcane Vinaigrette (see recipe below)
1 head	lettuce (such as bib, radicchio, or oak leaf)
4	eggs, hard-boiled, peeled, and quartered

Hearts of Palm Salad with New Potatoes and Herbs

One usually finds hearts of palm in a can, but if you are lucky enough to find them fresh, they are really something special. In Brazil, I've had fresh hearts of palm roasted over an open fire, and that was truly something unforgettable. For this salad the canned ones are fine, just quickly rinse them off to remove any "tinny" flavor.

Toss the ingredients together and season to taste. Serve over the lettuce leaves and garnish with egg wedges and herb sprigs.

2	onions, finely minced
½	garlic clove, finely minced
1 branch	fresh thyme
1½ c.	olive oil
1 T	Dijon mustard
¼ c.	lime juice
½ c.	sugarcane vinegar

salt, pepper, and hot sauce to taste

Caribbean Sugarcane Vinaigrette

I use this dressing on my hearts of palm, but it is wonderful on bitter greens or even on potato salad. Make a batch and you'll find a hundred ways to use it up and will soon be making more. You can change it up by using coconut vinegar, available in most Asian markets, where you would also find the sugarcane vinegar.

In a small saucepan, slowly cook the garlic, thyme, and onion in ½ cup of the olive oil. The mixture should cook over low heat until onion is tender, but without coloring or caramelizing. Remove from heat and cool. In a medium bowl, mix Dijon mustard, lime juice, and vinegar with the onion mixture and slowly add the olive oil, whisking constantly to emulsify the ingredients. Season to taste with salt, pepper, and hot sauce.

Note: You can also do this in a blender if you want a more emulsified dressing and don't mind cleaning up the equipment.

This sandwich honors the reggae great, Bankie Banx. Bankie is actually a folk singer who gets pigeonholed as a reggae star. You have to check him out at www.bankiebanx.net. He was my neighbor on the island and has visited Bloomington and shared his soul with southern Indiana. Buy at least one of his CDs and cook the recipes in this book while listening to him. They will taste even better.

The grape and grain salad stuffed inside the tortilla is also a great side dish or buffet salad. Super just on its own. Cooking many different grains is time-consuming, but don't let that keep you from making the dish. While preparing other items, I cook grains in large batches and freeze them individually in Ziploc bags. Grains are packed with gut-filling nutrients, and having them on hand will allow you to use them for easy meals in a snap.

Lay the tortillas down and spread bottom ⅓ with hummus and pesto.

Top with grains, eggplant, arugula, and carrot.

Roll tightly (like a Rastaman) and cut into 5–6 pieces and place in a circle on your plate. Make a ring around the wrap with the miso dressing and place pepper strips and olives in the center. Decorate with chives.

Miso/Tahini Dressing and Dipping Sauce

Combine all ingredients in a blender except the water, and blend until emulsified. Thin with water as needed. Season to taste with salt, pepper, hot sauce, and additional lemon juice, if needed.

MAKES ABOUT 2 CUPS

2 T	soy sauce	½ c.	olive oil
¼ c.	tahini paste	warm water as needed to thin	
½ c.	Japanese white miso paste	salt, pepper, and hot sauce to taste	
¼ c.	lemon juice		

Rasta Rap

(a.k.a. The Spa Wrap and Roll)

MAKES 4 WRAPS

FOR WRAPS

4	whole-wheat tortillas
½ c.	hummus
¼ c.	sun-dried tomato pesto
4 c.	Grape and Grain Salad (see recipe)
8 slices	grilled eggplant
8	arugula leaves
1 c.	grated carrot

GARNISH

Miso/Tahini Dressing and Dipping Sauce or your favorite salad dressing

pepper strips (slices of multi-colored peppers tossed in olive oil and lemon)

black olives

garlic chives for decoration

½ c.	rice vinegar
1 T	Thai fish sauce
1	garlic clove, minced
1 T	ginger, minced
1 T	honey
1	lemon, juiced
1	lime, juiced
1 T	sesame oil
2 T	olive oil
½ c.	Japanese seaweed salad (available in gourmet shops and Japanese restaurants)
1	chili pepper, minced (your favorite, depending on how hot you like it)
¼ c.	toasted sesame seeds (white, black, or a combination)
½	pineapple, peeled, cored, and finely diced
1	mango (slightly under-ripe), peeled and diced
1	medium cabbage (you can use red, green, savoy, Chinese, or a combination)

salt and pepper to taste

Athenia's Anguill-Asian Slaw

Athenia was our Jamaican bombshell. A real triple threat: gorgeous smile, great cook, and a wonderful teacher. This is her version of coleslaw that has tons of flavor without all the fat that you usually find in mayonnaise-based slaws. I put this out on all our buffets and served it with grilled fish and meats in our poolside restaurant. I usually dress it just before putting it on the table so the vegetables retain their crispness.

Combine the vinegar, fish sauce, garlic, ginger, honey, citrus, and two oils and whisk together.

Toss the remaining ingredients in the dressing and adjust seasoning to taste.

Baby Shrimp Ernise

Pre-cooked baby shrimp, called "TD shrimp" in the food service industry (meaning tiny deveined), are the easiest thing to prepare. Just thaw and toss in vinaigrettes and sauces and you're good to go. Ernise, our salad lady from Dominca, one of the Caribbean's most fertile isles, loved fresh fruit and vegetables. Both are incorporated into this wonderful lunch or brunch creation.

Mix together the sauce ingredients plus reserved orange zest and season to taste. Refrigerate until needed.

In a large bowl, toss together the shrimp, carrot, endive, and dressing, coating well. Add any additional herbs you may like and combine. Carefully add the citrus segments and gently turn the salad so you don't break them up too much. Season to taste.

FOR 6–8 FRIENDS

FOR THE SAUCE

½ c.	sour cream
½ c.	mayonnaise
1 T	Homemade Chili Vinegar (see recipe)
1	lime, zest and juice
1 tsp	ginger, minced
½	red onion, minced
½	bunch scallions, chopped

FOR THE SALAD

1½ lbs.	baby shrimp
1	carrot, julienned
2	endive, julienned
2	oranges, 1 tsp zest reserved for sauce, cut into segments
1	grapefruit, cut into segments

additional herbs if desired (Ernise used mint, dill, and tarragon)

salt and pepper to taste

Breadfruit Salad

1	small breadfruit
2 oz.	olive oil
2	carrots, cut into ½" dice
1	papaya, peeled and diced
1	red onion, diced
1 tsp	ginger, minced
1 c.	yogurt
¼ c.	mixed herbs (parsley, cilantro, and basil), roughly chopped

salt and pepper to taste

radicchio leaves (optional)

This dish uses one of the Caribbean's most adored ingredients. The breadfruit is known by most folks as the cargo Captain Bligh was carrying when he had that little misunderstanding with the boys on the boat. If you can find it, you will fall in love with it, too. If not, try this recipe with any boiled or roasted root vegetables. I love it with potatoes, parsnips, and carrots. Serve over radicchio leaves for a touch of color and the lovely bitterness they lend the dish.

Note: If you are in a hurry, you can cut the breadfruit into 6–8 wedges and toss it in the olive oil to cut down on the cooking time. Continue the remainder of the recipe as directed.

In a large bowl, rub the breadfruit with olive oil.

Place the breadfruit on a cookie sheet and bake in a pre-heated oven at 400° for 30–45 minutes or until tender when pierced with a knife. Allow it to cool to room temperature.

Remove the skin and center core of the breadfruit and cut into a large (½-inch) dice.

Toss with remaining ingredients and season to taste.

1½ lb.	chicken breast, grilled or poached and cut into small pieces
1 ea.	red, yellow, and green pepper, diced
3	ripe tomatoes, diced
2 ribs	celery, diced
1	small red onion, diced
½	pineapple, peeled, cored, and diced
1 bunch	mint, washed, stems removed, and roughly chopped
3–4	scallions, chopped
½ c.	Curry Vinaigrette (see recipe)

salt and pepper to taste

fresh chilies to taste (optional)

Good Vibration Chicken Salad

The chef who created this recipe is a dreadlocked speedster named Tyron. When he is not at work, he can be found either in his hotrod on the Anguillian roads or out on one of the local competitive sailing ships practicing maneuvers. The guy loves fast things, so as expected, this is a quick and easy salad to make that will get you out of the kitchen and back in the race. Great over lettuce leaves, in a wrap, or on a roll. Make extra for late night refrigerator raids.

Combine all ingredients and season to taste.

FOR THE VINAIGRETTE

½ c.	extra-virgin olive oil
1 T	coarsely cracked black pepper
1	garlic clove, minced
¼ c.	oregano, roughly chopped
1 T	honey
2 T	red wine vinegar
juice of 1 lemon	

FOR THE SALAD

1 lb.	pasta, cooked al dente (bow tie and wagon wheel work well)
1½ c.	feta cheese, diced
1 c.	pitted olives (mixed varieties)
½ c.	capers, rinsed
1 c.	green beans or peas (blanched al dente)
1	red pepper, cored and diced
1	green pepper, cored and diced
1	yellow pepper, cored and diced
1 c.	sun-dried tomatoes, roughly chopped
1 c.	mixed herbs, roughly chopped (basil, dill, tarragon, parsley, etc.)
salt and pepper to taste	

Greek Island Pasta Salad

The Greek islands are one of my other favorite "paradises." I love this dish for outdoor BBQs no matter where you are. You can add grilled chicken or fish to make this a one-dish luncheon. Add the herbs just before serving so they remain fresh and vibrant and keep their verdure. I love fresh oregano and it really gives a Greek flavor, but if you can't find the herb fresh, add a touch of the dried. Dried herbs can pack a punch, so add it little by little until it is just right.

Whisk together the oil, black pepper, garlic, oregano, honey, vinegar, and citrus and season to taste with salt and additional pepper as needed. Set aside.

Combine the remaining ingredients in a large bowl and toss with above vinaigrette. Season to taste.

MAKES 6–8 PORTIONS

FOR THE MARINADE

½ c.	extra-virgin olive oil
2 T	white wine vinegar
2 T	lime juice
2	garlic cloves, minced
1	small onion, minced
1 branch	thyme
½	Jamaican country pepper or Scotch Bonnet chili (or to taste)
1 ea.	red, yellow, and green pepper, julienned

salt and pepper to taste

FOR THE SALAD

1 lb.	bow tie or farfalle pasta (cooked until tender, tossed in a touch of oil to prevent sticking, and chilled)
½ lb.	mussels, cooked and chilled
½ lb.	squid rings, cooked
½ lb.	white fish (such as grouper), cooked and flaked
1	lobster tail, cooked and cut into nice chunks
5–6	scallions, chopped thin
½ c.	assorted herbs

Rosemary's Jamaican Sea Shells and Bow Ties

Nothing can bring a smile to my face quicker than hearing our friend and line cook Rosemary saying, "co co nut wa ta" with her sing-songy, Jamaican flare. Well, if there was something more cheerful, it would be this pasta salad she made for Sunday brunches and lobster BBQs.

Cook all seafood by either sautéing or poaching and refrigerate until needed.

Mix all the ingredients for the marinade and set aside.

Combine marinade with the pasta, seafood, and herbs 15–20 minutes before serving. If you add the seasoning too far in advance, the individual flavorings don't come through as brightly.

Adjust seasoning as desired.

2 lb.	steamed yams, peeled, cut into cubes, and chilled
1 c.	coconut milk
¼ c.	honey
1 T	curry powder
1	red onion, thinly sliced
¼ c.	cilantro, roughly chopped
¼ c.	mint, roughly chopped
¼ c.	scallions, chopped
¼ c.	Spanish sherry vinegar
2	limes, juiced
½ c.	toasted coconut

salt and pepper to taste

West Indian Slam'n Yam Salad

Another great buffet salad with the interesting twist of coconut milk to add the creaminess that mayonnaise usually gives a dish. You can use sweet potatoes or white yams for this. Their sweetness really becomes intensified with this dressing. Any root vegetables will work well.

Cook and reduce coconut milk, honey, and curry powder until the mixture is the consistency of heavy cream.

Cool to room temperature.

Combine remaining ingredients except the vinegar and lime in a large bowl and season with salt and pepper.

Add the coconut milk mixture, lime, and vinegar and toss to combine.

Adjust the seasoning and serve topped with coconut flakes.

ENeRGIZE YOUR AFTeR-NoONS

Anytime Energizing Vegetable Juices

Petal Rogers was my resident island juice master. To assemble our concoctions, we went into the garden and pulled up this and snipped that. We harvested fruits from the Caribbean orchard on the property and went back into the kitchen and got the juicers and blenders rolling. We had some laughs coming up with the names and you'll love to drink them as well. With a juicer they are simple to make. I always tell people to leave their juicer and blender close at hand, on the counter next to the sink. Juicing is like going to the gym—the hardest part of it is getting there. If you set your kitchen up for success, you'll be a winner. Juices and smoothies are a quick way to get lots of nutrients without sitting down for a big breakfast. Once you make them part of your routine, you won't be able to live without them.

Citrus Trio Master Recipe

One of my base ingredients in many of these juices, as with the recipes for smoothies. It is simply a blend of equal parts of freshly squeezed orange, lemon, and lime juices.

Vision Finder

Carrot, beets, celery, and citrus trio. Great for your eyes and Bugs Bunny's favorite!

MAKES 1 LARGE HEALTHY GLASS

2	medium carrots
½	beet
2 stalks	celery
splash of citrus trio	
1	baby carrot with top, washed well

Wash the vegetables well. Scrub any of the root vegetables with a green scrubby. Run carrots, beet, and celery through the juicer and add the citrus trio. Serve on the rocks garnished with a baby carrot sticking out.

Bush Dr. in da House

Our island "cure-all," with wild spinach, celery, ginger, carrot, beets, local bush herbs, and citrus trio.

MAKES 1 LARGE HEALTHY GLASS

1 c.	wild spinach (callaloo) or regular spinach, baby spinach, or other greens
½"	ginger
1	medium carrot
1	cucumber
organic herbs (some saved for garnish)	
splash of citrus trio	

Wash the vegetables well. Scrub any of the root vegetables with a green scrubby. Run through the juicer and add the citrus trio. Serve on the rocks garnished with a sprig of your favorite herb.

Jungle Juice

The island of Anguilla in a glass: pineapple, carrot, citrus trio, and papaya.

MAKES 1 LARGE HEALTHY GLASS

1	carrot
1 c.	fresh pineapple chunks, plus a slice for garnish
1 c.	papaya
¼ c.	citrus trio

Wash the vegetables well. Scrub any of the root vegetables with a green scrubby. Run through the juicer and add the citrus trio. Serve on the rocks garnished with a slice of pineapple.

Feel the Burn

Carrot, ginger, apple, and orange. Ginger's burn is a natural antibiotic. Great for seasickness, it also soothes sore throats.

MAKES 1 LARGE HEALTHY GLASS

½"	ginger
1	medium carrot
1	red apple, with a slice reserved for garnish
½ c.	orange juice
citrus trio to taste

Wash the vegetables well. Scrub any of the root vegetables with a green scrubby. Run through the juicer and add the citrus trio. Serve on the rocks garnished with an apple wedge.

Beet Sangria

No one will "whine" over this one, even folks who love the traditional wine-laced version.

MAKES 1 LARGE HEALTHY GLASS

1	green apple
½ c.	melon
1	ginger slice
¼ c.	grapes
2	medium carrots
½	beet
champagne grapes for garnish (optional)

Wash the vegetables well. Scrub any of the root vegetables with a green scrubby. Run through the juicer. Serve on the rocks garnished with a small bunch of grapes or champagne grapes if available.

Cucumber Cooler

Be cool as a cucumber with this hydroponic, supersonic blend of mint, cucumber, and citrus.

MAKES 1 LARGE HEALTHY GLASS

1	large cucumber
½–¾ c.	pineapple, with a slice reserved for garnish
1 handful	mint, with one sprig reserved for garnish
splash of citrus trio

Wash the vegetables well. Run through the juicer and add the citrus trio. Serve on the rocks garnished with a sprig of mint and a pineapple wedge.

Petal's Welcome Potion

When guests arrive for a weekend at my home, I like to treat them as if they are arriving at a resort. In summer, if they have been traveling, I offer them a refreshing chilled hand towel that I dampen, sprinkle with orange flower water, roll tightly, and place in the refrigerator. I also offer a cool drink. It can be as simple as a cold beer or champagne cocktail or this potion that I created with Petal while in the Caribbean. It can be made 15–20 minutes ahead and kept in the fridge.

MAKES 2 GLASSES

1	cucumber
2 stalks	celery
½	lemon, cut into quarters
1 c.	honeydew melon, with a wedge reserved for garnish
½"	ginger
1 handful	island bush herbs and greens (mint, basil, spinach, etc.)

Put through an extractor juicer starting with the herbs, greens, and ginger to extract as much juice from them as possible. Finish with the more watery vegetables.

Serve well chilled, garnished with a wedge of honeydew and a sprig of bush.

My slogan is "Maintain, don't gain." I created Regime Cuisine to make this possible even when consuming three meals, two snacks, and a zesty vegetable juice. Add a glass of wine or two, and you are still around 1,500 calories a day! Add a sensible amount of exercise and you've got a recipe for weight loss! In my first book, *Daniel Orr, Real Food*, I stressed this way of eating. Now I have to heed my own advice!

A Word about Your Waistline

Lavender Lemonade

Lavender adds a delightfully different dimension to this refreshing summer favorite.

Bring 1 cup of the water to a boil in a medium saucepan. Combine the boiling water and lavender in a medium bowl; cover and steep 30 minutes. Strain the lavender mixture through a fine sieve into a bowl; discard lavender leaves.

Combine 3 cups water and sugar in saucepan. Bring the mixture to a boil, then cook 1 minute or until sugar is dissolved. Combine lavender water, sugar syrup, and lemon juice in a pitcher. Cover and chill. Serve over ice. Garnish lemonade with lavender stems if desired.

FOR 6 FRIENDS

4 c.	water, divided, 1c. and 3c.
¼ c.	fresh lavender leaves, chopped
⅔ c.	sugar
1 c.	fresh lemon juice (about 6 lemons), several slices reserved for garnish
10–15	flowering lavender sprigs, some reserved for garnish
ice cubes as needed	

TaNGO with TaPaS

Tapas are those wonderful pre-dinner snacks that are so famous throughout Spain, they are almost a way of life. After work, one typically stops by a bar for a taste of a sherry and some snacks that are served on small plates that you rest on top of your glass between bites…hence the name tapas. Any red-blooded Spaniard would never eat dinner before 9 or 10 PM; if you've been in a restaurant in Barcelona or Madrid before then, you know the lonely feeling. The tapas bar is the equivalent to the English pub as a social hub for weary workers to rejuvenate themselves before heading home to the family. Whether in Indiana, New York, or on the islands, I love to make a complete meal of these intensely flavored dishes and find it a great way to entertain without the hassle of setting a formal table. My tapas are New World–inspired, with a few tips of the hat to the motherland. If Christopher Columbus had been a chef, this is what he would have been cooking when he returned to Spain. You can also serve them on platters as a buffet with small plates and little decorative appetizer forks set out on the table allowing your guests to serve themselves. Make a few of the recipes that follow and supplement the bounty with some warm Spanish almonds, cheeses, olives, and sliced meats and you'll have a party worthy of Ferdinand and Isabella.

Sweet Pea Guacamole

FOR 6–8 FRIENDS

This is a very versatile favorite of mine. Replace mayo with it on sandwiches and pita pockets, use it as a dip, use it on salads, use it as a sauce! You don't even have to tell your family and friends there's tofu in it! Make a batch and use within 3–4 days.

Puree ingredients together in a food processor or blender until smooth.

Season to taste with salt, pepper, and hot sauce.

1 lb.	sweet green peas (cook until skins are tender, about 2–3 minutes, shock in ice water, and drain well)
1 ea.	chili pepper (your favorite depending on how hot you like it), roughly chopped
1 T	ginger, minced
½ lb.	silken tofu
½ c.	olive oil
	salt, pepper, and hot sauce to taste

FOR THE BREADCRUMB TOPPING

6	garlic cloves, roughly chopped
¼ c.	olive oil
1 tsp	fresh thyme, chopped
1 T	fresh rosemary, chopped
½ c.	parsley leaves, packed
½ c.	assorted herbs (parsley, basil, cilantro, dill, tarragon, etc.)
1 tsp	Kitchen D'Orr New Regime Spice Blend (or ¼ tsp Chinese 5-spice powder)
3 c.	panko (Japanese breadcrumbs)
1 c.	toasted pine nuts, roughly chopped
1 c.	sun-dried tomatoes, roughly chopped

kosher salt and pepper to taste

FOR THE MUSSELS

50	New Zealand green-lipped mussels, cleaned, steamed, and chilled
10	cherry tomatoes, sliced
2 T	garlic, chopped
1 c.	basil leaves, chopped
¼ c.	olive oil

salt and pepper to taste

Stuffed Green-Lipped Mussels with Pine Nuts, Tomatoes, and Garlic

For this dish, you can use any type of mussel as long as they are big and plump. The breadcrumb mixture is a great thing to keep around as well. Store it in the freezer and use it as a crunchy topping on all your casseroles.

Note: These mussels are great the day you make them but can be a time-saver as well. Once you've got them made, keep the stuffed mussels in the freezer in Ziploc bags for quick entertaining.

Combine all ingredients for the topping except breadcrumbs, pine nuts, and tomatoes in the bowl of a food processor and run until smooth.

Add the crumbs to the herb mixture. Pulse to combine and adjust seasoning as necessary. This should be extremely green and very flavorful. Add the pine nuts and tomatoes and mix well to combine. Set aside.

Toss together the cherry tomatoes, garlic, basil, and olive oil.

Top the mussels with the tomato mixture, then pack on the seasoned breadcrumbs.

Bake at 375° as needed until hot and crunchy on top.

Red Bean Butter
with Garlic Pita Crisps

Do you like butter? What kind of question is that? We all love it, but it has a hideous way of ending up on our posteriors. Use this spread on bread and rolls at the lunch and dinner tables and you'll have something rich, satisfying, and, I think, even tastier than plain butter. I also use it in wraps and on sandwiches as a mayonnaise replacement, and even on bagels at breakfast. It is full of fiber as well, making it a no-brainer. Keep the butter for the occasional beurre blanc (I keep mine in the freezer at home to make it less tempting) and use the bean butter as your everyday spread. It's also a great hummus substitute.

Cook the onions and garlic in a little olive oil until tender.

Combine all ingredients in the bowl of a food processor and puree until smooth.

Season to taste with the salt, pepper, and hot sauce.

Reserve in refrigerator until needed; keeps well for 3–5 days.

Note: Also makes a healthy dip or sandwich spread in place of mayonnaise. You can change the flavorings to your liking with your favorite herbs and spices, such as basil or curry.

FOR 10–12 FRIENDS

2 15 oz. cans	red beans, rinsed and drained (or any other type of canned bean will also work)
½ c.	extra-virgin olive oil
1	medium onion, diced
5	garlic cloves, roughly chopped
1 tsp	lemon zest
1 tsp	rosemary, chopped
1 T	Paradise Kitchen Jerk Spice Blend (see recipe) or your favorite jerk seasoning
1 T	Kitchen D'Orr Mellow Yellow Spice Blend (or curry powder)
1 T	Kitchen D'Orr Mediterranean Spice Blend (or *herbes de Provence*)

salt, pepper, and hot sauce to taste

Saltfish Beignets with Sauce Creole

My *chef français*, David (Dah-veed), brought this recipe over the 15-mile waterway from St. Martin. I like the way he used fresh vegetables to lighten this fritter, which in other hands could become leaden. David left us for a nude beach on St. Martin. I'll have to make a note to visit him sometime soon. In Indiana, we can't skinny dip past the first of September!!!!

Note: Salt cod needs to be soaked several hours in frequent changes of cold water to remove the excess salt. This can be done overnight. To prepare the saltfish, cut up some onions and place in a pot with fresh water and bring to a boil. Cook through and flake. You can season the water with herbs, vinegar, and other flavorings depending on how you will be using the saltfish. Be careful when seasoning saltfish dishes because they are already salted.

Note: I like to accompany these fritters with Sauce Creole and a little grated cucumber, green papaya, or mango salad.

Note: Ají Dulce, "island seasoning peppers" or "flavor peppers," are small, thin-fleshed chilies that have the aroma of habanero peppers but don't have the wicked bite. My Brazilian friends call them "smell chilies." If you can get a hold of them, you'll fall in love.

FOR 10–12 FRIENDS AS HORS D'OEUVRES OR 6 AS AN APPETIZER

4 c.	flour	3	garlic cloves, chopped
4 tsp	baking powder	3	island seasoning peppers
2	eggs	1	chili pepper
1½ c.	milk	3 c.	flaked saltfish (see note above)
½ c.	tomatoes, diced		
½ c.	scallions, chopped		salt and pepper to taste
½ c.	sweet peppers, diced		frying oil as needed
½ c.	onion, diced		

Serve piping hot with Sauce Creole (see recipe, right).

Mix together the flour, baking powder, eggs, and milk to form a batter.

Fold in the remaining ingredients and season to taste (remember that the fish itself is salty). Chill until ready to cook.

Heat frying oil to 350–375°. Carefully drop spoon-sized fritter into the oil. Do not make them too big or they will be too dark on the outside and raw on the inside.

Sauce Creole

This is a light, fresh mixture that may be used as a dip for the beignets, left, or as sauce for grilled fish, chicken, or pork. Cooking the Scotch Bonnet chili, one of the hottest on earth, whole gives you its wonderful flavor with surprisingly little heat. If you want it hotter, mash a bit of the pepper up after cooking and add it back to the sauce to taste. Make it as spicy as you like! Serve hot or cold. Keeps for several days in the refrigerator.

MAKES 1½ CUPS

¼ c.	olive oil
1	garlic clove, minced
¼ c.	yellow onion, diced
¼ c.	green bell pepper, diced
¼ c.	red pepper, diced
5	plum tomatoes, ripe, diced
1	Scotch Bonnet or your favorite chili, whole
¼ c.	fresh lime juice
2 tsp	granulated sugar
½ tsp	salt
¼ tsp	ground black pepper

Heat the olive oil over medium heat and add the garlic, onions, peppers, tomato, and Scotch Bonnet chili. Sweat for 8–10 minutes until tender but not colored. Add remaining ingredients; simmer for 15–20 minutes. Cool to room temperature and refrigerate until needed.

Back to Nature from the Gec-Ko

Paradise isn't just for you and me. Nature abounds and shows up in the least expected places. Geckos and lizards not only sun on stones and scurry away on paths and trails but become houseguests hiding between shower curtains and spending evenings watching silently from the rafters. You really need to learn to be a good sharer.

In the garden I've had to deal with fire ants, white flies, aphids, and cabbage-worms as pesky little insurgents, and I've become my own little "Chemical Ali" following Franklyn's natural remedies (see p. 46). I'll share, but enough is enough.

Then there is the nightly ritual of mosquito repelling with spray, lemon basil, or vitamins. Anti-ant warfare is carried out with ground cinnamon. You'll also have to learn to keep many of your dry goods in the freezer. Flour, pasta, biscuits, and cookies become weevil fodder.

New Yorkers know about roaches, but one night early in my Anguillian tenure I was freaked out by the size of the one that showed up in my living room. After catching it in a paper towel I told my horror story to one of the guys at work and he said, "That's just a water bug." Although I've seen them only rarely since, I now just shoo them out the door. They don't travel in packs like the Manhattan variety.

Being from the Indiana outback, I grew up accustomed to the sounds of the night and I loved having them back in my life in Anguilla. Dogs barking, cats mating, roosters crowing, and crickets fiddling throughout the night are welcome evening music that just sings me to sleep. Much more sleep-inducing than the subway that rattled below my 42nd Street apartment or the all-night sirens screaming up 10th Avenue that Manhattan tried to sing me to sleep with.

In Anguilla, birds attacked my papayas and got to the guavas before I did. Although that was aggravating, I also got to watch the white egrets do their long-legged dance in my backyard, and hordes of little finches ate sugar from a bowl on my terrace and sang in the trees while I ate my breakfast. I'll take the tradeoffs any day.

Fruit rats and bats can be pests if you have an orchard going, but if you pick your fruit before it is fully ripe and move it inside, you won't be bothered . . . much.

Once you've accepted that nature was here before you and appreciate that it is we who are definitely getting the better end of the deal, you'll allow yourself to calm down and get with her rhythms. Let go of your control issues and learn to go with the flow. Mother Nature is the one you want to be behind in this eco-friendly Caribbean conga line.

2–3 c.	assorted olives such as cerignola, arbequina, sun-dried black, picholine, sicilian, and kalamata
¼ c.	large cocktail onions
¼ c.	Greek pepperoncini
2 T	balsamic vinegar
¼ c.	olive oil
1 branch	fresh thyme leaves
1 branch	fresh tarragon leaves
1 branch	fresh rosemary, coarsely chopped
4	garlic cloves, crushed with the back of a knife
1 T	fennel seed, toasted and cracked
1 T	crushed black pepper
1 T	chilies, chopped (use your favorite variety)

juice and zest (julienned) of 1 lemon

Marinated Mixed Olives

These are great pre-dinner snacks with cocktails. You can spice them up with your favorite chili or some chili flakes if you want added kick. Great for packing up in a picnic basket or for the beach. Accompany with nice chunks of Parmesan and some crusty baguette slices. They also make a good semi-non-perishable holiday gift, jarred up and tied with a bow.

Drain and rinse all olives, peppers, and onions. Marinate with the remaining ingredients for at least 24 hours and up to 3 days. Store in the refrigerator until needed.

To serve, toss them well to coat and allow to come to room temperature before serving. I also like these warmed slightly.

The Green Professor

My friend "Professor" Franklyn Brooks runs an organic arable farm at the CuisinArt Resort and Spa. He grows okra as one of his core crops and always has several varieties on display. Okra is a member of the hibiscus family and has beautiful yellow flowers, which hide the infant vegetables. If you think of okra as "that slimy stuff of the South," you need to try it again this way. The biggest mistake is over-cooking. In classic gumbos long cooking is needed, but try it in your everyday recipes cooked quickly like a green bean and you'll be happily surprised. It is also wise to add a touch of acid like lemon juice or vinegar to your okra to lessen its slipperiness. Baby okra can even be eaten raw if it is young enough. One of the highlights of my farm tour is when we hand out these little guys. A little-known fact is that these are power-packed protein pods. The okra seeds are said to have more accessible protein even than soy. Choose medium-size okra for this recipe, but if you see the extra small fresh baby okra pods in the market, buy them for adding whole to stir-fries and your other favorite vegetable dishes, or even for raw munching.

Cornmeal and Okra Rellanos with Sauce Creole

FOR 6–8 FRIENDS

4 oz.	Monterey Jack cheese with chilies
1 lb.	fresh okra (nice fat ones about 4" long but still tender)
1 c.	self-rising flour
⅓ c.	self-rising cornmeal
1	large egg
½ c.	buttermilk
½ c.	dark beer
½ tsp	salt
corn oil, for frying	
Sauce Creole (see recipe)	

Okra rellanos, you've got to be kidding me. No, Dorothy, you're not in Guadalajara any more. Anyone with a garden knows what it is like to be inundated with produce when a vegetable comes in to season. I came up with this as a way to use our jumbo okra. Sauce Creole is a lightly spicy sauce from the French Caribbean islands that I like to serve with them, but any salsa would work just as well. If you can't find extra-large okra that are still tender (they shouldn't be full of stringy fibers and should easily snap at the pointed end), you can use the same batter and sauce with Italian banana peppers, squash blossoms, or any other stuffable vegetable.

Cut Monterey Jack cheese into 3 × ¼ × ¼-inch sticks.

Cut a lengthwise slit in each okra pod, being careful not to cut all the way through. Push seeds aside. Stuff pods with cheese sticks and set aside.

Combine flour and cornmeal in a large bowl and make a well in center of mixture.

Stir together egg, buttermilk, and beer; add to dry ingredients, stirring until smooth.

Pour oil to depth of 3 inches in a Dutch oven; heat to 375°. Dip stuffed okra in batter, coating well; fry, a few at a time, in hot oil until golden. Drain on paper towels. Sprinkle with salt and serve immediately with Sauce Creole.

2 c.	plain yogurt, drained to remove excess liquid
1	shallot, minced
2	scallions, sliced thinly
2 tsp	ginger, grated
½ c.	mayonnaise
¼ c.	tamarind concentrate (available in Asian and Latin markets)
2 tsp	Thai fish sauce (available in the Asian aisle of your supermarket)

salt and pepper

Yogurt Dip with Tamarind Ginger

This versatile dip is killer with everything from crudités to fried foods. I especially like it with chicken sate skewers and for dipping chilled shrimp. You can also spoon it over chilled or grilled chicken or fish. Even dress up boring leftovers with it.

Drain yogurt in a cheesecloth in the refrigerator for 4 hours.

Place shallot, scallion, and ginger in a bowl of a food processor and pulse until finely chopped. Add drained yogurt, mayonnaise, tamarind, and fish sauce, and pulse to combine. Season to taste.

1 lb.	yellow lentils
2	Spanish onions
6	garlic cloves
½ c.	olive oil
1 qt.	water
2 T	Don't Let Your Man-Go Hot Sauce (see recipe)
1 tsp	freshly ground black pepper
1 T	kosher salt

OPTIONAL SEASONING

1 tsp	hickory-smoked salt
1 T	Kitchen D'Orr New Regime Spice Blend (or Chinese 5-spice powder)

Yellow Lentil Spread

Throw that French onion dip out the window and try this dip that is full of both flavor and fiber and packs a powerful punch from hot sauce and spices. Yellow or red lentils will fall apart and almost puree themselves, creating a dip-like consistency.

Note: I recently started using a bacon-flavored kosher salt as a seasoning. Can you believe it??? It is great stuff. Give 'er a try.

Pick through and wash lentils and set aside.

Finely mince onions and garlic and sauté until tender in a medium-sized soup pot.

Add lentils and water and bring to a boil. Skim off impurities.

Add desired seasonings and cook until lentils are tender. Reduce heat and cook, stirring often, until it reaches the desired thickness.

Daniel's Spicy Nuts

MAKES 5 POUNDS

1 lb.	pecans
1 lb.	cashews
1 lb.	walnuts
1 lb.	almonds
1 lb.	peanuts
5	egg whites
1 T	cornstarch
2	garlic cloves, minced
5 T	Kitchen D'Orr New Regime Spice Blend
1 T	Kitchen D'Orr Aux Poivres Spice Blend
½ c.	superfine sugar
1 T	cayenne pepper
¼ c.	kosher salt

This recipe is another highly requested one. People always ask if there is some controlled substance sprinkled on them . . . they're so addictive. Well, there are no coco leaves, but I do use some of my signature spice blends! This makes a 5-pound batch, so you'll be covered just in case you wake up jonesing in the middle of the night. They make great gifts around the holidays when put in decorative jars and tied with ribbons or some raffia.

Note: I use a non-stick sheet pan for roasting the nuts. If you don't have one, spray a little non-stick spray on your sheet pan or cook on a sheet of parchment paper.

Mix nuts and bake, stirring often, on a non-stick sheet pan at 425° until lightly browned, about 10 minutes.

While the nuts are roasting, mix the remaining ingredients in a large bowl and whisk well. Pour the hot nuts into the egg mixture and stir well to coat.

Return the coated nuts to the same hot sheet pan, spread in a single layer, and return to the oven. Do not overcrowd the sheet trays, so the nuts will cook evenly.

Bake until golden, stirring often and scraping the bottom of the sheet pan, about 8 minutes at 375°.

Cool and store in airtight containers.

CaRIB-BEAN CoCK-TaiLS

Whether you are poolside in Atlanta or on a rooftop in Manhattan, you can change your latitude with a few Caribbean cocktails. These are some of my favorites. I've included some that you make in large batches for parties, others to bottle for holiday entertaining or to give away as gifts, and still more for shaker drinks and martinis that you can make by the glass. A few contain unusual ingredients, like carrots and ginger, that are popular in the islands but have yet to make their way into home bars. Give them a try for novelty's sake; who knows, you may fall in love them. I like to have a theme drink when I throw a party. It keeps things easy for the host and makes the event more memorable for your guests. You can always have some beer in the fridge and vodka in the freezer for those who don't want to play by the host's rules.

The Bush Garden

This is a play on a mojito using herbs from the garden. In the Caribbean, herbs are called "bush." It may sound a bit strange, but they are addictive. Try it with other herbs for your own unique blend.

Muddle the herbs and sugar in a cocktail shaker.

Add the remaining ingredients and shake.

Strain over ice into a highball and top with soda water.

Garnish with fresh herbs.

MAKES 1 GLASS OF GOODNESS

15	mint leaves
2 sprigs	thyme
2 sprigs	lemon basil
1	lime leaf
2 tsp	raw sugar
2 oz.	vodka
1 oz.	fresh lime juice
1 oz.	simple syrup

The 3 Cs (Caribbean Coconut Cooler)

Fill 4 glasses with ice.

Pour 3 oz. cold coconut water and 2 oz. orange liqueur into each glass.

Squeeze ¼ lime into each glass.

Stir, garnish with lime wedge, serve.

MAKES 4 GLASSES OF GOODNESS

	fresh coconut water from 2 coconuts, chilled (or 1 12 oz. can Goya unsweetened coconut water, chilled)
1 c.	orange-flavored liqueur, such as Curaçao
1	lime, juiced
	lime wedges, for garnish

1 can	Thai coconut milk or homemade (see Got Coconut Milk? recipe, p. 81)
1 can	condensed milk
1 can	evaporated milk
1 can	Coco Lopez
1 T	Kitchen D'Orr Sweet Seasons Spice Blend (or Chinese 5-spice powder)
1	pinch of salt
1 bottle	dark rum
1 c.	coconut rum

OPTIONAL GARNISH

2	vanilla beans, cut in half lengthwise (one for each bottle)

Coconut Martini

I was inspired by a Puerto Rican holiday drink called a coquito when a guest asked me to make a coconut martini. I now make it by the bottleful and keep it in the fridge for all occasions. The Puerto Rican cocktail is richer and thicker and is more closely related to eggnog than to a martini. I leave out the egg yolks, shake it over ice, and pour it into a long-stemmed martini glass. Great to take to Christmas and holiday parties.

Combine coconut, condensed and evaporated milks, Coco Lopez, spices, salt, and rums.

Mix well and pour back into empty rum bottles.

Add one vanilla bean (2 halves) to each bottle for garnish and perfume.

To serve, pour approximately 4 oz. into an ice-filled martini shaker and shake well. Strain into chilled glasses and garnish with freshly grated nutmeg.

Note: If you ever make the homemade coconut milk on page 81, you can rim your glasses with a bit of toasted coconut flour.

It is easy to buy canned coconut milk imported from Thailand or the Caribbean, but for a special treat try making your own. It isn't difficult to do and yields a clear, nutritious coconut water, coconut milk, and cream. You also get a wonderful coconut flour you can use to coat fish and chicken fillets, bake with, use in place of breadcrumbs, or use to thicken stews. Coconut milk will keep for 3–5 days in the refrigerator. You can freeze the coconut flour until needed.

Put cleaned coconut meat in a blender. Pour boiling water over the meat. Carefully blend until smooth and thick. (Use caution when blending hot items as they have a tendency to explode. Blend on slow speed or in small batches.)

Let stand for 10 minutes. Place a colander over a large bowl. Line the colander with cheesecloth or a kitchen towel. Pour liquid through cloth. Once drained, wring any remaining liquid from the coconut. As the liquid settles, the extra-rich coconut cream will rise to the top. It is wonderful to spoon over fresh berries or to use in dessert recipes. Simply stir before using and the water and cream will combine for use as desired.

MAKES 3 CUPS

2	fresh coconuts, opened, meat scooped out, and peeled (keep coconut water for other uses; see note under Coconut Martini recipe)
3 c.	boiling water

MAKES 2 (750 ML EACH)
BOTTLES

1 bottle	red rum
2 c.	freshly squeezed lime juice
2 c.	Spice Syrup (see recipe, right)
1 c.	water
2 T	Angostura bitters

freshly grated nutmeg, sugarcane skewers, and lime wedges to garnish

Island Rum Punch

I learned this recipe from a bartender in Port of Spain, Trinidad. We usually think of rum punch as being that fruity red libation that I find too sweet. The spice syrup and lime in this version make it a more sophisticated cocktail. It packs a punch, so it really lives up to its name. Don't forget the freshly grated nutmeg over the surface of each glass. It really isn't optional. This recipe makes 2 bottles so you can keep it in the refrigerator ready for unexpected guests. It will last 2–3 weeks if you have good self-control.

Combine ingredients, except the garnish, and stir to combine.

Taste and adjust with additional bitters or lime.

Pour into 2 empty rum bottles and store in refrigerator until needed.

To serve, pour into rocks glasses packed well with ice and grate nutmeg over the top. Garnish with fresh sugarcane skewers and lime wedges.

SPICE SYRUP
MAKES 2½ CUPS

2 c.	water
1 c.	sugar
1	lime, cut into slices
2	star anise, crushed
1	cinnamon stick, crushed
2 branches	thyme
5	black peppercorns, crushed lightly
1	fresh bay leaf
2	medium ginger roots, sliced thinly on the bias
2	cardamom pods, lightly crushed

Combine and bring to a boil.

Remove from fire and allow to cool slowly.

Strain out solids and refrigerate until needed.

Note: This syrup can be used to toss with fresh fruits for a great fruit salad or to poach pears, guavas, peaches, or other stone fruit.

Tropical Pineapple Mango Frappé

This rich "shake-like" drink is great when you are entertaining a crowd. You can leave it alcohol-free for the kids and spice it up with your favorite booze for the others. I found it interesting that Anguillian belongers spike this with the anise-flavored French Pernod.

Roughly chop the fruit and combine with all the remaining ingredients.

Bring to a boil and reduce heat to a simmer.

Simmer for 30–45 minutes.

Cool to room temperature, remove spices, and blend.

Strain through a medium strainer and flavor to taste with your favorite sweetener.

Chill until needed.

Serve over ice with rum or Pernod to taste.

MAKES 1 GALLON

2	pineapples, very ripe
2	mangoes, peeled
1 gal.	water
2	cinnamon sticks
4	cloves
2	star anise
3	bay leaves
1 T	fresh ginger, chopped
1 c.	sugar or Splenda (or sweeten to taste with your favorite honey)

ice as needed for serving

rum (or Pernod) to taste

The Big Bamboo

This one is in honor of a funny tune sung late at night in rum bars throughout the Caribbean. If you make it to Anguilla, track down Sproka to play it for you and you'll understand. A little hint for you: ginger is thought to be an aphrodisiac.

MAKES 1 GLASS OF GOODNESS

2 ½ oz.	Ginger and Honey Rum (see recipe)
1 oz.	fresh lime juice
3 oz.	ginger beer (available at Caribbean markets)
1	sugarcane stirrer
1	lime wedge, for garnish

ice as needed for serving

Fill a glass with ice. Add ginger rum and lime juice and top with ginger beer as needed. Serve garnished with cane stir stick and lime.

Passionate Bubbles

Lots of lovers make their foray into married life with a trip to paradise, so I created a few celebratory cocktails to help put them in the mood. This is one of our most popular cork poppers.

MAKES 1 GLASS OF GOODNESS

1	lemon slice
1 oz.	passion fruit nectar
1 oz.	passion fruit rum
3 oz.	chilled champagne

Muddle the lemon, nectar, and rum with ice and strain into a chilled champagne flute. Slowly top with champagne.

Old Time Cuba Libre

Rum-and-Cokes have made rum a huge seller worldwide, but the traditional name "Cuba Libre" is often forgotten. In Hemingway's time, the drink was a little more elegant mixture. Some say it had up to 6 ingredients. Digging through old cocktail books from the forties and fifties, I found this recipe and love the added complexity that the various ingredients give the drink.

MAKES 1 GLASS OF GOODNESS

1½ oz.	light rum
¾ oz.	gin
2 dashes	Angostura bitters
½ oz.	fresh lime juice
5–6 oz.	Coke
1	lime slice for garnish

Fill a highball glass with ice and add the rum, gin, bitters, and lime. Give the glass a swirl. Top with the Coke and garnish with lime.

1	fresh soursop (see note below)
1 c.	water
½ tsp	nutmeg, freshly grated
½ tsp	cinnamon
½ can	condensed milk
	vanilla extract to taste
	ice as needed
	rum to taste (optional)

Pucker and Kiss

Another lover's cocktail popular on an island full of lovers. The name says it all, so get ready.

MAKES 1 GLASS OF GOODNESS

1 oz.	sour apple liqueur
½ oz.	chilled cranberry juice
	splash of fresh lime
4 oz.	chilled champagne
1	green apple slice

Chill the apple liqueur, cranberry juice, and lime in a shaker. Pour into a chilled champagne flute and top with champagne. Garnish with apple slice.

Oh Be Joyful

This is a non-alcoholic punch served at family events and holiday celebrations. I had it first at a little girl's christening and fell in love with it. As I sipped on mine, my friend John came up and offered to spike it up. "A splash of rum never hurt nothin'," he said with a smile.

Note: Soursop is a Caribbean fruit that rarely makes it to the States. It is beloved throughout the islands and is a favorite craving fruit for pregnant women. It looks like a green alligator bag. Leathery with many spike-like points, it doesn't come off as being very hospitable, but peel it, remove the seeds, and puree the flesh and you have a smooth and comforting fruit that you can use in drinks, shakes, and frozen confections. The leaves of the soursop tree are also used in bush tea. Goya makes a canned nectar of soursop but it doesn't have the velvety consistency that the fresh fruit has. If you have a Caribbean market in your town, ask about it.

Blend all the above ingredients until smooth and taste. Adjust as needed. Serve over ice.

Frozen Mojito

This was one of our signature cocktails. Guests always asked me what makes it taste so good. The fresh key lime juice and mint picked each day in our gardens made a big difference, but so did the setting. It also helps to have a really good blender. So grow a garden in the summer and pack it full of good spicy mint.

MAKES 1 GLASS OF GOODNESS

8–10 sprigs	fresh mint
1 oz.	fresh lime juice
½ oz.	simple syrup
2 oz.	light rum
1 dash	Angostura bitters

crushed ice, as needed

mint and lime wedge for garnish

Combine all the ingredients in your blender and whiz until smooth, green, and delicious. Serve in a rocks glass with a mint sprig and a wedge of lime.

Caribbean Passion Fruit Punch

Passion fruit is one of the intoxicating perfumes that make island drinking and cooking so addictive. If you are unable to find fresh passion fruit, you can use the bottled or canned nectar with good success. Passion fruit is used to add an acidic note to vinaigrettes, sauces, and desserts as well, so if you find a good source buy a few extra bottles and enjoy. This may be spiked with booze, shaken, and served as a shot in fresh passion fruit "shells."

MAKES 4–6 GLASSES OF GOODNESS

8–10	passion fruit (depending on size and flavor, or 1 c. of bottled nectar)	3	cloves
		1	bay leaf
1	vanilla bean, cut in half, seeds scraped	¼–½ c.	sugar (or to taste)
		4 c.	water
1	cinnamon stick	rum or vodka to taste	

Combine all ingredients including the vanilla seeds and pods and bring to a boil.

Reduce heat and simmer for 20–30 minutes.

Chill well.

Taste and adjust flavoring. If the mixture is too sweet for your tastes, add some water or lime juice, and if it is not sweet enough, add more sugar.

May be strained if you don't like the vanilla seeds.

Serve over ice. Garnish with citrus fruit and mint if desired.

Also good with a bit of rum or vodka!

Anguillian Roasted Tomato Bloody Mary

This is more time-consuming than those easy-to-make Bloody Marys where all you have to do is open a can. But the time is definitely well spent! Make the complete gallon recipe and freeze it in small containers for future use or simply cut the recipe in half.

Note: I use this recipe to make a wonderful Bloody Mary Granité that I serve with my Pepper and Chili Carpaccio and Red Hot Gazpacho Soup (see recipes). Simply add ¼ cup each of vodka and olive oil to every 2 cups of Bloody Mary mix, combine well, and freeze in a baking dish. Once solid, rake with a fork and . . . Voilà! A wonderful spiced ice.

Toss tomatoes, onions, celery, herbs, and sliced garlic in bowl with enough olive oil to coat the ingredients, and season with salt and pepper.

Roast in oven until golden brown and caramelized around all edges.

Puree the roasted vegetables in a blender with the tomato juice.

Add the lemon zest, lemon juice, horseradish, Worcestershire sauce, and black pepper.

Adjust thickness with additional tomato juice or water as needed.

Check and adjust seasoning with salt, pepper, and hot sauce. Add booze, if desired.

MAKES 1 GALLON BLOODY MARY BASE

12	plum tomatoes, halved
1	medium Spanish onion, thinly sliced
2 stalks	celery, thinly sliced
2 T	garlic, sliced
1 T	rosemary and thyme, chopped
1 T	black pepper
½ c.	prepared horseradish
½ c.	Worcestershire sauce
1 T	hot sauce
1½ cans	tomato juice (48 oz. ea.)
2	lemons, zested and juiced

4	cucumbers, cut into chunks
¼	fresh pineapple
3–4 sprigs	mint
2 T	simple syrup

juice of 2–3 limes (or to taste)

ice as needed

Pineapple and Cucumber Limeade (a.k.a. Agua de Pepino)

I love scuba diving and have made many trips to Mexico and other Caribbean locales. After a strenuous morning of diving, I love to make healthy citrus cocktails. My favorite is this refreshing, traditional south-of-the-border libation. Sounds weird, but trust me, it's totally addictive.

Sometimes my farmers would have a bumper crop of cucumbers and fill our refrigerator with them. When life gives you cucumbers, make Agua de Pepino!

Put cucumbers and mint through the juicer. Add remaining ingredients and blend well.

Serve over ice. Garnish with mint sprigs and a cucumber slice.

Pineapple Wine

MAKES 1 GALLON

There may be no "Caribbean" section in your local wine store, but Caribbeans *are* winemakers. Pineapples, oranges, and ginger fill the role of grapes in the making of their lighthearted holiday libations such as this one. Give it a try. My friend Lindsey and I made this and boy, was it an interesting process.

Chop pineapple and ginger in a food processor until smooth.

Add pineapple mixture to a large pot with water, dates, sugar, cinnamon, and black peppercorns.

Place over high heat. When it reaches a boil, lower temperature and simmer for 10 minutes.

Remove from heat and cool.

Transfer to a large non-reactive container.

Add yeast and mace. Cover loosely and let stand at room temperature.

After 2 weeks, strain through a cheesecloth.

Return to storage vessel for another 2 weeks.

Re-strain into bottles and store in refrigerator.

Note: Metal-clasped French lemonade bottles make excellent storage vessels for this wine.

2	pineapples, peeled
1 T	ginger, peeled and roughly chopped
8 c.	water
1	cinnamon stick
10	black peppercorns
½ lb.	dried dates
2 lbs.	sugar
1 tsp	active dry yeast
½ tsp	ground mace

1 lb.   fresh ginger, peeled
2   limes, zest and juice
12   black peppercorns
1 T   cream of tartar
2½ c.   boiling water
3 c.   sugar
2 tsp   active dry yeast
¼ c.   white rum (optional)

Ginger Beer

Sometimes we all get into a gastronomic rut. The same things to eat and drink, day in and day out! Mix it up a bit! Not just drinking but *making* drinks can be a social event. Have the neighbors over for a Dark and Stormy made with this homemade Ginger Beer. Life is short, drink it up!!! This is a bit of a chemistry project like the previously mentioned Pineapple Wine, so if you are up for it, give it a try.

In a food processor, roughly chop ginger.

Remove to a large non-reactive jar or bowl.

Add lime zest, lime juice, peppercorns, and cream of tartar.

Bring 2 quarts of water to a boil. Pour over top and allow to sit overnight.

Strain ginger mixture through cheesecloth or a well-rinsed kitchen towel.

Make a simple syrup by heating remaining cup of water with sugar until it dissolves.

Add syrup to ginger mixture.

Stir in the yeast and let stand 10 minutes.

Add rum.

Pour into bottles with tight seals and let stand at room temperature.

When carbonation is evident, serve over ice.

Note: *French lemonade bottles with clasp closures work well for this, too. Fill a few and it makes an attractive gift.*

1 oz.   pomegranate juice
1 oz.   mango nectar
½ oz.   key lime juice
2 oz.   white rum (Clément works well)
1 oz.   club soda
orange wheel as garnish

Da Pom Pom

"Pom pom" is another name for a beautiful derrière, and a Caribbean man never misses a chance to stop and show his respect with a smile and a whistle. This one's for all the ladies. Lavon, our resident mixologist, made this one up, and he was a true connoisseur.

Shake over rocks and pour in a chilled martini glass. Garnish with orange wheel.

Ginger Rat

Lavon, our mixologist extraordinaire, brought me this non-alcoholic drink he created for the "Taste of the Caribbean" culinary competition. "Chef, it tastes great, but what do we call it?" he wondered. The banana gave it a rich, almost mousse-like consistency, so I came up with a funny little banana mouse with clove eyes and a banana skin tail hanging out of the glass and told him to call it a "Banana Mouse." Lavon turned to me and said, "It looks more like a ginger rat to me." His name stuck.

In a martini shaker, combine the ingredients and shake over ice. Strain into a hurricane glass.

Make your ginger rat (see photo above, left) by placing the 2 cloves as eyes at the end of the banana. Cut a little mouth just below and place 2 rounds of thinly sliced ginger behind the eyes as the ears. Cut a slit on the opposite end and slide onto the glass. Take a strip of banana peel and make a rattail to stick out the other end of the glass. What fun!!!

MAKES 1 GLASS OF NON-ALCOHOLIC GOODNESS

2 oz.	fresh-squeezed ginger juice
3 oz.	banana, freshly pureed
2 oz.	pineapple juice
2 oz.	fresh-squeezed orange juice
½ oz.	lime juice
½ oz.	simple syrup

garnish with sliced ginger rounds, ½ banana, 2 cloves, 1 strip of banana peel

Rainy Days
A Good Thing

Living in the sun-drenched islands, one longs for that rainy day to cool off the sand and give ya a break from the monotony of beauty. Watching a storm roll in, making the other islands in the distance disappear like a David Copperfield trick, is one of the joys of the Caribbean lifestyle. Rainy days are a good time to do your chores and have friends over to make ginger beer or pineapple wine. The garden looks better and the animals are happy. Rainy days, as long as they aren't accompanied by hurricanes, are a good thing.

Be Irie Cocktail

To "be irie" means to be contented. Stop and enjoy yourself. Don't stress. "Everythin' irie mon?" is both the question and the answer. This is a perfect drink to take you to that "special place" any time life seems overwhelming.

MAKES 1 GLASS OF GOODNESS

3 oz.	coconut water (fresh is best, but Goya makes a good unsweetened canned product)
1 oz.	key lime juice
1 oz.	coconut rum
1 oz.	white rum (Clément works well)
2 oz.	ginger ale
1	lime wedge
1	sugarcane stir stick

Combine, shake on the rocks, and serve in a tall tumbler with a lime wedge and a sugarcane stir stick.

Athenia's Jamaican Carrot Juice

This rich Jamaican drink is almost like a milkshake. The pureed carrot gives it a richness that makes it seem more fattening than it is. In Jamaica, Guinness is added to this drink, which is said to make it an aphrodisiac. I haven't needed to try that . . . yet.

MAKES 6 GLASSFULS OF GOODNESS

1 lb.	carrots, peeled, chopped, cooked until very soft and cool (save water for blending)
1 can	condensed milk
1 shot	amaretto
1 pinch	nutmeg
1 pinch	cinnamon

In a blender, combine all ingredients and puree until smooth.

Pour over ice and enjoy.

Salt Pond

Most Caribbean islands have murky, greenish-blue salt ponds on them, and Anguilla is famous for hers. They were a major revenue source for the island for most of the last century. Now with most salt coming from mines, there is little left of this old way of life. It was hard, nasty work harvesting salt. After a day of it anyone would need a drink!

MAKES 1 GLASS OF GOODNESS

1 oz.	blue Curaçao
2 oz.	orange vodka
1½ oz.	Carib vodka
1 oz.	peach puree
3 oz.	orange juice
½ oz.	lime juice

GARNISH

Rim glass with salt

2 slices of lemon floating in glass

Fill a shaker with ice. Add ingredients and shake. Pour into chilled, salt-rimmed martini glass and garnish with lemon slices floating on top like lily pads.

John's St. Kitts Cooler

Big John was a lifesaver for Christopher and me. You'll never meet a harder-working or more giving person. John loved to demonstrate his island heritage during his quick classes held poolside every afternoon at the resort. This is one of the drinks our guests were lucky enough to learn. If you like ginger ale you'll love this. You can also use the ginger syrup in the kitchen over fresh fruit salad. A shot of rum is never a bad thing, but I'll leave that up to you.

FOR 6–8 FRIENDS

FOR THE GINGER BASE SYRUP

½ lb.	fresh ginger, peeled and thinly chopped	2	bay or allspice leaves
½ c.	sugar	1 tsp	almond extract
1 c.	water		club soda as needed
3	cloves		lime wedges and mint sprigs for garnish
1	star anise		rum (optional)

Combine all the ingredients except the almond extract in a heavy-bottomed stainless steel saucepan and bring to a boil.

Simmer for 20–30 minutes on low heat.

Set aside and allow to cool.

Strain syrup, reserving some nice pieces of ginger for garnish.

Fill iced glasses a quarter full with the syrup and a slice of the reserved ginger.

Top with chilled soda water and garnish with candied ginger, a lime wedge, and a sprig of mint.

Alligator Daiquiri

Everyone is afraid to try an avocado cocktail, so I call it by its other name, the alligator pear. Maybe it is even more frightening? Anyway, it's become a real favorite. Most Americans think of avocados in guacamole, but try it sweet sometime. In Brazil and other South American countries, the avocado is almost always eaten with sweetener, so don't be scared to try it. It won't bite you.

MAKES 2 GLASSES OF GOODNESS

4 oz.	Brazilian cachaca or other light rum
2 oz.	simple syrup
1 oz.	lime juice
¼	avocado, ripe
1 T	half and half
1 c.	crushed ice
2	lime slices

Put ingredients in a blender and whiz until smooth. Pour in hurricane glasses and garnish with a slice of lime.

HoME-MaDE FLaVORED RUmS

I love making flavored rums. In many of St. Martin's restaurants, a waiter will bring you a bottle with a few glasses at the end of your meal and let you pour what you like. These hospitable spirits, dressed with the flavors of local fruits and spices, warm you and leave you with a wonderful taste in your mouth, even when you get the bill. I make them with all types of ingredients, from ginger and black peppercorns to an incredible combination of kumquat and star anise. Don't stop at drinking them; try cooking with them. Splash some ginger rum in a sauté pan with some shrimp and lemongrass, try rum on a chicken breast, or sprinkle pineapple rum over a warm vanilla cake and you've hit culinary gold. Putting flavored rums together is a great Saturday afternoon project and will make memorable gifts around the holidays. You don't need to use expensive rums for these. In fact, I use one that is only one step above gasoline! No, it's really a wholesome preservative. But there is no reason to use a high-quality product that a rum master has spent years and passion creating, only to overpower it with sugar and strong aromatic flavors. These embellished rums will store for a couple of months in a cool dark place. Tied with raffia or a decorative ribbon, these bottles make wonderful holiday gifts.

Note: Gather liquor bottles as you empty them or go to a kitchen store and purchase some decorative bottles to have around. My recipes are for 4 bottles each, so you need a few empties to pour the stuff in. Any of the following recipes may be cut in half or quartered.

Pineapple and Vanilla Rum

MAKES 4 BOTTLES

2	pineapples, cut into 1½" pieces
1	vanilla bean, cut in half lengthwise
5	peppercorns
2 c.	water
4½ c.	sugar
2 liters	white rum
1 liter	dark rum

In a large pot, mix the pineapple, vanilla, pepper, water, and sugar together. Bring to a boil on medium-high heat until sugar syrup is thick. Remove from the heat. When the pineapple syrup is cool, add the rum. Soak and scrape labels off the bottles and dry well. Stir well to incorporate the syrup and the rum. Place pieces of the fruit and spices in each bottle and top with the flavored rum. Screw cap back on and store until needed.

Kumquat and Star Anise Rum

MAKES 4 BOTTLES

2 c.	water
4½ c.	sugar
1 qt.	kumquats, cleaned and pricked well with a fork
1	vanilla bean, cut in half and seeds scraped out
5	star anise pods
2 bottles	white rum
½ bottle	dark rum

This rum is wonderful around the holidays. Makes a great handmade gift when placed in a decanter or interesting bottle.

Combine the water, sugar, kumquats, and vanilla and simmer until the mixture makes a nice syrup (reduce by about half).

Add the star anise and mix well. Cool to room temperature.

Soak and scrape labels off the bottles and dry well. Stir well to incorporate the syrup and the rum. Place pieces of the fruit and spices in each bottle and top with the flavored rum. Screw cap back on and store until needed.

Makes a great after-dinner drink and is wonderful with cigars.

Rum Runner

Rum runs through the veins of the Caribbean like chlorophyll through a plant, giving color and vitality. After the image of the beaches with their seven shades of blue, the second image, for me at least, is of a tall, cool rum drink and the shade of a palm tree. What would Carnival be without rum? Just another party.

Over the past 40 or 50 years, rum has developed a reputation for being common. Rum-and-Coke and other sweet drinks have made it the #1-selling alcohol, but in the minds of food snobs it has ranked significantly lower. Artisanal rum makers have been working to bring rum back to the forefront of sophisticated palates over the last 10–15 years with carefully crafted spirits.

Rum can taste extremely different from island to island and from maker to maker, just like a cognac or Armagnac. The difference has a lot to do with the method used to extract the sugar. The French islanders first make a clear *"vin"* from the fresh juice they squeeze from the cane. The *vin* is then distilled and aged in a manner much like a French brandy. This method makes the rum a clearer vehicle for the flavors of the cask to ride on. There is no molasses to muddle the intricate and subtle caramels and vanillas that come from the burnt oak barrels, which are French, of course. The English and Spanish islanders tend to make their rum from molasses, a sugar production by-product. Molasses was a conundrum to the early Europeans until they figured how to turn it into "kill devil." These rums are more straightforward and sweet, with a nice, round finish.

Then there is the question of white versus dark rum. I like to think of white rum as the more masculine drink. It is sharp and aggressive and can be a bit hard to take. It often needs something sweet or fruity to tame it. Dark rum, on the other hand, is more feminine. It takes the extra time in the changing room (oak barrel) and comes out perfumed with vanilla and caramel. Rounder and more voluptuous, it's worthy of a beautifully shaped snifter and after-dinner conversation. With white rum, it's straight to the bedroom.

I spent a couple of afternoons with some of our mixologists putting together the rum list for the Tapas Lounge and Rum Bar. I found it fascinating how different the flavors could be. We tasted rums from producers from Guyana, Brazil, Trinidad, Puerto Rico, Cuba, Honduras, Martinique, Guadalupe, and, of course, St. Martin and Anguilla. Like many others, I had a lack of appreciation for the drink that I have now turned into a passion. Next time you're in your favorite bar, restaurant, or liquor store, rummage through the rum section and you might find a new friend.

Banana Black Peppercorn Rum

MAKES 4 BOTTLES

2	vanilla beans, split in half
5	coarsely cracked black peppercorns
2 c.	water
4½ c.	sugar
4	bananas, peeled and cut lengthwise into 4 pieces ea. so they fit in the neck of the bottle
2 liters	white rum
1 liter	dark rum

Scrape the vanilla bean to release the seeds.

In a large pot, mix the vanilla bean pods, seeds, peppercorns, water, and sugar together. Bring to a boil on medium-high heat until sugar syrup is thick.

Add the banana and remove from the heat.

When the banana syrup is cool, add the rum.

Soak and scrape labels off the bottles and dry well. Stir well to incorporate the syrup and the rum. Place pieces of the fruit and spices in each bottle and top with the flavored rum. Screw cap back on and store until needed.

Ginger and Honey Rum

MAKES 4 BOTTLES

1 lb.	ginger, sliced
2 c.	water
3½ c.	sugar
1 c.	honey
2 strips	lemon peel
5	black peppercorns
2 liters	white rum
1 liter	dark rum

In a large pot, mix the ginger, water, sugar, lemon peel, and peppercorns together.

Bring to a boil on medium-high heat until sugar syrup is thick.

Remove from the heat and add honey.

When the ginger syrup is cool, add the rum.

Soak and scrape labels off the bottles and dry well. Stir well to incorporate the syrup and the rum. Place pieces of the fruit and spices in each bottle and top with the flavored rum. Screw cap back on and store until needed.

Cooking with rum is also fun. Nothing says "party" like a flaming dessert! But rum has a deeper place in the Caribbean kitchen. It cures and keeps fruits; adds depth to soups, sauces, and stews; marinates raw fish; and flavors all sorts of mousses, cakes, and creams. I even like to store my chopped ginger in a jar of dark rum and use both the root and liquid in all kinds of dishes.

Orange Spice Rum

In a large pot, mix the orange zest, orange juice, cinnamon sticks, peppercorns, water, and sugar together. Bring to a boil on medium-high heat until sugar syrup is thick.

Remove from the heat.

When the orange syrup is cool, add the rum.

Soak and scrape labels off the bottles and dry well. Stir well to incorporate the syrup and the rum. Place pieces of the fruit and spices in each bottle and top with the flavored rum. Screw cap back on and store until needed.

2	oranges, juiced and zested with a vegetable peeler
6	cinnamon sticks
10	black peppercorns
2	cardamom pods, lightly crushed
2 c.	water
4½ c.	sugar
2 liters	white rum
1 liter	dark rum

Lemongrass Rum

In a large pot, mix lemongrass, lemon peel, water, and sugar together.

Bring to a boil on medium-high heat until sugar syrup is thick.

Remove from the heat.

When the syrup is cool, add the rum.

Soak and scrape labels off the bottles and dry well. Stir well to incorporate the syrup and the rum. Place pieces of the lemongrass in each bottle and top with the flavored rum. Screw cap back on and store until needed.

1 lb.	lemongrass, half cut thinly on the bias, the other cut in half into batons
5 strips	lemon peel (cut with a vegetable peeler)
2 c.	water
4½ c.	sugar
2 liters	white rum
1 liter	dark rum

iSLaND STaRTeRS

Appetizers can be the best part of a meal. Restaurant chefs often feel compelled to restrict their main course selections to mundane meat and seafood entrees. Think beef, chicken, and tuna. Appetizers are where their creativity can really shine with bites that challenge guests' taste buds. Diners are willing to take a chance with a starter. They want to be sure that the main dish is something that they are really going to like and are less likely to experiment.

On the island we created great dishes from a completely new palette of ingredients. To name just a few, we discovered mini-wini chilies, christophene, island pumpkin, hearts of palm, cane sugar, green bananas, bread nuts, green coconut, assorted roots and beans, breadfruit, and many varieties of local seafood. Christopher and I became culinary Van Goghs, with chef's knives instead of paintbrushes and rum instead of absinthe. Luckily, we still have all four ears between the two of us.

I love to make a meal of starters for just this reason. You get to taste so much more of the chef's creativity and often the dishes are more interesting and daring. Appetizers usually include fun salads, interesting sauces, and intriguing accompaniments without the standard "two veg and a starch" pattern that main course dishes often fall into. This also makes a combination of a couple (or three) starters a healthier choice if you are concerned about calorie intake. Ceviches, grilled jerked quail skewers, salads, and soups are all great ways to get started . . . but not a bad way to finish a meal, either. I'm not huge on sweets, so send me over some jerked chicken heart skewers, please.

Put on some calypso, reggae, merengue, or good French Caribbean jazz, sip a rum punch, and get into a creative spirit. Bang some pots and pans together and get started on some culinary adventures by trying some of these tasty recipes for "small plates." It is a great way for modern man to de-stress and get happy.

Anguillian Jerked Quail

Most folks don't think of wild game when they think of the Caribbean, but there are lots of things to hunt and gather down there. Game birds are plentiful on some islands, not to mention iguana, wild boar, and others. True "jerk" is slow-cooked on a bed of allspice leaves until it melts off the bone. This is a modern version that uses the jerk rub as a marinade. Use it on any meat or even tofu! Nice served with the Athenia's Anguill-Asian Slaw on page 54.

Rinse quail and pat dry with paper towel. Cut in half. Combine remaining ingredients and mix well. Taste the marinade and adjust to taste.

Marinate quail for at least 15 minutes, or overnight in the refrigerator.

Place 2 half quail on each brochette or skewer so the skin is on the same side. Grill skin side down until the skin becomes nice and crisp and most of the fat cooks out, about 4–6 minutes. Be careful not to burn; move away from coals if birds start getting too dark.

Turn quails to flesh side and quickly sear. Do not over-cook or they will become dry. I like them cooked about medium rare.

While the quail are grilling, bring the leftover marinade to a boil. Cook for several minutes. Remove to a warm serving dish, brush quail with the warmed marinade, and squeeze a little fresh lime over them.

FOR 4 FRIENDS

4	boneless quail
1½ T	Jerk Rub—Wet Style (see recipe)
1 T	freshly cracked black pepper
3 branches	thyme, roughly chopped
2	garlic cloves, minced
½ T	ginger, minced
2	key limes, sliced into thin rounds
2	allspice berries, crushed
¼ c.	olive oil

additional chilies if desired

salt and pepper to taste

Pepper and Chili Carpaccio with Wild Herbs and Bloody Mary Granité

Carpaccio, the much-loved dish, is named after an Italian artist who smattered his canvases with layers of red paint. The owner of Harry's Bar in Venice created the first edible Carpaccio in the artist's honor. Beef is classically used in this dish, but creative chefs soon started using other red meats and tuna. Nowadays, anything that is served sliced thin and served raw, red or not, is a "Carpaccio." I wonder what the artist would think about becoming more famous for a recipe he never ate than for his work with a brush.

Note: Partially freezing the tenderloin after searing makes slicing easier.

Note: A word on spices: When cooking with whole spices such as fennel, coriander, and cumin, it is best to lightly toast them before using. This releases a pungent and more exotic flavor. To do this, put them in a sauté pan and cook over medium heat, stirring often until you smell the toasty aroma. Quickly pour them out of the pan or they will burn. They can then be ground with a mortar and pestle or put in a Ziploc bag and coarsely crushed with a rolling pin or coffee mug.

FOR GRANITÉ

Combine the Anguillian Roasted Tomato Bloody Mary mix with the vodka and olive oil and pour into a Pyrex baking dish. Freeze until solid and scrape with a fork to make the granité.

FOR CARPACCIO

Combine first 5 ingredients in a coffee grinder and pulse until coarsely ground.

Rub 1 tablespoon oil over beef, then coat beef with spice mixture. Let stand 1 hour at room temperature.

Heat 3 tablespoons oil in heavy large skillet over high heat. Add beef and sear on all sides, turning every 2 minutes, about 12 minutes total (beef will be darkly seared on the outside and rare in center).

Chill quickly uncovered in the refrigerator for 1 hour, then wrap in plastic until ready to serve. One hour before slicing put meat in the freezer to firm it up and make it easier to cut. Slice meat as thinly as possible. Place it between layers of plastic wrap and pound until paper-thin. Place meat on plates, cover with plastic wrap, and refrigerate until ready to serve. This can be done several hours in advance.

TO SERVE

Toss salad greens with olive oil and lime juice and mound a little in the center of each plate. Sprinkle with sea salt, top with granité, and garnish as desired.

FOR 6–8 FRIENDS

FOR THE GRANITÉ

2 c.	Anguillian Roasted Tomato Bloody Mary (see recipe)
¼ c.	extra-virgin olive oil
¼ c.	vodka

FOR THE CARPACCIO

2 tsp	whole black peppercorns
1 tsp	white peppercorns
1 tsp	red chili flakes
2 tsp	toasted fennel seeds
2 tsp	toasted coriander seeds
1 tsp	coarse kosher salt
4 T	olive oil
1 T	lime juice
1–1¼ lb.	trimmed beef tenderloin
½ lb.	wild greens, watercress, or arugula

sea salt as needed

garnish with cherry tomatoes, radishes, and herbs (optional)

8	bamboo skewers
4	portobello mushroom caps, quartered
4	cremini mushrooms, halved
2	bell peppers, cleaned and cut into hunks
2	garlic cloves
2 T	olive oil
2 tsp	thyme leaves, minced
salt and pepper as needed	
4 c.	purslane (or watercress or arugula)
¼ c.	olive oil to drizzle
2 T	lemon juice
sea salt as needed	

Mushroom and Sweet Pepper Skewers with Purslane Salad

These skewered treats make a simple yet elegant salad. They may be cooked on the grill or under a hot broiler. Use whatever big, chunky mushrooms you can find. You can even use wild mushrooms such as porcini or chanterelles. I've even been known to replace the olive oil with a drizzle of truffle oil.

Note: Purslane is a wild herb or salad that grows rampantly in sandy soil almost anywhere. I even had it growing uncultivated on my rooftop on New York's 42nd Street! In the islands it is pulled up and fed to the pigs. On Anguilla they even call it pig weed. On the internet I found that it is used throughout the Caribbean in soups and sauces. It has a wonderful lemony crunch and is extremely high in omega-3s. I found it at the Union Square Market selling for $10 a pound, so don't turn your nose up at it. If it is out of season, or otherwise unavailable, try watercress or arugula as a substitute.

Soak skewers in water as you get started, to avoid burning.

Skewer mushrooms and peppers, alternating between portobellos, peppers, and creminis.

Season with garlic, thyme, olive oil, salt, and pepper.

Grill or roast skewers until mushrooms are tender.

Toss the purslane in lemon juice, salt, and olive oil.

Place two skewers on each plate.

Sprinkle with a bit of crushed sea salt and lemon juice.

6   bamboo skewers,
        soaked in water to
        prevent burning

18   jumbo tiger shrimp,
        shelled and deveined

3   bananas, ripe, cut into
        ½" chunks

¼ c.   Papaya Banana Catsup
        (see recipe)

sea salt to taste

1   lime

¼ c.   cilantro, coarsely
        chopped

¼ c.   red pepper, cut into
        fine strips

banana leaves or other
decorative leaves for garnish,
such as flowering kale or
colorful lettuce

Grilled Tiger Shrimp with Papaya Banana Catsup

Shrimp's briny sweetness loves to dance with the spicy richness of this homemade condiment.

Prepare charcoal fire or place your rack on the top level of the broiler closest to the heating unit.

Alternate shrimp and banana pieces on skewers (3 shrimp and banana pieces per skewer). Cover with Papaya Banana Catsup. Grill over high heat until shrimp is cooked, about 4 minutes (shrimp should still be slightly translucent at center). Remove from grill and arrange on a platter lined with fresh banana leaves. Finish by sprinkling with sea salt, cilantro, red pepper, and squirt of lime juice.

Serve with additional Papaya Banana Catsup as a dipping sauce.

Marinated Island Conch
with Citrus and Coconut Milk

Curtis was one of our line cooks at the restaurant and this is his recipe for marinated raw conch. Curtis was a man of few words, but he loved flavor. He used the extremely spicy cherry peppers and lots of herbs from the garden, but you can use Scotch Bonnets or your favorite chili pepper. Remember, the veins and seeds are where most of the heat of a chili is, so remove them if you are a wimp.

Note: This same marinade can be used on sushi-quality octopus or calamari or any other sushi-quality raw fish for a ceviche or crudo. I also like it spooned over raw clams or oysters.

Whisk together ingredients for the marinade and taste. Adjust seasoning as needed. Refrigerate until needed.

Toss together the conch, onions, celery, and the marinade and refrigerate overnight or at least 3 hours. Add herbs and serve garnished as desired.

FOR 10–15 FRIENDS

FOR THE MARINADE

1½ c.	extra-virgin olive oil
½ c.	white vinegar
½ c.	fresh lemon juice
¼ c.	fresh orange juice
¼ c.	fresh grapefruit juice
1	mini-wini or hot cherry pepper (or your favorite chili to taste)
2	garlic cloves, finely minced
2 T	ginger, minced
1 T	fresh thyme
¼ c.	Thai fish sauce
½ c.	coconut milk

salt and pepper to taste

5 lbs.	fresh conch, cleaned and sliced as thinly as possible (save tough parts for another use)
1	large red onion, thinly sliced and rinsed in cold water
1 c.	celery, minced
2 c.	fresh herbs, chopped (mint, basil, tarragon, parsley, and cilantro)

garnish with citrus segments, toasted coconut, fresh herb sprigs, avocado (optional)

Ya Mon: Caribbean Handshakes

Every island has a handshake that the local men use to greet one another; it's kind of an entrance fee to the real heartbeat of the place. When you arrive, spend some time with the bartenders and ask them to show you the local shake; then practice with your companion back in the room. We northerners sometimes are a bit reserved when it comes to greetings, but in the Caribbean, the shake can be made up of four or five parts. If you take the time to learn it, new doors can open and you'll feel a bit more a part of the surroundings.

Irie Conch Salad

FOR 2 FRIENDS

½ lb.	tender conch meat, sliced thin
1	garlic clove, minced
1 tsp	ginger, minced
1 tsp	Tabasco (or your favorite hot sauce)
¼ c.	yellow onion, finely diced
¼ c.	olive oil
1	small red seasoning pepper, minced (red bell pepper will work just fine)
1	small green seasoning pepper, minced (green bell pepper will work just fine)
2 T	scallion, finely sliced
½ c.	lime juice
salt and freshly ground pepper to taste	

Here is another version of conch salad. For those of you who recoil at the thought of chewy stewed conch, I promise you'll be amazed at the delicacy of the mollusk served raw. It was inspired by my friend Dale Carty, the owner of Tasty's Restaurant in Anguilla. His conch has a sweet, ocean-clean taste with a pleasing crunch. It is my favorite treatment for a fresh haul of conch. Frozen conch will not be quite the same, but often you can't even find that. Don't despair—you can try this recipe with any impeccably fresh seafood such as raw scallops, tuna, squid, whelks, abalone, clams, oysters, or prepared Japanese octopus.

Mix all ingredients.

Taste for seasoning. Serve in a bowl over crushed ice with fresh lime and additional chili sauce on the side.

FOR 4 FRIENDS

FOR THE MARINADE

1½ tsp	lemon zest
2 tsp	fish sauce
½ c.	extra-virgin olive oil
1 T	honey
1 T	coconut water (from the fresh coconut)
1 T	Scotch Bonnet pepper, finely minced (adjust to taste)
¼ c.	cilantro, roughly chopped
1 T	mint, roughly chopped
1 T	tarragon

salt and pepper to taste

1 lb.	yellowfin tuna, sushi quality, cut into ¼" dice
1½ T	white balsamic vinegar

juice of 2 limes

juice of 2 lemons

garnish with Asian chives, toasted shredded coconut, and grated citrus zest (optional)

Island Tuna Crudo, Coconut Water, and Scotch Bonnets

If there is one dish from our kitchen that really defines what we call contemporary caribbean cooking, it's this *crudo* (Italian for raw). We toss the tuna with home-grown herbs, chilies, and coconut water just prior to serving. It stays sashimi red because of the extremely short marinating time. Light, fresh, and beautiful. This was on my first menu at FARMbloomington, my Indiana restaurant.

Combine all ingredients, except for the acid and the fish, in a bowl and mix well. Taste and adjust the seasoning as needed with salt and pepper.

Cut the cleaned tuna into small-size pieces.

To serve, add the white balsamic vinegar, the juice of the lime and lemon, and the fish to the marinade and toss to coat.

Finish with sea salt and decorate with the toasted coconut, chives, and lemon zest.

Note: At the resort we serve this ceviche in a cracked coconut on crushed ice.

FOR THE MARINADE

1½ tsp	lemon zest
2 tsp	fish sauce
½ c.	extra-virgin olive oil
1 T	honey
1 T	coconut water (from the fresh coconut)
1 tsp	Scotch Bonnet pepper, finely minced (adjust to taste)
¼ c.	fresh herbs, roughly chopped (any combination of cilantro, fresh dill, mint, or tarragon)

salt and pepper to taste

1 lb.	snapper fillet, boned and skinned
1½ T	white balsamic vinegar

juice of 2 limes

juice of 2 lemons

thinly sliced vegetables, red onion, and lime slices for garnish

Sashimi Salad of Island Snapper with Fresh Herbs and Scotch Bonnets

Sushi and sashimi have finally made it to our little island of Anguilla. I was driving back home to Old Ta one evening and noticed a Japanese restaurant that seemed to have popped up overnight on "da big road."

I stick to the more Western ways of serving raw fish. This recipe for ceviche using the Anguillian big-eyed snapper is one example. You can use any type of sushi-quality fish for this dish. We like to toss everything together at the last minute so the citrus juice doesn't "cook" the pristine ingredients. You really have to trust your fishmonger to give you the freshest fish because there is no hiding behind a big ball of wasabi.

Root vegetables add a nice crunch to this. Try carrots, parsnips, or radishes, thinly sliced.

Combine all ingredients, except for the acid and the fish, in a bowl and mix well.

Taste and adjust the seasoning as needed with salt and pepper.

Cut the cleaned snapper into small-size pieces.

Toss the fish in the marinade and serve quickly on chilled plates. Garnish with two herb sprigs and root vegetables, red onion, and lime slices.

Shrimp Quesadilla with Cilantro and Scallions

FOR 2 FRIENDS

1 c.	small shrimp, peeled, deveined, and cooked
½ c.	Monterey Jack and cheddar cheese mix
1	roasted pepper, roughly chopped
1	garlic clove, minced
1	scallion, chopped (some reserved for garnish)
10 sprigs	cilantro, roughly chopped (some reserved for garnish)
2	plain tortillas (or try red pepper or spinach-flavored)

accompaniments: sour cream, hot sauce, and salsa

Everyone loves quesadillas. We played around to make this one somewhere between a fish taco and a slice of heaven. Baked in our famous pizza oven, poolside, I can't think of anything better as an afternoon snack. You can use any type of seafood in this recipe. Try crab or lobster, or if you have some leftover fish from last night's dinner, this is a fun and easy way to get another meal from it without the family knowing!

Preheat oven to 450°.

Toss together the shrimp, cheese, peppers, garlic, scallions, and herbs. Season with salt and pepper.

Lay out the tortillas. Place half the filling on half of each tortilla and fold over.

Bake on a pizza stone or preheated sheet pan until brown on the bottom, about 7 minutes, and flip over and cook the second side, about another 3–5 minutes.

Remove to a cutting board and slice each quesadilla into 3 triangles and serve garnished with herbs, scallions, sour cream, and your favorite hot sauce and salsa.

Crab Fritters with Lemon Zest and Parmesan

You can use the same recipe and replace the crab with shrimp, salt cod, or even ground cooked chicken for a change of pace. Serve with my Hearts of Palm Salad with New Potatoes and Herbs on p. 52.

1 T	butter, melted
½ can	coconut milk
1	egg, beaten
½ tsp	lemon zest
½ tsp	curry
½ tsp	red pepper, finely diced
1 T	paprika
1½ T	garlic, chopped
½ c.	grated cheddar
¼ c.	grated Parmesan
1 c.	scallion tops, chopped
½ T	Tabasco
1 c.	breadcrumbs
¼ c.	flour
¼ c.	grated coconut
½ T	baking powder
1 lb.	picked lump crabmeat
salt and pepper to taste	

Combine the first set of ingredients and mix well. Add the second set of ingredients and mix well. Adjust thickness with additional flour if needed. Add in half of the crabmeat and mix well. Season to taste. Gently fold in the remaining crab so as not to break up the lumps. Form into small cakes. Fry one and sample, then adjust with seasoning and flour if needed.

3	eggs
1½ c.	sour cream
½ c.	cornmeal
1 c.	flour
1½ c.	fresh corn kernels
1 T	olive oil
3	scallions, finely chopped
1 tsp	lemon zest
1 tsp	garlic, minced
½ tsp	ground black pepper
1 tsp	baking powder
1 tsp	salt (or to taste)

Johnnycakes with Sour Cream and Corn

Johnnycakes are the local quick bread of Anguilla. They range from a cornmeal griddlecake to fried pizza dough. For this version, I went back to a recipe I learned as a *stagier* at Marc Meueau's L'Espérance in Saint-Père-sous-Vézelay, France. He served a corn crepe topped with foie gras that I can still close my eyes and taste. I think you'll love these any time of the day. They are great for an elegant breakfast with smoked salmon and sour cream, or as an accompaniment with any meat entree. I even like them as passed hors d'oeuvres topped with crab salad, avocado, or even sturgeon roe.

Whisk the eggs and sour cream together and set aside. Measure the cornmeal and flour and fold in until incorporated. Add the baking powder and the remaining ingredients and incorporate. Make a small crepe and adjust seasoning and thickness as needed.

Refrigerate at least 30 minutes before using.

Cook on a lightly oiled griddle or pan as you would your favorite pancake mix.

3 lbs.	baby octopus
¼ c.	white miso
¼ c.	extra-virgin olive oil
¼ c.	sherry vinegar
¼ c.	lime juice
¼ c.	shallots, minced
¼ c.	ginger, minced
¼ c.	Thai fish sauce
¼ c.	honey
1 tsp	garlic, minced
1 tsp	red chilies, minced

"Sea Cat" in Ginger Miso Sauce

Sea cat, Anguillian vernacular for octopus, is one of the most under-rated of sea creatures. Octopus is wonderful when cooked tender and dressed while still steaming. Dressing anything while warm, from steamed potatoes to seafood, coats the ingredients and keeps the moisture from escaping. This dish can be served warm over greens or cooled to room temperature. If you have chilled leftovers, allow them to come to room temperature. Cold foods are often a bit chewier and their flavors muted.

Note: A pressure cooker will greatly cut the cooking time.

Cover baby octopus with cold water in a pressure cooker and seal the top. Cook until tender, about 45 minutes.

Mix remaining ingredients together in a mixing bowl and set aside.

Toss warm octopus directly in marinade and cover. Allow to rest in marinade until the octopus is room temperature. Adjust seasoning as needed. Best served straight away; if made ahead, allow to warm to room temperature before serving.

Callaloo and Black-Eyed Pea Fritters

Callaloo is the wild local spinach used throughout the Caribbean. It is different in various islands. Some "callaloo" is dashine, which has large elephant ear-shaped leaves. Its root is taro, the root used for those colorful high-end potato chips. These leaves should be eaten very young and always cooked thoroughly. New Zealand spinach is called callaloo in Dominica. In Anguilla, polk weed, something that we actually have growing on our farm in southern Indiana, is the Anguillian callaloo. Any of these greens can be used in this recipe, but you will be equally successful with more common Swiss chard, collards, or kale.

FOR 10 FRIENDS	
2 c.	Callaloo, shredded (Swiss chard, kale, or other toothsome greens may be used)
1	small onion, finely chopped
½ c.	fresh black-eyed peas (or drained canned peas)
3	garlic cloves, minced
1	tomato, finely chopped
1 T	butter, melted
¼ c.	water
1	large egg, beaten
1½ c.	flour
1 T	baking powder
½ tsp	salt
1 tsp	Paradise Kitchen Jerk Spice Blend (see recipe)
oil as needed for frying	

In a large saucepan, melt butter and add the garlic and cook until lightly brown and toasty smelling. Do not over-brown or garlic will become bitter. Quickly add the onion, peas, callaloo, and tomato, mixing all the time. Add the water, reduce the heat, and cover to steam until tender, about 5 minutes. (*Note:* If using canned peas, add them when you add the eggs.) Remove cover and reduce remaining liquid until practically dry. This will intensify the wonderful flavors. Cool. Add beaten egg.

In a large bowl, combine the flour, baking powder, salt, pepper, and jerk seasoning. Mix in the vegetable mixture and add additional water if the batter is too stiff. Fry at 360° in a deep fryer or sauté until golden on all sides. (*Note:* Always test a small amount of any batter by making a small "test" portion. Taste it and adjust seasoning as needed.)

Chef's note: Try thinning out the batter and using it to make crepes. They bring this simple fare to new heights when topped with smoked salmon, caviar, or herbed chèvre.

Serve with Athenia's Anguill-Asian Slaw (see recipe).

Hungry for a Soul

Windy Weather in the Caribbean

When you live in the Caribbean, you enjoy the changes of seasons just as you do up north, except maybe in late summer when the heat is stifling and the TV and radio are tuned in to the hurricane report. There are subtle changes that vacationers may not even notice.

I've learned to love the rain. It is a great break from the painfully beautiful days to which you normally wake up. Expats and tourists down for a few days of sun in the islands try to keep a brave face, but you can easily read their disappointment. I, on the other hand, smiled. I didn't have to wear a hat and my tube of sunscreen got a break on rainy days. I especially loved when it rained on a sunny day; those unexplainable fleeting showers refreshed and surprised us all and allowed us to stop for a minute or two.

The windy season was a bit different; I didn't like it much. It wasn't like a hurricane, but it did keep the boats from sailing, and that meant I didn't get my fresh fish, lobsters, crayfish, whelks, and conch . . . not to mention my deliveries from the United States and Europe. They called these "ground seas" and no one would be going out, at least not anyone in his or her right mind. Cooking on an island has its difficulties; windy weather and rough seas are a couple of the most frustrating conditions. However, during these times of year something spiritual seems to fill the air. It's a strange, achy uneasiness that creeps into your joints and stays. After a day or two you just want it to pass, but it doesn't. You don't want to complain, you want to assimilate into the culture and act as if it is normal. You try not to ask, but finally it just slips out . . . "When is this wind gonna stop?" When I finally asked, I was told, "You see, the sea is hungry for a soul and she won't calm 'til she takes one. Sooner or later a fool-headed fisherman or sailor will hit them seas and won't be heard from again. Only after she's satisfied will she let up. Then the winds will pass and the old sea, she'll calm."

Then I understood and decided that I wouldn't complain about not having fish for a couple of days. Getting the tourists (especially those east-coasters) to understand—that wasn't so easy. I'm talkin' fish . . . don't even ask about my banana stories!!! There were mornings when the boats couldn't make it over the rough seas with my bananas, but don't even try to explain that to a grumpy New Yorker. Breakfast time without his or her favorite fruit brings out a guest's . . . challenging side!

Quick Caribbean Blood Pudding

For the real thing, the first directive in the method section of this recipe would read, "Go to your backyard and slaughter a pig." Since I don't think many of you will be doing that, I make this pudding with fresh liver and store-bought spicy Italian sausage. I've also cut out the step of forcing the sausage into casings. I figure if you're game enough to try blood pudding, I shouldn't punish you with too much work. You will have to serve this with my signature papaya and lemon hot sauce, though; it makes it sing.

Note: This mixture freezes well and may be used to stuff boneless quail. You can also form into patties, grill them, and serve with grilled pineapple or apples. I also make this into little meatballs and pass them around with bamboo toothpicks.

Blend liver and rice in food processor until it forms a smooth paste. Add the Italian sausage, rum, seasonings, garlic, and spice and pulse to incorporate. Fold in the diced dates and cilantro. Cook a small amount as a tester, sample, and adjust seasoning as needed.

Warm a large non-stick sauté pan over medium heat and add oil. Form small oval patties of the pudding mix using two large oval soup spoons (these are called quenelles in French). Dip the spoons in ice water between each process to lessen sticking.

Carefully place the puddings into the oil as you form them, turning them as needed. Repeat until pan is full. Brown well on all sides. Deglaze pan with water and allow to cook down. When cooked through, remove from pan and cover. Keep warm until serving.

Arrange puddings on plates or a platter and serve with hot sauce and fresh lime segments.

Note: I also feel this cries out for some fried sweet plantains and the simple Kale Salad (see recipe below).

Kale Salad

FOR 4 FRIENDS

2 c.   kale, sliced thin
2 T   extra-virgin olive oil
2 T   lime juice
salt and pepper to taste

Toss all ingredients together and season to taste.

FOR 6–8 FRIENDS

1 lb.	calf's liver
1 c.	cooked white rice
1 lb.	hot Italian pork sausage, casing removed and crumbled
¼ c.	dark rum
¼ tsp	allspice, ground
1 T	salt
¼ tsp	ground cloves
1 tsp	Kitchen D'Orr Sweet Seasons Spice Blend (or Chinese 5-spice powder)
3	lime leaves, cut into thin strips (or fresh lime zest)
1 T	ginger, minced
1 or 2	chilies, your favorite depending on desired spiciness, chopped
3	garlic cloves, chopped
5	dry dates, pitted and diced small
¼ c.	cilantro, roughly chopped with stem

TO COOK

¼ c.	olive oil, for frying
¼ c.	water

TO SERVE

accompaniments: lime segments and Don't Let Your Man-Go Hot Sauce (see recipe)

LiMiNG It UP uNDeR PrEssuRE

Making Your Gramma's
Pressure Cooker Your Friend

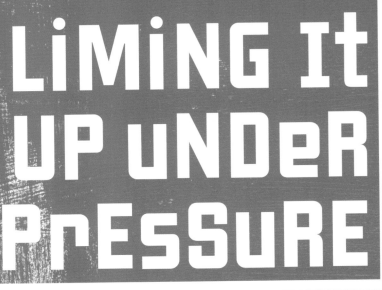

Although most of us have about 30 seconds a day to spend in the kitchen, there are those rainy days and Sundays that you should give yourself the gift of a good, home-cooked meal. Better yet, give yourself the gift of a good, slow-cooked meal. Stews, braises, and pot roasts warm a place deep inside. A primal place that a cup of ramen noodles just can't reach, no matter how much fresh cilantro and minced chilies you doctor it up with. No, these are times to bring out the pressure cooker and lime. "To lime" is Caribbean for "chillin', relaxing, and letting the time go by." Your worries will still be there when you push away from the table, but you may have a fuller perspective. Your belly certainly will.

My gramma had a pressure cooker on her farm in southern Indiana. I don't remember her using it much, but it looked well worn. I think by the time I was old enough for memories, my gram had renounced "those foods," the odd and tough cuts of meat that sustained her family and farmhands during the Depression. Oxtails, old roosters, pig tails, and tripe went into the back reaches of the recipe file as chicken breasts and tenderloins moved to the front. The pressure cooker was a souvenir of the past that made her remember times she didn't want to relive—a dusty trophy on the top cabinet.

The more things change, the more they stay the same. New Yorkers now relish oxtails, beef cheeks, saltfish, and tripe in their fancy-schmancy restaurants. For them it's an adventure, not a hardship, and restaurateurs are raking in the profits from the "mystery meat" section of the menu. The good news for the home cook is that most of these ingredients are inexpensive and the recipes easy. The pressure cooker cooks them up faster and intensifies flavors, pushing them into every fiber of the food. You will be eating up a bit of the history and folklore of the Caribbean that rarely make it to a restaurant menu. You'll have to try these at home.

The dishes that follow are made for "limin'." Nothing is precisely cut, weighed, or measured. The recipes are guidelines. Some of the ingredients do require advance soaking, such as beans and salted meats and fish, so make sure you plan ahead. Once you've got it in the pot, though, you can commence with the "limin'." Turn on the ball game, read a book, open a good bottle of wine or rum, and relax. Let the aromas drift throughout the house. Hell, open the windows and make all the neighbors jealous, too.

1½ lb.	pigs' trotters, cut into chunks
2 tsp	salt
1	Spanish onion, medium dice
½ stalk	celery, medium dice
1	carrot, peeled, medium dice
1	parsnip, peeled, medium dice
2	lime leaves, thinly sliced
1 T	ginger, small dice
5	garlic cloves, roughly chopped
1 sprig	thyme
2	hot chilies
¼ c.	cilantro, roughly chopped with stems
1	lime, zest and juice
enough	water to cover
¼ c.	assorted fresh herbs, chopped (such as cilantro, Thai basil, scallion)

Pigs' Trotters

Don't be afraid to try this recipe. I know it might sound a bit scary, but pigs' trotters (all right, pigs' feet) are wonderfully gelatinous. West Indian spices cut the fat, rendering them finger-licking good. I had a young couple over from St. Martin, and halfway through a plate of these, a pile of well-cleaned bones in front of her, the girlfriend said, "I don't eat pork, but I do love pigs' feet." That's how good they are!

Place all ingredients into a pressure cooker.

Cook on high until stew comes to boil.

Simmer 2 hours or until meat is very tender and not at all chewy.

Allow to cool. Serve at room temperature in their "jelly," topped with chopped fresh herbs, lime wedges, coarse sea salt, and your favorite hot sauce.

1½ lbs.	saltfish, soaked and cut into 2" dice
½ c.	olive oil
2	large Spanish onions, sliced
1 c.	water
1 sprig	thyme
1	cayenne pepper
½	lemon, for zest
1	red bell pepper, cut into strips
1	yellow bell pepper, cut into strips
6	garlic cloves, finely chopped
¼ c.	extra-virgin olive oil
¼ c.	assorted chopped herbs (basil, cilantro, and scallions)
1	lemon, for juice
1 T	chili vinegar (optional)

Saltfish Salad

This salad can be served over greens as a main course but is also great as part of a mixed appetizer plate with other items such as hummus, eggplant caviar, and a mixed grain salad.

Note: Saltfish must be soaked in plenty of water for at least 12 hours before using. Change water frequently to get the most salt out of the fish. It is a delicate balance not to over-soak the fish, which will remove its entire namesake flavor. You can also use poached fresh cod if you are in a hurry (no pressure cooker needed), but the flavor and texture will be slightly different.

Put saltfish, olive oil, onions, thyme, pepper, lemon zest, and water into a pressure cooker.

Cover and seal your pressure cooker. Bring to a boil.

Lower to a simmer and cook over medium heat for 30 minutes. Remove from heat and carefully open pressure cooker.

Add bell peppers and garlic.

Cover, return to heat, and cook an additional 15 minutes or until all the excess liquid has evaporated.

Remove from heat and cool to room temperature.

Using a fork, break apart the fibers of the fish until no large chunks remain.

Dress the fish with extra-virgin olive oil, herbs, chili vinegar, and a fresh squeeze of lemon.

Stewed Whelks with Fresh Coconut Dumplings and Scallions

TO POACH WHELKS

2 lbs.	fresh whelks (a.k.a. *scungilli* in Italian)
1 qt.	water or as needed
1	large onion
1 stalk	celery
2	garlic cloves

FOR THE STEW

1 oz.	olive oil
1	onion, large dice
1 stalk	celery, large dice
1	carrot, large dice
3	garlic cloves, sliced
1 T	tomato paste
3	tomatoes, roughly chopped
½ qt.	stock (poaching liquid)
2 T	thyme
3	scallions, chopped
salt and pepper	

In the Caribbean, whelks, also known as turbans, are an old local favorite. They are gathered and roasted in the coals at beach BBQs, as well as long-braised in soups and stews back home. It is rare that you will find them on restaurant menus, though. They are too much work for most kitchens. If whelks are not available try this recipe with clams, octopus, calamari, or even canned escargot. If using a canned quick-cooking substitute you will not need the pressure cooker. Just follow to stewing part of the recipe.

Note: Coconut Dumplings are a traditional accompaniment (see recipe, right).

TO POACH WHELKS

In a pressure cooker, place the whelks, onions, celery, and garlic and cover with water. Cover and simmer over medium heat until whelks can easily be pulled out of the shell, about 30–45 minutes. Remove from heat and strain the stock, being careful to leave any sand at the bottom of the pot. Reserve stock for stew.

Separate the whelks from the shell and remove the stomach and "the foot" from the meat with a knife.

FOR THE STEW

In a large sauté pan on high heat, add the olive oil, onions, celery, and carrots. Cook the vegetables until tender. Add the garlic, tomato paste, tomatoes, and whelks.

Continue to cook for 5 minutes, then add the stock and simmer until reduced by half. Finish with thyme and scallions. Add the Coconut Dumplings (see recipe, facing page), and toss to coat with the sauce. Taste and adjust seasoning with lemon juice, salt, and pepper.

Fresh Coconut Dumplings

Combine all the ingredients. Knead the dough with your hands and pat out to about a half-inch thickness. Cut dough into 1-inch pieces and poach in boiling salted water until cooked through or approximately 7–10 minutes.

Add to the pan with the whelks and toss to coat with the sauce. Serve immediately.

2 lbs.	flour
1	fresh coconut, grated (save water for another use)
1 T	butter, unsalted
¼ c.	vegetable oil
¼ c.	water
salt	

1½ lbs.   goat meat, cubed

FOR MARINADE

1	Spanish onion, roughly chopped
2	garlic cloves, roughly chopped
3	seasoning peppers, roughly chopped
2	banana peppers, roughly chopped
1	Jamaican country pepper, roughly chopped
1 T	Kitchen D'Orr Mediterranean Spice Blend (or *herbes de Provence*)
2 T	Kitchen D'Orr Mellow Yellow Spice Blend (or curry powder)
2 T	sweet paprika
¼ c.	olive oil
¼ c.	white vinegar
1 T	salt

FOR STEW

½ c.	olive oil
4 c.	water
2	bell peppers (red and yellow)
2	green bananas, cut into 2" pieces
1	large sweet potato, cut into 2" pieces
1 can	coconut milk
¼ c.	assorted fresh herbs, roughly chopped

salt, pepper, and hot sauce to taste

Pressure Cooker Goat Stew

Goat has kind of a strong lamb flavor that is balanced by the spices and coconut milk in this recipe. Although not often eaten at home in the United States, it is a prized dish in many countries from Greece to the Middle East to Central and South America. If goat is not available you can use lamb shoulder in its place. Most Caribbean cooks would never think of using boneless meat. Half the fun is sucking it off the bones. I make a rich and hearty stew, but if it is less thick, Anguillians would call this dish "goat water" and serve it as a brothy soup. As with all stews, this is even better reheated the next day.

Mix marinade ingredients with goat cubes. Marinate for at least 2 and up to 10 hours in refrigerator. Remove goat meat from marinade, setting marinade aside.

Heat olive oil in the bottom of a pressure cooker. Add goat meat and brown on all sides. Add marinade back to the pan along with water. Cover and seal your pressure cooker. Bring stew to a boil, then lower heat and simmer. Cook until goat is tender, about 1½–2 hours.

Add sweet potato, bell, and banana peppers, re-seal pressure cooker, and cook an additional 15 minutes.

Open and adjust seasoning with salt, pepper, and hot sauce to taste. Pour into a warm serving dish and finish with chopped fresh herbs.

Caribbean Cassoulet

This is a twist on a French classic. It is "slow food" at its best, but I speed it up a little by using a pressure cooker. Using the frozen beans in place of dried beans is a way to get this to the table a little quicker as well. It is still a weekend dish but one you don't have to stand over much. The salted meats may be found in any good Latin bodega or ethnic market. They have a much deeper flavor than fresh meats. If you can't find the frozen beans you can use soaked dry beans in their place, but the cooking time will be longer.

Chop the pig tail and snout into medium-size pieces. Place in a pressure cooker and cover with water. Bring to a boil and reduce heat to a simmer. Cook until tender, approximately 1–1½ hours. Remove both the meat and the liquid and set aside. Wash pressure cooker.

Return cooker to high heat and pour in olive oil. Add the garlic and cook until toasty and lightly browned. Do not over-cook.

Quickly add the onions, bouquet garni, and the sausages and cook, stirring, until onions have softened but not colored. Add the ginger, celery, red pepper, tomatoes, and chilies and continue to cook for 3–5 minutes until they begin to soften as well. Add a splash of water if needed.

Toss in the beans and collard greens and stir to coat. Add enough water to create a stew-like (not soupy) mixture and bring to a boil. Cover with lid and cook for 10–15 minutes and season to taste with cracked pepper. Additional salt will probably not be needed because of the pork products. Remove chilies when you feel the dish has the desired spiciness. Serve immediately.

This may also be baked and served in individual casseroles.

FOR 8–10 FRIENDS

4	salted pig tails, soaked 24 hours and rinsed
1	salted pig snout, soaked 24 hours and rinsed
¼ c.	olive oil
6–8	garlic cloves, roughly chopped
2	large Spanish onions, diced
1	bouquet garni
1 lb.	pork sausage links
2 T	ginger, minced
2	large carrots, diced
2 stalks	celery, diced
1	red pepper, diced
5	tomatoes, diced
2–3	chilies (your favorite), left whole
1 lb.	frozen butter beans
1 lb.	frozen black-eyed peas
1 lb.	frozen chopped collard greens
water as needed	
cracked black pepper to taste	
4 legs	duck confit, cut into 2–3 pieces each (optional: see note at end of recipe)

Note: To make a more classic cassoulet, you can add confit of duck legs to the dish. I place duck confit pieces in the bottom of a large casserole or baking dish. Spoon out the sausages and arrange evenly with the confit. Pour the bean mixture over the confit and cover. Bake in a 350° degree oven for 1 hour until tender.

¼ c.	olive oil
1	Spanish onion, large dice
5	garlic cloves, chopped
1 lb.	salt beef, cut into ½" dice
1 lb.	red kidney beans, soaked
1	bay leaf
2 sprigs	thyme
1	Jamaican country pepper
2	Roma tomatoes, chopped
1 tsp	black pepper, freshly ground
1 T	Kitchen D'Orr Mediterranean Spice Blend
1 c.	water
½	lime, for juice
5 pieces okra, cut crosswise into ½" slices	

Boiled Salt Beef and Beans

Although almost mindlessly easy to prepare, this dish does take a little advance planning. Both the salt beef and the beans should be soaked overnight. Soak the salt beef in ample cold, fresh water for 12–24 hours. Change water frequently to remove the maximum amount of salt. The beans should be soaked separately, also in ample co ld water. If you forget to soak the beans, plan on extra cooking time for the stew. Serve this dish over simple white rice with a salad or stewed greens.

Note: For the beef, there can be no forgetting! On the Spanish-speaking islands, this meat is called carne secca, and you can most often find it in Latin and ethnic markets. It is very different from bresaola, the less salty dried beef from Italy, which is eaten sliced "as is," like prosciutto. It is essentially a less dried version of the beef jerky found in the States. It is sold in large, beefy chunks and is coated with salt crystals. You'll find it next to the salted pig tails, snouts, and ears if you're lucky enough to have a good Caribbean market nearby. If you can't find the real deal in your local bodega, buy a good-quality beef or bison jerky and soak it until soft. Don't purchase the reconstituted snack in "stick" form found in your local gas station or you will be greatly disappointed. It is best purchased from a meat market or butcher that makes its own.

Combine all ingredients except okra and lime juice in a pressure cooker. Seal pressure cooker and bring to a boil over high heat. Reduce to medium heat and simmer 1 hour. Open and taste beans for doneness and seasoning. If ready, remove from heat and stir in okra and lime juice.

Spicy Caribbean Tripe Stew

For gutsy gourmets only! This is one of those deliciously slurpy stews that takes both time and passion to prepare. Tripe, now a favorite of mine, took me a while to appreciate. I knew the great chefs of Lyon, France, would order up bowls of it after shopping in the glorious markets there, but I had to learn to coax the delicate flavors out of this humble ingredient, which in inexperienced hands can be tough, chewy, and rank. I love it served with Island Cornmeal Fungi with Okra (see recipe; fungi is Caribbean for polenta) or with plain white rice and a salad. This is soul food with a Creole accent.

Note: Even better reheated.

Cut the tripe into thin ribbons, removing any fat that may be attached.

Place in a pressure cooker and cover with water. Cover and seal and bring to a boil. Cook 30 minutes and turn off heat. Once the pressure cooker has stopped hissing, carefully remove the top. Place a colander in the sink and drain. Rinse under cold water and repeat. Drain and rinse again. The tripe should be tender at this point.

Rinse pressure cooker and dry well. Return to stove and heat well over medium-high heat. Add olive oil and garlic. Cook until garlic starts to lightly color and smell wonderfully nutty. Add onions, tomatoes, chili, ginger, orange zest, spices, thyme, salt, and pepper and sauté until onions start to become tender. Return tripe to the pot and add the tomato juice. Cover and cook over medium-low heat for 30–45 minutes, until tripe is meltingly tender. Turn off heat and allow the pot to stop hissing.

Carefully remove the lid and add the three colors of sweet pepper. Stir to incorporate. Season to taste with additional salt and pepper if needed. Return to the stove uncovered and cook, stirring, over medium-low heat for 15–20 minutes until peppers are tender. Turn off fire and do a final seasoning adjustment.

Note: I like to make this even more of a meal by adding a can of well-rinsed white beans or garbanzos to the stew at the same time as the sweet peppers. Hominy kernels are also sometimes added.

2 lbs.	tripe, sliced thinly (this is easily achieved if semi-frozen)
¼ c.	olive oil
5	large garlic cloves, thinly sliced
2	large onions, coarsely sliced
4	large tomatoes, seeded and roughly chopped
½	Scotch Bonnet pepper (or your favorite chili depending on how hot you like it), seeded and sliced thinly. Remember you can add more, but you can't take it out once you add it!
1 T	fresh ginger, chopped
2 thin strips	orange zest
1 tsp	Kitchen D'Orr Sweet Seasons Spice Blend (or Chinese 5-spice powder)
2 branches	fresh thyme, roughly chopped
1 T	kosher salt
1 tsp	freshly ground pepper
1½ c.	tomato juice
1	large red pepper
1	large green pepper
1	large yellow pepper
½ bunch	cilantro
3	scallions
salt and pepper to taste	

4 lbs.	fatty pork such as shoulder, leg, or belly, cut into cubes
1	Spanish onion, roughly chopped
20	garlic cloves
1	lime, zest and juice
1 stalk	lemongrass, thinly sliced
¼ c.	Thai basil leaves
1 tsp	thyme
1 c.	chili vinegar (or 1 c. white vinegar plus 1 habanero)
1 T	salt
1 T	Kitchen D'Orr Sweet Seasons Spice Blend (or Chinese 5-spice powder)
¼ c.	raw sugar
¼ c.	olive oil
2 c.	water

Stewed Garlic Pork with Lime and Chilies

Stews were often cooked in the community ovens after the bread was pulled out. Covered Dutch ovens were pushed under the dome and left until the meat was cooked tender from residual heat.

Note on chili vinegar: I use chili vinegar in this recipe, which is made by pouring boiling vinegar over your favorite fresh whole chilies and letting it sit at room temperature for a week or two. I like adding a touch of salt, sugar, and dried spices such as allspice, cinnamon, bay, coriander, and fennel. It is great in dressings, marinades, or just in a cruet on the table to drizzle on greens and other goodies. You can make different flavors with different levels of spiciness.

Note: Mexican *piloncillo,* or raw sugar, is pure, unrefined sugar pressed into cone shapes. It is about the closest thing that you can use for the flavor of the Old World. The name is Spanish for "little python." There are two categories: "blanco" is milder, while the darker "oscura" is deeper and richer. Both may be replaced by conventional brown sugar, which is granulated sugar flavored with molasses.

Toss pork cubes with all the spice ingredients. Marinate at least 2 hours or overnight. Remove pork from marinade, drain, and pat dry. Reserve marinade for later.

Heat olive oil in the bottom of a pressure cooker. When hot, add pork and cook to dark brown on all sides. Pour marinade over pork and cook over medium-high heat until all liquid evaporates. Add water. Seal pressure cooker and return heat to high. When it boils, lower the heat to a simmer and cook until pork is tender, about 1 hour. Reduce, uncovered, until sauce thickens.

WAHOO, KINGFISH, TUNA, SNAPPER.

Fish

Brain Food

As a child growing up in the Midwest, the extent of our fresh "seafood" was what we caught in the nearby lake or pond. Things like catfish, crappie, blue gills, red ears, and the occasional large-mouth bass were all we knew about fresh fish. Those who had extremely good luck might come home with a meal of snapping turtles, pike, or frogs' legs. What did a barefoot boy from Columbus, Indiana, know about the sea? For us, saltwater seafood began and ended with Mrs. Paul's fish sticks and frozen cod fillets. Usually we were told we had to eat this imported stuff because it would make us smart; it was "brain food." The few times a year that we got to taste true seafood were true celebrations.

I remember Cole's Market next to the strawberry patch on State Road 46. It was an old-timey supermarket with a creaky wooden floor, a cat in the window, and piles of just about anything reaching up to the rafters. The owner, Clyde Cole, would usually be behind the register meeting and greeting. Jim Williams was manning the meat counter cutting steaks and pounding cutlets, but at Christmastime he brought in fresh oysters. Folks from all around the area would make an annual pilgrimage for those succulent bi-valves.

The only lobster in my hometown was brought in yearly as an Episcopal Church fundraiser each summer. For that event, we'd have the grand-parents over and spend hours around the table sucking every last little leg of its saline sweetness. The adults talked for hours while we kids usually fell asleep at the table, not wanting to admit defeat. Home-made ice cream usually followed! Now almost every supermarket has a lobster tank and sushi-grade tuna. I think it's fantastic, but I look back sentimentally to that "pre-seafood time," thinking of family, friends, and special moments that are now memories.

Many years later in New York City, where you can get just about any-thing at the snap of your fingers, I learned a lot more about seafood. Much of my education came from early morning visits to the great, old open-air fish market on Fulton Street. It was a real eye-opener for a guy from the Midwest. Living and working in France also taught me a trick or two. Each fisherman, fishmonger, and chef showed me new tech-niques for buying, preparing, and serving an array of sea creatures.

By the time I was back in New York at the helm of the wonderful La Grenouille, I was the biggest purchaser of Dover sole in New York. When you buy that amount of fish, a "fish guy" will bend over backward to keep your account. Nothing but the freshest ever arrived at our door.

Later, at Terence Conran's Guastavino's under the 59th Street Bridge, I was buying tons (literally) of fish for our "little" 700-seat bistro! I was rarely unhappy with the freshness of the products. After 15 years, I'd blindly thought that I'd never given my dear guests any experience less than perfect. Little did I know the true vibrancy that exists when you live on the sea.

The first thing Christopher and I realized when we got to Anguilla was that we were going to get to "play" with the freshest fish we'd ever seen. The big-eyed snappers were so pristine that you could see yourself reflected in their peepers. They were brought up from depths of up to 150 feet and had the cleanest, most succulent flesh, perfect for raw dishes like tartars, carpaccios, and Italian crudos. The Anguillian fishermen introduced us to potfish, the reef fish brought up in lobster pots during harvest. Our new culinary territory also included hines, doctor fish, red mon, butterfish, porgies, buffalo head, old wife, and angelfish. The freshness was what really made them so special. The fishermen would drive their pick-ups brimming with their daily catch straight to the restaurant. No blast chilling, no shipping, no overnight transport; these critters were still kicking, especially the spiny lobsters and saltwater crayfish.

Upon our arrival, we learned the folklore, too. Avoid certain reefs or your dinner might be poisoned. Don't eat certain fish when the cedar tree is dropping flowers. Never eat barracudas unless you're starving, and even then, throw the head on an anthill and see if the ants eat it before you try. Stay away from the covalie and black jack and think twice about the dogtooth snapper. Reefs near shipwrecks should not be fished because of the large amount of copper found in old boats.

Not all "fish moments" threatened to be harrowing: dropping fresh armored trunkfish onto glowing coals, then cracking them open 20 minutes later and eating them seasoned with a splash of ocean water and a squeeze of local lime; grilling sea lice (which we re-christened slipper lobster for obvious reasons) and dipping them in Caribbean chili and herb butter; snorkeling with a flashlight after sunset to bag crayfish and spear sleeping butterfish; laughing about how big Christopher's eyes got when a huge puffer fish accosted him.

We had what should be an illegal amount of fun collecting and experimenting with the local fish to create the recipes that follow. The great news is that they are very adaptable to the northern table. Each recipe will offer you other varieties of fish and shellfish you can use with equal success. Remember, recipes are guidelines; don't allow them to be a ball and chain. Use them for inspiration to help you get a wonderful meal on the table and have a great deal of fun doing it.

1 lb.	whitefish fillet
2	eggs, whisked well
½ T	garlic, minced
1 T	ginger, minced
1 T	lime zest
1 T	chilies, minced
1 T	curry powder
¼ c.	mascarpone cheese
1½ lbs.	jumbo lump crabmeat (picked clean of shell and membrane)
1 c.	island herbs (a combination of cilantro, basil, dill, and mint)

salt and pepper to taste

Paradise Kitchen Caribbean Crab Burgers

An imaginative twist on the crab cake, these burgers are the bomb. I like to grill them up and serve with spicy mayonnaise and seaweed slaw. You can also use this same mixture for mini-burgers during cocktail hour.

Combine the fish, eggs, garlic, ginger, lime zest, chilies, curry, and mascarpone cheese in a food processor. Add a bit of salt and pepper. Blend until fish is smooth, but do not over-mix. Remove from processor to a medium-size stainless steel bowl.

Mix in half of the crabmeat and herbs, being careful not to overwork. Fold in the remaining crab carefully to leave it in lumps. Cook a little of the mixture as a sample and taste for seasoning. Adjust as needed.

Form into 6 patties and refrigerate until needed.

Pan sear as needed and serve on soft buns with sweet potato fries.

FOR 2 FRIENDS

FOR THE FISH

2–6 oz.	fish steaks
2 T	Paradise Kitchen Jerk Spice Blend (see recipe)
2 T	olive oil

FOR THE SALAD

2	beefsteak tomatoes, ripe, washed and sliced into rounds
1	medium cucumber, washed and cut julienne

olive oil, as needed

lime juice, as needed

favorite fresh herbs (optional)

sea salt and freshly cracked pepper, as needed

Anguillian Jerked Fisherman's Steak

This is one of my favorite recipes because it is so easy and so good. You can vary the type of fish according to the market's supply. I like tuna, swordfish, grouper, or salmon. You can even try the same recipe with chicken breast or pork medallions. Nothing could be simpler.

Place fish in a Ziploc bag and add olive oil and spices. Rub around to evenly distribute the seasonings and refrigerate until needed. Can be done several hours in advance. Remove fish from refrigerator about 15–20 minutes before cooking.

Heat a non-stick pan over medium heat. Place the steaks in the pan and cook until medium-rare, about 5–7 minutes on the first side and 3–5 minutes on the second, depending on thickness. Remove to a plate (if left in a hot pan they will over-cook).

Place the tomatoes in a circle in the middle of plates and season. Place fish in the middle and top with the cucumbers. Sprinkle with salt and pepper and drizzle with olive oil and lime juice. Sprinkle with fresh herbs if desired.

Blanquette de la Mer au Curry (Shark or Monkfish Stew with Curry)

FOR 6 FRIENDS

Shark has had a bad reputation ever since the movie *Jaws* came out. Many of these animals are not man-eaters but are quite tasty when eaten by man. There are many types of shark that are good to eat. Some are tender and good for the grill, but others are tougher and good for longer cooking, as this recipe calls for. Most shark is better when soaked overnight in milk to tenderize. Serve with some white rice or buttered noodles.

Note: Monkfish makes wonderful seafood stews and may replace the shark if shark is not available. It will have a quicker cooking time, so be sure to test occasionally. This should be a chunky stew, not overly flaky.

3 lbs.	shark or monkfish
seasoned flour as needed with salt, pepper, and a touch of sugar	
1	onion
1	clove
1 or 2	carrots, peeled and cut into ¼" rounds
18	white pearl onions, peeled
½ lb.	mushrooms
2 T	green curry paste
2	egg yolks
½ c.	whipping cream
juice of 1 lemon	
butter	
salt	
herbs: 2 sprigs thyme, 3 parsley, 1 rib celery, ½ bay leaf	
6–7 c.	white chicken stock, fish stock, or water
chopped mint and toasted pine nuts as garnishes	

Cut the fish into 2-inch cubes. Stick the onion with a clove. Tie together the celery, thyme, bay leaf, and parsley in a bouquet garni.

Melt 3 tablespoons of butter with oil in a heavy-bottomed saucepan. Toss the cubed shark in the seasoned flour to coat. Add the shark to the pot and brown on all sides, then add the carrots, onion, herbs, curry paste, and salt. Add water to cover the fish. Cook over high heat and bring to a boil. Reduce the heat, cover, and simmer for 45 minutes, skimming as needed.

Peel the white pearl onions. Clean the mushrooms and cut them into quarters. Add to the shark the last 15 minutes of cooking. Combine the egg yolks with the cream and half of the lemon juice in a bowl. Set aside until needed.

Carefully remove the shark, mushrooms, and onions with a slotted spoon and place them in a warm serving dish. Cover and keep hot. Reduce the cooking liquid until slightly thickened.

Pour the cream and egg yolk mixture into the cooking liquid. Cook over very low heat for 10 minutes. Do not let the sauce boil. Add the lemon juice, salt, and pepper to taste as needed. Strain through a fine chinoise (fine strainer) over the fish.

Sprinkle with chopped mint and toasted pinenuts.

4–6 oz.	mahimahi fillets
2 T	olive oil
2	garlic cloves
2	lemons, juiced, plus zest of 1 lemon

sea salt and cracked black pepper to taste

Green Papaya Slaw (see recipe, facing page)

Curry Vinaigrette (see recipe, facing page)

Pan-Roasted Mahimahi with Thai Green Papaya Slaw and Roasted Peanuts

Don't let the fact that you don't have green papaya stop you from cooking this dish; instead try jicama, crisp pear, Chinese cabbage, or raw pumpkin. This is an example of the wonderful flavors that come together in the Caribbean when East meets West.

Make the Green Papaya Slaw and Curry Vinaigrette.

Place the fish fillets in a baking dish and season with the olive oil, garlic, and lemon zest. Allow to marinate for at least 30 minutes. Season with salt and pepper.

Heat a non-stick pan over medium-high heat. Place the fillet in and cook until well browned on the first side, about 3 minutes. Flip and lightly color the other side. Do not over-cook. The fish should be lightly pink on the interior.

Remove to a clean dish and drizzle with a touch of olive oil, a sprinkle of sea salt, and a little lemon juice.

Place some of the salad in the middle of each dinner plate and top with the fish. Add a bit more salad on top and sprinkle with chopped peanuts. Spoon a little of the vinaigrette around and serve.

Green Papaya Slaw

FOR 4–6 FRIENDS

1	green papaya, shredded (if you don't have papaya try jicama, crisp pear, Chinese cabbage, or raw pumpkin)
1	large carrot, shredded
1	red pepper, fine julienne
½ c.	mint, roughly chopped
¼ c.	pineapple juice
1 T	sugar
juice of 2 limes	
1 T	fish sauce
1 pinch	crushed red pepper flakes or fresh chilies to taste
1 tsp	garlic, minced
½ tsp	ginger, minced
2 T	olive oil
¼ c.	roasted peanuts, roughly chopped
Tabasco and salt to taste	

Toss papaya, carrots, peppers, and mint. Combine remaining ingredients and season to taste. Toss together and allow to sit at least 10–15 minutes. Sprinkle with peanuts.

Note: If making in advance, don't add green herbs until you are ready to serve.

Curry Vinaigrette

MAKES 1 CUP

¼ c.	shallots, chopped
½ T	garlic, finely chopped
2 T	curry powder
½ T	turmeric
¼ c.	cider vinegar
1 T	honey
1 c.	vegetable oil
½ T	salt
1 tsp	pepper
2	lemons (juiced) + ½ zested

Chill and store in the refrigerator until needed. I like to keep mine in a squeeze bottle to use to flavor and decorate many dishes. Great on just about everything. Pretty too.

Heat the olive oil in a heavy-bottomed saucepan and add the shallots and garlic.

Cook slowly until transparent but uncolored.

Add curry and turmeric and continue to cook to bring the flavors together.

Deglaze with cider vinegar and add remaining ingredients. Puree in blender until smooth. Thin as needed with hot water. Season to taste.

2	shallots, sliced thinly into rounds
2 T	flour
vegetable oil as needed for frying shallots	
4	grouper fillets (5–6 oz. ea.)
4–6 T	Tamarind Glaze (see recipe, facing page)
8 heads	baby bok choy (depending on size), cut into wedges (or your favorite stir-fried vegetables)
1 T	olive oil
1	garlic clove, minced
1 T	ginger, minced
½ c.	Beet and Balsamic Emulsion (see recipe, facing page)
2	lemons
salt and pepper as needed	

Tamarind-Glazed Grouper Fillet, Baby Bok Choy, Crispy Shallots, and Beet Emulsion

I use this glaze to perk up grouper, which tends to want the extra zing that tamarind has. Adding the Thai fish sauce makes it a bit Asian, so I like to serve this with quickly sautéed bok choy. A little-known fact is that there is a lot of Chinese food in the Caribbean. Most smaller islands don't have fast food restaurants, but they will have a roadside Asian restaurant that sells quickly prepared foods and ice-cold beers. They are usually local hangouts that the tourists drive by. Not me, as they were open late at night when I got off work.

Note on tamarind: Tamarind is originally from the Far East and was brought to the Caribbean many years ago. The Caribbean varieties usually take a bit more sugar to balance out the acid than the imported Thai varieties often found on the shelves in ethnic markets and even supermarkets nowadays, so just add the sugar to your taste. In the islands there are all types of recipes using tamarind, from sodas to sorbets, candies, and creams. I use this savory glaze, more Asian than Caribbean, for all types of dishes, and even as a dip for hors d'oeuvres and baby back ribs. You'll love it over pork, chicken, or game birds. Also, you can spice it up with some fresh or dried chilies if you like. I'll never forget a Thai candy I ate, a gumdrop of sweet-and-sour tamarind with hot-as-hell chilies rolled in granulated sugar. What a contrast of explosive flavors.

Prepare the Tamarind Glaze and the Beet and Balsamic Emulsion.

Separate the shallot slices and toss in the flour with a little salt and pepper. Fry in oil at medium temperature until crispy and light brown. If they become too dark they will be bitter. Remove to paper towel and allow to drain. Season with a sprinkle of salt.

Marinate the fish fillet in a tablespoon or so of glaze for 20–30 minutes. Place fish on a non-stick sheet pan and broil for 7–10 minutes, depending on size, until just cooked through.

While the fish is marinating, stir-fry the bok choy in the olive oil with the garlic and ginger. Season to taste with salt and pepper. Add a touch of water to the pan to create steam and cover lightly until vegetables are cooked. Cook the vegetables al dente, or nice and crunchy and very green. Do not over-cook.

Carefully place bok choy on warm dinner plates, arranging it in a circle. Place the fish in the middle and spoon over a little more glaze. Top with crispy shallots and spoon around the vinaigrette. Serve accompanied by half lemons.

Tamarind Glaze

MAKES ¾ CUP GLAZE

2 T	tamarind paste (seeds removed)
2 T	Thai fish sauce
1 T	fresh ginger, minced
1 T	garlic, minced
3 T	honey
3 T	dark molasses
2 T	ketchup
2 T	fresh lime juice
1 tsp	freshly ground black pepper
1 T	Kitchen D'Orr Aux Poivres Spice Blend
1 T	Kitchen D'Orr New Regime Spice Blend

In the bowl of a food processor or blender, combine the tamarind paste, fish sauce, ginger, garlic, honey, molasses, ketchup, lime juice, pepper, Aux Poivres, and New Regime Blend, until smooth. Pour into a saucepan and bring to a boil. Remove from heat and place in a storage container. Refrigerate until needed.

Beet and Balsamic Emulsion

I like to keep this vinaigrette in a squeeze bottle and use it to add flavor and color to all sorts of dishes.

MAKES 1 CUP

1	small beet, boiled until very tender and peeled
1 T	ginger, minced
¼ c.	balsamic vinegar
½ c.	olive oil
½	lemon, juiced
salt and pepper to taste	

Place all ingredients in a high-speed blender and puree until smooth. Add hot water as needed to thin to a smooth and pourable sauce-like consistency. Season to taste with salt and pepper. Chill until needed.

Lost at Sea

Whether you're a chef or energy trader, you still need to get away every now and then to clear your head and escape your everyday pressures. For me, a busman's holiday is the best way. I like to go visit the critters that will eventually make their way to my table. A day of fishing, spearing, hunting, and gathering takes me to a different world. As my buddy "Nature Boy" says, "If it feels like work, you must not be fishin.'" He's a fisherman/tour guide out of Island Harbour. If you're lucky enough to catch him on a free day, he will take you out and show you the ropes, lines, and sinkers of what being an island fisherman is all about.

Grab a picnic basket of snacks, some water, and drinks and meet him at the pier around 7 AM. It is a late start for him, but you've probably had a couple of rum punches the night before and you're on vacation! Don't forget to bring the ladies! Nature Boy loves the ladies. Its fun to watch this rough-and-tumble guy turn into a real gentleman when the fairer sex is around, gently escorting them onto the boat and caring for their every need throughout the day. If they are lucky, he may even dive for some flamingo shells for them. The day we went out, he was gathering those for some lucky lady. Besides the ladies and the beer, bring some snorkeling gear, towels, hats, and sunscreen. Don't forget the sunscreen! And if you are balding, like me, bring a hat.

We went to Scrub Island (think Gilligan's Island) to gather whelks and lobsters. Whelks are a sea snail, an underwater escargot that hides along the rocks just at water's edge. They can be as big as a fist with beautiful black-and-white spiral shells. Once anchored, we started out along the rocks stopping at each edible example of sea life. We saw, and ate, "longback" barnacles that adhere to the exposed areas of the reef. Nature Boy pried them off with a screwdriver, exposing the smoked-salmon-colored muscle that you peel off and eat. It is sweet and crunchy like a Japanese clam. It would take a lot of them to make a meal. We also harvested sea urchins, known as "sea eggs," carefully picking up the white ones and leaving the black, dangerous-looking spiny ones behind. When harvesting sea eggs, I like to let them rest in my hand for a few seconds until all their little feelers stick to you. It feels really cool/creepy. Check it out if you get a chance.

If you're lucky, you'll find some lobsters peeking out from under the rocks. Nature Boy is always ready for them with his lobster stick—a broom handle fitted out with thin wire loops on both ends that he gingerly coaxes around their tails then quickly tightens. As any good sportsman, he always carefully stalks his prey, in this case making sure that none of the lobsters he harvests are either undersized or carrying eggs. He respects the rules, but even more so, he understands the environmental issues. We saw about eight lobsters that day, some up to 6 or 7 pounds. It was my fault we got only one in the bag though; I let the lobster stick float away during an exciting "whelk moment."

After a few hours of underwater foraging, we headed for terra firma and took a walk in the "bush." We found a coconut tree that Nature Boy scrambled up to harvest three young coconuts—with one hand! He also taught us a riddle: "What has three eyes but can't see? A coconut!" Later, when we found a large rock, he demonstrated how to de-husk and drink them. This was the best coconut water I'd ever had. Nature Boy said it would be even better with a bit of gin splashed in. I always wonder at moments like this if it is the setting or the actual experience that makes things taste so damn good. In this case it was both, plus the company. Later we cracked open the shells and scraped out the tender "jelly" and ate it like some exotic vegetal foie gras quivering on our tongues.

Back on the boat, we headed east to Shoal Bay, stopping on the way to harvest some conch. Whereas whelks and barnacles fasten themselves to the rocks, conch are like sea cows at pasture. They slowly meander on the low-growing grass of the seabed. From above they look like abandoned old shells, but don't let that fool you. Dive down 20 or 30 feet and turn them over. They are fluorescent pink with a hard razor-like foot that guards its inhabitant. I found three and headed back to the boat to listen to some reggae-styled Dylan tunes and await Nature Boy's return. We could see him snorkeling and diving and swimming. I couldn't believe it when he surfaced with eight big conch. The guy didn't even have a bag with him! He dove, gathered, swam, and, let's not forget, breathed, all with 25 pounds of cargo. Impressive.

I may have forgotten to mention that Captain Morgan was on board as well, so when it came time for spear fishing, I chose to let it be a spectator sport. It was amazing to watch as well. Nature Boy swam down 15 or 20 feet, then got into a sniper's pose. "Zip" (that's underwater for "Bang"), and he got a parrotfish, then a red belly, then a doctor, then a butterfish. In a matter of minutes, we had a bag of fish that would have taken me hours to catch. He said on a good day he can bag 100 pounds of fish in a couple of hours. Not a bad day's work.

Back at the pier our education wasn't over. We learned how to clean conch and skin triggerfish. We also spoke about the best way to prepare our catch. I asked Nature Boy what he did with the conch and he said with a smile, "I sell it." Some of the other locals came over to see what we had caught. One of the guys wanted a bit of conch "to chew on." We headed back home to try some recipes and salve our sunburns. Nature Boy headed back to Gwen's, a beachside reggae bar, to study some other natural wonders he had spotted waving to him on the way back to port. As I said, Nature Boy loves the ladies.

2 T	olive oil
2	onions, roughly chopped
2	carrots, peeled and cut on a bias or into little flowers
3	garlic cloves, minced
2	bay leaves
1 piece	orange peel
1	bouquet garni
3	cloves
1	allspice berry, lightly crushed
2 tsp	Kitchen D'Orr Aux Poivres Spice Blend
1½ qt.	fish stock
8	vine-ripe tomatoes, roughly chopped
½ lb.	okra, roughly chopped
½ lb.	bok choy, well cleaned and roughly chopped
2 lbs.	fish fillet, cut into bite-size chunks (big-eyed snapper, pompano, or other mild whitefish)
3 T	salted butter
¼ c.	lime juice (plus 1 tsp of the zest)
1	red pepper, cut in fine julienne
1	yellow pepper, cut in fine julienne
1	fresh chili, minced fine (I like using a chili such as a fresh cayenne or serrano)
½ c.	parsley, basil, tarragon, culantro or cilantro, purple basil, roughly chopped

Snapper in Chili and Ginger Broth with Island Vegetables [a.k.a. Island Fish Water]

I love this simple fisherman's soup that shows the blending of cultures in T&T (Trinidad and Tobago) with Asian and Western ingredients. I learned it from a bartender who worked in a small stall next to the central food market in Port of Spain. Use whatever fish looks freshest in the market, and you can add many other mollusks and crustaceans as well.

Heat the olive oil in a large sauce pot and add the onions, garlic, bay leaves, orange peel, bouquet garni, and spices. Add fish stock, bring to a boil, and simmer 15 minutes.

Season to taste with salt and pepper. Add the tomatoes, okra, and bok choy and bring to a boil, reduce to a simmer and add fish, then cook 1–2 minutes more. Remove from heat and gently stir in the butter, lime juice, julienne peppers, and chilies. Adjust the seasoning, add the fresh herbs, and serve.

Full Moon Rising

Full Moons, Moonlight Nights, and Midnight Picnics

The full moon on an island like Anguilla creates a sense of lunacy. The light is bright and all encompassing. Locals say you can see things on a Moonlight Night that you can't see during the brightest day. It was one of the things that made Christopher and me decide to make "the big change" and take our cooking to Anguilla. On our first visit, we were at Bankie Banx's Dune Preserve next door to CuisinArt having a gingery rum punch he calls "Duneshine" and looking out at the sky full of moonlight. "This does it for me," said Chris, and we were hooked. The full moon is that intoxicating!

Manhattan nights are pretty much the same as the days only with darker corners, cooler sidewalks, and, of course, the glaring streetlights. You can get anything you want 24/7 as long as you know where to look for it. The neon and halogen obliterate the stars; you may not even know if there is a full moon hiding behind those skyscrapers. Don't get me wrong, I love New York nightlife, but I have learned not to miss it too much. You need to learn to distill the essence of the moonlit night Caribbean-style. It is true that Anguilla can be pretty quiet after the sun goes down, but on special nights she can also be the island that never sleeps. Take that New York, New York!

Islanders see full moons as welcome visitors . . . a special time to share with family and friends. A time when the kids can stay up late and wander the small hamlets and port villages with siblings and family friends and fantasize about what is lurking behind the cemetery walls, the abandoned house, or the old cedar tree. Often there are nighttime chores that can be done in the moonlight, like gathering dried wood from the bush to bring home for an outdoor cookout. These, too, are perfect outings for pranks and mischief. Once the tasks are completed, it's likely the younger kids, spooked, will run back to the yard for some crisp johnnycakes, or charcoal-grilled ears of corn, or potfish, a shared pot of fish stew cooked outside in a simmering "firestone" cauldron.

Families call these Moonlight Nights, and they are a celebrated connection to the past.*

Games of "dog and da bone" and the sound of dominoes slapping the table animate the evening as sweetly as the playing of music on handcrafted instruments. The older folks entertain the young with jokes and stories of the old

days and the old ways. No moon-filled night would be complete without a ghost story or two.

Of course the full moon smiles down on lovers of all ages. It is the perfect time to grab the one you love and head to the beach for a Midnight Picnic. Simple foods are what are called for: trunkfish tossed on the remnants of a bonfire until lightly charred, then cracked open and eaten with a sprinkling of seawater and local lime, or roasted breadfruit cooked on the same coals with a pot of stewed fish, or even some whelks cooked in their shells until tender and eaten with melted butter and local hot sauce. Most of these items are also considered "island Viagra," so make sure you carry along a big beach towel in case you get lucky!

Moonlight Nights and Midnight Picnics are special and should be cherished. With so-called progress comes some undesirable trappings. We become distracted by what is new and need to be plugged into something to be stimulated. With electrical lights, boom boxes, TV, microwaves, and fast cars whisking us into the future so fast, we often forget the joys of sharing simple times with those right next to us.

*Bankie Banx has created a full-on celebration of the full moon with a yearly event called Moonsplash, where he collects the best Caribbean talent for three nights of great music, culture, and fun with an emphasis on the fun. The dates change with the moon, so check the web for dates and times. A word to the wise on times: if it says your favorite act will start at 10 PM, show up at midnight. "Island time" doesn't become more accurate with the full moon.

2	1 lb. blue runners, whole, scaled, and gutted (mackerel or any other firm fatty fish works well in this recipe)
1	banana leaf, torn into 6 × 6" sections
2	bell peppers, sliced
1	medium onion, sliced
3	garlic cloves, roughly chopped
2	Roma tomatoes, sliced ¼" thick
1 stalk	lemongrass, green part only
3	scallions, chopped into 2" sections
¼ c.	olive oil

assorted herbs, such as dill, cilantro, Thai basil

salt and pepper

fresh lime wedges, for garnish

Whole Blue Runner Roasted in Banana Leaves

The "blue runner" I call for in this dish is a richly flavored fish that I first met on Anguilla. It is not widely available on the mainland, but the recipe works well with almost any whole fish. You can also try it with fish fillets, especially if the fish has a little fat to it like salmon or wahoo. Remember the fat in fish has all those great omega-3s, so you should eat it at least twice a week. In the absence of fresh banana leaves, use fresh horseradish greens or large collards or the slightly less romantic parchment paper or aluminum foil to lightly wrap your baking dish.

Preheat the oven to 400°.

Line a 12 × 9" baking pan with banana leaf sections, leaving two aside.

Stuff body cavity of each fish with lemongrass, half of the garlic, and some of the herbs. Place stuffed fish on top of banana leaves. Put remaining herbs, garlic, onion, scallion, and peppers in a bowl. Pour olive oil over vegetables, season liberally with salt and pepper, and gently toss vegetables. Divide and arrange half over each fish and cover with remaining two banana leaves. Weight down with coral or a foil-wrapped brick or stone.

Bake until fish is cooked through, approximately 35 minutes.

Serve whole with fresh lime wedges and herbs.

1 tsp	olive oil
1 T	Sofrito de Carlos (see recipe)
2 tsp	garlic, chopped
1 T	shallots, chopped
1 branch	fresh thyme
1	cherry pepper, whole (known as mini-wini, or use your favorite chili)
1 c.	white rice
½ c.	white wine
1 tsp	Kitchen D'Orr Mellow Yellow Spice Blend or curry powder
3–4 c.	fish stock, hot
1 T	saffron
6	Anguillian saltwater crayfish or langoustines, cut in half lengthwise
2	lobster tails cut into medallions, shell on
6	clams
	mussels, beards removed and scrubbed (discard any open ones)
4	chicken thighs, each cut in half
4 oz.	chorizo sausage, cut on a bias in ½" pieces
15	large shrimp, peeled and deveined
12 oz.	fish fillets
4 oz.	squid, cut into rings
½ c.	mixed herbs (basils, fennel tops, garlic chives, and tarragon are in the mix I use)
	salt and pepper as needed
	parchment paper or foil

Anguillian Paella, Sofrito de Carlos, Local Crayfish, Spiny Lobster, and Island Hen

This Spanish classic has been a favorite of mine since a junior high school trip to its motherland. I love the intensely deep flavor that is obtained through the layers that you build into the dish. I've made this Caribbean by using my friend Carlos's Puerto Rican recipe for sofrito and by using the bounty of the local reefs. The touch of curry and the hot chili are a tip of the hat to the West Indies. You can use this as a base and add whatever seafood is the freshest you can get. I've even made paella with bluegills from my parents' lake in Indiana!!!!

Note: Don't forget fingerbowls afterward. They are a nice touch even in an informal family setting. I like to put warm water, a squeeze of fresh lemon (to remove the oils from your fingers), orange flower water (for a beautiful scent), and a slice of lemon in my fingerbowls. You can also use rose water and rose petals.

Pre-heat a wide shallow pan over medium heat. Add the oil and follow with the garlic, shallot, thyme, cherry pepper chili, and sofrito. Remove with a spoon and set aside.

Add the chicken and sausage and cook until the chicken has browned and the oils from the chorizo have been released. Return the sofrito mix to the meats and add the rice, saffron, and curry and sauté until rice is translucent. Deglaze with the white wine and cook until the liquid has evaporated.

Season the seafood with salt and pepper and add to the rice. Top with the fish, hot fish stock, cover with parchment paper or foil, and place in a 350° oven for 25–30 minutes or until liquid is cooked off and rice is tender. If stock evaporates before the rice is cooked, simply add a bit of water and return to the oven. Remove from oven, gently fold in the herbs, and adjust seasoning if needed.

Serve straight away with wedges of lemon and a large empty bowl for your guests to throw their picked shells into.

2	trunkfish, split, with all innards removed except the liver
2	garlic cloves, roughly chopped
2 sprigs	thyme
½	lime, sliced
2 tsp	salt

freshly ground black pepper

Sea Urchin and Scallion Butter (optional; see recipe)

Grilled Trunkfish

This fish is one of the oddest-looking creatures you'll see coming out of Anguillian waters. Trunkfish, also called "shell fish," has an armor-like exoskeleton that protects its dense, meaty flesh. The same hard outside also shields and steams the flesh when you throw it on the fire. The rich liver is a local delicacy. Trunkfish are hard to find, but you can wrap any fish in a collard leaf and then in foil and throw it on the fire and you'll have something good to eat. You can try this with African lobster tails, which can be found frozen in many grocery stores.

Note: To glam up this fisherman's dish, try adding a compound butter to melt over the top. I like my Sea Urchin and Scallion Butter.

Prepare a hot charcoal fire in your grill.

Season the inside of the fish with salt, pepper, lime, thyme, and garlic.

Grill 10 minutes per side.

Crack open and remove the fillets and liver.

Serve with fresh lime and Sea Urchin and Scallion Butter.

Grilled Potfish "en Papillotte"

Delicate potfish caught in local waters are an Anguillian favorite. Any smallish whitefish, such as snapper, bass, or porgy, would make a good substitute. Also, if you're without a grill, a 400° oven works as well, but you'll be losing the smoky flavor of the charcoal.

Build a hot charcoal fire in your grill.

Place cleaned potfish on top of foil sheets.

Stuff empty body cavity with thyme, garlic, ginger, and some lime slices.

Top fish with onions, bell pepper, salt, olive oil, vinegar, and remaining lime slices.

Seal foil on all sides and place on the grill.

Cook until foil packages "balloon" and fish cooks through, about 15–20 minutes for a 2-pound fish.

Carefully open foil to release steam.

Serve with fresh herbs and lime.

2	potfish, approx. 1–2 lbs. each, cleaned
2	garlic cloves, minced
1	onion, sliced thin
1	bell pepper, sliced thin
1 T	ginger, minced
1	lime, cut into rounds
2 sprigs	thyme
2 tsp	sea salt
2 T	olive oil
1 T	chili vinegar
2	foil sheets

2 T	olive oil
2	onions, roughly chopped
2	carrots, peeled and cut on a bias or into little flowers
3	garlic cloves, minced
2	bay leaves
1 piece	orange peel
1	bouquet garni
3	cloves
1	allspice berry, lightly crushed
2 tsp	Kitchen D'Orr Aux Poivres Spice Blend
1½ qt.	fish stock
8	vine-ripe tomatoes, roughly chopped
½ lb.	okra, roughly chopped
½ lb.	bok choy, well cleaned and roughly chopped
2 lbs.	fish fillet, cut into bite-size chunks (snapper, pompano, or other mild whitefish)
3 T	salted butter
¼ c.	lime juice (plus 1 tsp of the zest)
1	red pepper, cut in fine julienne
1	yellow pepper, cut in fine julienne
1	fresh chili, minced fine (I like using fresh cayenne or serrano)
½ c.	parsley, basil, tarragon, culantro or cilantro, purple basil, roughly chopped

Potfish (Island Bouillabaisse) with Tomatoes, Fennel, Saffron, Chilies, and Lime

This is a simple fisherman's soup that blends cultures in a pot. I first created this dish after visiting Trinidad and Tobago (or T&T, as they call them). I love the combination of Asian and Western ingredients. When Christopher and I first made this dish for our staff, they said it tasted like home. That is just the compliment a chef lives for.

This recipe calls for fish, but you can throw in any other sea fodder of your choice, such as crayfish, spiny lobster, clams, or mussels.

Heat the olive oil in a large sauce pot and add the onions, garlic, bay leaves, orange peel, bouquet garni, and spice. Add fish stock, bring to a boil, and simmer 15 minutes. Season to taste with salt and pepper. Add the tomatoes, okra, and bok choy and bring to a boil. Reduce to a simmer and add fish; cook 1–2 minutes more. Remove from heat and gently stir in the butter, lime juice, julienne peppers, and chilies. Adjust the seasoning, add the fresh herbs, and serve.

GRiLLeD LoBSTeR 101

Go to almost any beachside shack in Anguilla and you'll find a simple grilled spiny lobster or ocean crayfish on the menu. This is not always the case on other islands, where crustaceans have been over-fished. Many places now only have lobster seasonally and no crayfish. So if you are a lobster lover, you may want to check to make sure they are available on the island of your destination before you go. Caribbean lobster is more difficult to cook than its northern cousin. It is meant for the grill or to be poached gently in butter. It often needs to be tossed in a creamy sauce afterward or it will tend to be dry. To me, Maine lobster is much more versatile and forgiving to the cook. Caribbean spiny lobster (*Metanephrops binghami*) has more chew to it and the saline flavor profiles tend to be highlighted, whereas the *Homarus americanus* is generally sweeter and more tender. I have also included in this chapter some compound butters and a marinade. They are great on grilled shellfish and seafood.

Here are a few tips on grilling Caribbean lobster or crayfish. These tips work just as well for the northern cousins.

- Always purchase lobsters from a reputable fishmonger, or, if you are lucky, from local lobstermen.

- Build a good hardwood charcoal fire on half of your grill and allow the "black" to cook out, leaving pieces covered with white ash.

- Cut lobster in half, from head to tail.

- Pre-season your lobster with a favorite seasoning. The recipe for mine is given below.

- Start with your lobster shell side down and cook until the meat begins to turn white and pull away from the shell on the outside. The shell should give off a nice "roasted, toasted" smell, but do not allow the shell to burn. This is a major mistake that shows the fire was too hot or that the lobster was cooked too long.

- Turn lobsters over and cook until the meat is white and firm at its thickest part between the tail and the body.

- Remove lobsters to the slow side of the grill, turn them cut side up, and top with your favorite compound butter. Cover and heat until butter is melted.

- Finish with freshly squeezed lemon juice and a pinch of sea salt.

½ c.	good-quality extra-virgin olive oil
2–3 branches	thyme leaves, roughly chopped
1	lemon, zested and juiced
¼ c.	shallots, minced
2	garlic cloves, minced
2 tsp	curry powder
1 tsp	freshly cracked black pepper
1 tsp	kosher salt

Paradise Kitchen Wet Marinade for Lobsters and Seafood

Whisk ingredients together and pour over lobster halves. Allow to marinate 10–15 minutes before grilling.

A Few of My Favorite Compound Butters

Compound butter is a mixture of room-temperature butter and flavorings. It is melted over grilled fish and meats. The classic is "maître d'hôtel" butter, a French recipe served over everything from filet mignon to fillet of trout. These are some more modern versions you can use over anything you grill or roast. You can make up the butter in advance, spoon it into the middle of a sheet of plastic wrap, and roll it up into a log. The butter can be refrigerated or frozen until needed. It is a great way to use up extra herbs, scraps of ginger, and chilies you have around the house. These butters are extremely versatile and can be used on everything from your breakfast brioche to your movie-night popcorn. You'll soon come up with your own favorites.

Tarragon and Ginger Butter

½ lb.	butter, softened
½ bunch	tarragon, picked from the stems and roughly chopped
2 T	ginger, grated
2 T	lime juice (or to taste) plus 1 tsp of the zest
1 tsp	crushed black peppercorns
salt and pepper to taste	

Combine all ingredients into a small mixing bowl. Mix together until creamy and fully incorporated. Roll between plastic into logs, then chill in the refrigerator or freezer.

Sea Urchin and Scallion Butter

½ lb.	butter, softened
¼ c.	sea urchin, mashed with the back of a spoon
2 T	red flying fish roe (small red caviar)
¼ tsp	freshly ground black pepper
¼ tsp	lime zest, finely grated
1	lime, for juice
2 T	scallion, minced
salt and pepper to taste	

Combine all ingredients in a small mixing bowl until creamy and urchin is fully incorporated. Season with salt and pepper to taste.

Sea Eggs

Sea urchins are the pungent yellowish feather-shaped "tongues" found most often in sushi bars garnishing rice. They are a delicacy that the French adore and the Japanese are crazy about, but one that few Americans have discovered. In the English-speaking Caribbean they are known as "sea eggs" and are relatively unknown as well, eaten only by fishermen and foragers of the waterfront. They are in abundance, though, as any scuba or skin diver will attest.

Making a compound butter with this rich seafood is a great way to stretch and preserve your fresh sea urchin roe, or sea eggs. Rolled and frozen, this butter will be ready for use whenever a fresh grilled lobster or fish demands it. You can also serve it melted as a decadent dipping sauce or add it to other sauces.

Jamaican Chili and Lime Jerk Butter

½ lb.   butter (room temperature)

1 T   Jerk Rub—Wet Style (see recipe)

1 T   fresh chili pepper, minced (use your favorite pepper to taste)

¼ c.   lime juice, plus the zest

1 T   paprika

1 T   fresh thyme leaves

¼ c.   scallions, chopped

salt and pepper to taste

Combine all ingredients into a small mixing bowl. Mix together until creamy and fully incorporated. Roll between plastic into logs, then chill in the refrigerator or freezer.

Puerto Rican Cilantro Butter

½ lb.   butter (room temperature)

½ bunch   cilantro, finely chopped

2 tsp   crushed coriander seeds

1   shallot, finely minced

1 T   lemon zest

1 tsp   cracked black pepper

salt to taste

Combine all ingredients into a small mixing bowl. Mix together until creamy and fully incorporated. Roll between plastic into logs, then chill in the refrigerator or freezer.

T&T Shallot and Curry Butter

T&T is the nickname of Trinidad and Tobago. This butter gives that country's West Indian flavor to anything you put it on. In T&T, they like it spicy.

½ lb.   butter (room temperature)

¼ c.   Italian parsley, chopped

1 T   green, red, or yellow chili paste (available in Asian and Caribbean markets)

¼ c.   lemon juice

salt and pepper to taste

Combine all ingredients into a small mixing bowl. Mix together until creamy and fully incorporated. Roll between plastic into logs, then chill in the refrigerator or freezer.

CooKiNG for CaRNi-VOReS

Getting to the Meat of It

Driving the roads of Anguilla with the windows down, you quickly understand that the soul of the Arawaks is still alive. As I said before, the early tribes of the island invented BBQ by cooking over hot coals on "grills" made of green wood branches. An updated version of this cookery is still one of the most popular ways of preparing food there.

There are also many traditional slow-cooked dishes that use inexpensive cuts of meat and pressure cookers. Using island-raised goat, pork, or imported meats, traditional Ameridian Taino *barbacoa* is still king. Before the tourist culture came to the islands, many of the indigenous and post-slave culture folks had been struggling for years. Many still are. The dishes that have developed show the creativity and ingenuity of a people fighting to nurture their families as well as to celebrate nature's bounty that the colonials left them. For me, a bowl of curried goat stew (locally called goat water) brought me a spiritual connection to the past as well as a warming hope for the future.

Daphine, one of my cooks, explained to me that until the 1970s, many Anguillians cooked outside on fire rocks (three large, level stones placed around hot embers used to cook soups, stews, and boiled dumplings) and in oil drum ovens. "The foods were 'sweet' and tasted better than most anything cooked today," Daphine remembers. The old ways weren't easy. Meats were salted and dried on the roof. When pigs were slaughtered, everything but the "oink" was utilized. Everyone had chickens for meat and eggs. Keeping up with the family's water needs was a full-time job of carrying.

For most people raised in the Caribbean, a meal isn't a meal without a nice big hunk of meat. Yes, there are those who are happy with some fish stew, but for most locals you need meat to feed both their stomach and their inner Arawak souls. Rastas and Adventists abstain from meats, and there are others who are so connected to the sea that meat doesn't interest them, but for most, pork, chicken, beef, lamb, and goat are the fuels that keep their engines running.

Some of the best charcoal I've cooked over is made right on the island by smoldering hardwood in charcoal pits. The resulting black nuggets are packed into burlap sacks ready to be lit with gathered twigs and cardboard. Lighter fluid is frowned upon. The coals burn extremely hot yet are long lasting, making them perfect for the pork ribs and chicken thighs that are so popular. One of the first things we did when we moved to Anguilla was buy a handmade BBQ and a bag of coals. The Anguillian

grill is a seemingly simple but ingenious contraption made from old metal gas tubes cut in half, then hinged. Chimneys and handles are added, and a metal grill is put in place. Of course, being on an island that loves to party, it's made portable with removable legs. Mine was a sky blue model.

I believe the hearth of an Anguillian home is its BBQ grill . . . at least it is at my house. Even when "eating out" in paradise, grilled foods are the way to go. In fact, there's probably not a local restaurant on the island that doesn't offer grilled ribs and chicken. You can pick up a couple of chicken thighs at the blue food wagon on "da big road" on the way to work, or if you're hungry leaving Johnno's on a Friday night, there is a roadside stand at the speed bump in Sandy Ground offering up grilled meats, hot dumpling-filled chowders, and cold drinks late into the night. Just look for the crowd.

Simple grilled, roasted, and stewed dishes are what people call "FOOD." The fancy stuff that tourists eat isn't really a meal for a "belonger." They want meat and provisions and a few dumplings thrown in to fill the plate. The dishes I've included in this tome are a mix of both "FOOD" and the fancy stuff. Please don't hold it against me. I encourage you to try both the homely dishes and the fancier "chef" dishes. This way you'll be able to experience the soul of modern island cooking.

Paradise Kitchen Grilled Chicken with Chilies, Garlic, and Lime

The advance marinating of the chicken is key to its deep, soulful flavor. I use Scotch bonnet peppers (seeds and veins removed), but you decide how much heat you can take and use your favorite pepper accordingly. Make sure you "finish" the chicken as I describe at the end of the recipe. It really makes it POP!

Prepare the grill; place an oiled rack 4–6 inches above medium coals.

Combine the oil, lime juice, rosemary, garlic, spices, and salt. Brush the chicken inside and out and marinate for 3–4 hours before grilling. May be done the day before and refrigerated overnight.

Place the chickens on the grill, bone side down. Baste chicken halves frequently with marinade mixture and turn every 10 minutes. Once nicely caramelized, move to the cool side of your grill and cook until done, about 30–40 minutes. When done, chicken should be tender and juices will run clear when the meat is pierced with a fork.

Finish by drizzling with olive oil, sprinkles of crystals of sea salt, coarsely ground pepper, and squeezes of fresh lime over the crispy chicken just before taking it to the table. Small things like this will make a huge difference.

Oh, and toss some lime wedges and big sprigs of cilantro around it as well.

FOR 4–6 FRIENDS

2	broiler chickens, split, about 5–6 lbs. total
3 T	extra-virgin olive oil
⅓ c.	lime juice
4	kaffir lime leaves, cut into thin ribbons
1	fresh chili pepper, minced—use your favorite depending on heat
2 branches	fresh rosemary, crushed
2 T	Kitchen D'Orr Mediterranean Spice Blend
1 T	Kitchen D'Orr Mellow Yellow Spice Blend
2	large garlic cloves
2 tsp	salt
2 tsp	freshly ground black pepper, to taste
additional olive oil as needed	
sea salt as needed	
1	whole lime cut in half

Parler Français?

Filet mignon is French, of course. *Oui, Oui!!* With *filet* meaning "thick slice" and *mignon* meaning "dainty," the word appeared in America around the 1890s and is now used nationwide.

Buy whole tenderloin when it's on sale and slice into filet mignon yourself. That way you control the thickness. Wrap unneeded slices tightly in plastic wrap, seal in a Ziploc bag with all the air removed, and freeze for later use. When properly trimmed, the filet mignon is extremely lean and perfect for healthy cookery. Filet mignon is boneless, but you get a taste of it whenever you eat a T-bone steak.

FOR 4 FRIENDS

1½ lb.	filet mignon, cut into 4 steaks, each 1¼–1½" thick
2 tsp	Paradise Kitchen Jerk Spice Blend (see recipe) or your favorite spicy rub
2 tsp	olive oil
sea salt and cracked black pepper as needed	
4 c.	finely chopped kale, calalloo, or other greens
1	red pepper, cut into thin strips
2 T	olive oil
2	garlic cloves, minced

BALSAMIC VINEGAR PAN SAUCE

2 tsp	garlic, minced
¼ c.	dry vermouth
¼ c.	beef or chicken stock
2 tsp	soy sauce
1 T	balsamic vinegar
salt and freshly ground black pepper	

Jerk-Rubbed Filet Mignon with Steamed Kale and Calaloo

Filet mignon is a tender cut of meat but often is lacking in flavor. I love to spice it up with a jerk rub and sear it until nicely caramelized. You can serve this with any number of dishes in the side dish and accompaniments chapter, but I like bitter greens especially well.

I often serve it with crispy shallots and top it with a chutney.

Season the meat generously with jerk rub, salt, and cracked pepper.

In a medium-size heavy skillet, heat the oil over medium-high heat. Put in olive oil, followed by the steaks, and sear them for 3–4 minutes per side until medium-rare. Remove and cover loosely to keep them warm while you prepare the vegetable and sauce.

Meanwhile, in another pan heat the olive oil and add the garlic. Cook until it begins to brown and add the peppers and the greens. Sauté the greens until they start to wilt, and add 2 tablespoons of water to create steam. Cook until tender. Season to taste with salt and pepper. Set aside with the beef.

Pour off all but 1 tablespoon of the fat, leaving any meat juices in the pan. Reduce the heat to medium and sauté the garlic for 15 seconds, stirring constantly. Add the vermouth and scrape up any browned bits from the bottom of the pan. Raise the heat to high and reduce the vermouth to a syrup. Pour in the stock, soy sauce, and vinegar. Boil until the sauce just begins to thicken. Remove from the heat, swirl in the butter, and taste for salt and pepper. Pour over the steaks and serve.

Bush = Anything Green

In the islands, "adding a little bush" means going to the garden or scrub (untended land out back) and finding some aromatic herbs to put in the pot you have going on the stove. It will be a step in most recipes from cocktails to after-dinner tea. Bush is what gives the depth and soul to a dish. Whether it is a long-cooked stew or a quick sauté, there is an herb that will bring all the flavors together and give a great finish to what you are cooking. Every traditional Caribbean household has a bush garden out back growing herbs for all purposes. There are medicinal herbs, kitchen herbs, and herbs used for other domestic purposes like repelling pests and cleaning and scenting laundry, and even the body as well.

Most culinary bush have folkloric values as well as being flavor enhancers. These dual purposes make cooking with herbs a must for Caribbean recipes. The age-old wisdom handed down from generation to generation makes the scent of fresh herbs part of what makes a house a home. I've found that a simple fish cake becomes a family classic when you add a bit of minced lime leaf and some homegrown mint to the poached and shredded parrotfish. Add some lemongrass to your fish water and it won't taste like the neighbor's.

Both the Caribs and the Arawaks used wild herbs in their cooking, and the Europeans took them back home along with the chilies and other vegetables they stole from the New World. Thanks to the horticultural influence of the African slaves, Asians, and East Indians, the Caribbean has become a culinary melting pot of flavors. Thai and lemon basils, thyme, cilantro and culantro, garlic chives, and scallions are all found in backyard gardens and farmers' markets throughout the islands. Stingy thyme (Mexican oregano), allspice leaves, and bay leaves also play a large part in local cooking; this is the stuff culinary dreams are made of.

On many islands you'll find bouquets of bush already bundled together for specific uses. Stew bush, soup bush, curry bush, fish bush, and meat bush are frequently found "pre-packaged," if that's what you call a variety of herbs tied tightly with string. These are bundles of bush tied tightly with string in a masochistic fantasy that Julia Child would call a bouquet garni.

Fresh herbs and dried herbs are important in most cultures and cuisines, but somehow even more so in the islands. In the Caribbean, "bush" is not just a flavoring but a cultural connection to the past. The toil and hunger of slavery in most islands has left a ghost who whispers to us, even if we are just visiting.

One evening, I dined on a lovingly prepared dish of a friend's grandmother's fish stew. It was full of vibrant herbal tones but was missing something. His "passed" granny's voice seemed to be whispering in my ear, suggesting that he may have forgotten something from the bush garden out back . . . maybe to add a few more chilies? I left his house feeling spooked; she should talk to him.

Spice-Crusted Rack of Lamb

1	18 oz. rack of lamb (Frenched by your butcher)
1	garlic clove, cut into 8 pieces
1 sprig	fresh thyme
1 sprig	fresh rosemary
1 sprig	fresh sage
1 T	Paradise Kitchen Jerk Spice Blend (see recipe) or your favorite dry rub
1 T	crushed black pepper
2 T	olive oil

Rack of lamb is a festive dish that I think is very romantic. Just think of all the nibbling and bone-sucking goodness that you get when you have it on your plate. A full rack is definitely meant to be shared and is a perfect splurge whether you are cooking for a longtime love or a prospective new one. I suggest serving this dish with one of the lighter vegetable dishes found in the side dish section of the book. You won't want to feel heavy on a romantic night.

"Pick" the rack of lamb with garlic, 1 piece of garlic next to each bone. This is done by puncturing the meat with the tip of a knife and inserting the garlic. Chop half the herbs and mix with the other seasonings. Rub lamb with 1 tablespoon of the olive oil and follow with the herb and spice mix. Refrigerate until ready to cook. This can be done up to 24 hours in advance.

Pre-heat oven to 450°.

Heat a large, oven-proof, metal-handled sauté pan over high heat. Add the other tablespoon of olive oil to the pan and sear the lamb until golden brown on both sides. Place in oven, fat side down, and roast 5 minutes. Turn over, put remaining herb sprigs under lamb, and roast an additional 5 minutes, spooning some of the cooking fat over the lamb. Roast a final 4–5 minutes. Cooking time will depend on the size of the rack, so if it is smaller it may take less time.

Take the lamb out of the pan (if you leave it in it will continue to cook). Cover and allow to rest for 7–10 minutes before carving.

2	legs of lamb
½ c.	olive oil
5	key limes, sliced thinly
¼ c.	brown cane sugar
1 bunch	thyme, roughly chopped
1 bunch	rosemary, roughly chopped
2 heads	garlic, roughly chopped
1	red onion, sliced thinly
1 T	cracked black peppercorns
1 T	crushed red pepper flakes
1 T	cracked allspice berries
2 T	Kitchen D'Orr Mellow Yellow Spice Blend (or curry powder)
1 T	whole mustard seeds
4	bay leaves, crushed
1 T	whole bird peppers, dried
1	fresh red chili, roughly chopped
2 T	fresh ginger, chopped
2 T	sea salt

Grilled West Indian Leg of Lamb

This is a great marinade for lamb, goat, or other red meat and works equally well with poultry, pork, or even thick fish steaks. Marinate for 12–24 hours, then grill, roast, or put on the rotisserie and cook to desired doneness. Serve with simple side dishes like white rice and lentils and, as always, a handful of cilantro or mint and some lime wedges.

Note on bird peppers: There are many types of bird peppers, but usually one thinks of Thai and Chinese dishes. Bird peppers are one of the smallest chilies, but they pack one of the biggest bites. Two well-known varieties are tepin and pequin. You can find them fresh in green and red, the red being the ripe variety or dried in Asian markets. I like to use them whole to give flavor, but remove them before serving. It is when you cut them that they truly roar.

Place the leg of lamb in a large baking dish and remove any white fat that feels hard to the touch.

Mix the remaining ingredients to create a marinade and rub into meat on all sides, cover, and refrigerate. Turn the meat over every several hours.

Grill or roast on a hot grill until crusty on the outside, about 10 minutes on the first side and 8–10 minutes on the second side, depending on the thickness of the leg.

Move to the slower side of the grill, covered, an additional 8–10 minutes. A quick-read thermometer should register 125–135°. Rest for 8–10 minutes, lightly covered with aluminum foil. Slice thinly against the grain of the meat; it should be well caramelized on the exterior and a rich, rosy red on the inside.

1	fresh ham, weighing 5–7 lbs., large center bone removed and scored along the skin side with a sharp knife
1 c.	lime juice
1 T	sea salt
¼ c.	Paradise Kitchen Jerk Spice Blend (see recipe)
½ c.	coriander, roughly chopped
2 T	thyme, roughly chopped
1	Holland red hot chili sliced in thin rings (or your favorite chili)
1 c.	Goya tomato and chili sauce (or tomato sauce with some green chilies added to taste)
½ c.	olive oil
1 c.	water

Anguillian Jerked Fresh Ham

This is a great dish to cook for a group when you want to free yourself up from last-minute work while entertaining. It takes 3–5 hours in the oven (depending on the size of the ham), so pop it in and you'll have plenty of time to get into that party dress, throw on the pearls, and practice that Latin dance step. If you don't boogie, at least you'll have time to jump in the shower.

Wash the ham inside and out with the lime juice and sea salt, rubbing in both with your fingers. Allow to sit at least 15 minutes and up to several hours. Massage the inside of the ham with the jerk seasoning, herbs, and chilies; then roll it back to its original shape. Tie it if you wish, but it will take longer to cook if you do.

Fifteen minutes prior to roasting, pre-heat oven to 450°.

In a roasting pan just large enough to hold the roast, combine the tomato sauce and water and mix well. Place the ham with the skin side down and rub with the olive oil. Season with a little more sea salt and roast for about 30–45 minutes or until well browned. Turn over, skin side up, and reduce the temperature to 325° and cook an additional 2 hours, basting every 30 minutes or so, until the skin is nice and crisp. Add additional water as needed. The liquid should reduce to a sauce-like thickness.

Take the temperature of the roast in the thickest part; it should read 165° at this time. Do a final basting, turn off the oven, and let the meat rest an additional 20–30 minutes inside the oven, covered lightly with aluminum foil.

Serve thinly sliced with the natural juices spooned over.

Great with polenta, tomato salad, and greens.

3 racks	baby back ribs, approximately 2 lbs. ea.
¼ c.	Homemade Chili Vinegar (see recipe)
¼ c.	cane syrup
¼ c.	Paradise Kitchen Jerk Spice Blend (see recipe) or your favorite spicy rub
1	lime, juiced
1 T	crushed black pepper
1 T	garlic salt
1 T	fresh thyme

Jerked Island Ribs

Ribs are a way of life in Anguilla. They are at every beach shack and are even sold along the road. Carnival wouldn't be Carnival without them. If you visit the island, make sure you go to B&D's for a rib and chicken combo. Also, head downtown on Saturday, where some of the top ribs on the island can be found across the street from the People's Market.

Rub ribs with jerk spices, garlic salt, and black pepper. Mix chili vinegar, cane syrup, and lime juice and pour over seasoned ribs. Let marinate 2–3 hours.

Start hardwood charcoal fire on one side of your grill. Allow the coals to burn until "da black cooks out of 'em" and they are coated with white ash.

Grill over medium heat for 30–45 minutes, until tender and slightly charred. If the fire is too hot, move ribs off the hot side and cover so they continue to slowly cook and smoke until tender. Once cooked through, you can wrap them in aluminum foil and keep them warm on the grill until you have the rest of the meal ready. They will slowly steam in the foil and continue to cook and get nice and moist.

Serve with Don't Let Your Man-Go Sauce (see recipe) and a squeeze of fresh lime.

Carnival, Summerfest
Whatever You Call It, It's a Party!

Carnival comes from the Latin word meaning meat. Historically, carnivals were held throughout Catholic Europe as a final feast and celebration before the long, meat-deprived season of Lent. Think Mardi Gras. The Spanish brought the energy and excitement of the yearly event to the Caribbean as they slowly converted the indigenous peoples to their religion. The Caribbean region was known as the "Spanish Lake" during the early years of European domination, a title that bitterly upset the Anglicans.

Caribbean carnivals or festivals are now held throughout the year with different themes on each of the islands. Many isles are not Catholic, so they hold their festivals at times other than before Lent. The French and Spanish isles, also Brazil and New Orleans, continue to have them in mid-February, while islands with greater British and Dutch influence are a bit more liberal about when they time their celebrations. Anguilla's 2-week Summerfest is held in late July and early August. It celebrates both the rich cultural history of the island and its modern vitality. Events feature new and traditional music, local beauty and talent competitions, and, most importantly, Anguilla's national sport, boat racing!

Days before the party commences, you can literally feel the energy building, especially if you are leeward of the town center and the music drifts into your open bedroom windows late into the night. The events are a needed break for all those living on the island; they rejuvenate and re-energize everyone. It's a time to "lime," to kick back with family and friends and enjoy some free time without a lot of hassle and pretense.

The party starts on Thursday night with all the local dignitaries opening the event with positive speeches (politicians never change no matter what country you are in) and fireworks. But skip these and head to the real action of the food stalls. There are cauldrons of cow's foot soup, goat stew, braised conch, fish water, grilled chicken thighs, pork skewers, and ribs. That's great gutsy food that speaks to the roots of the people and their past struggles, history, and folklore, as well as their bright outlook for the future. No politician can beat that. I suggest picking up several different dishes and passing them among friends so you can more fully immerse yourself in the spicy stew that is a Caribbean carnival.

"August Monday," the first Monday in August, is a national holiday that launches a week of daily boat races as well as nightly events in The Valley (the

protected capital town in the middle of the island). These events include calypso competitions, reggae and soca nights, and the crowning of Miss Anguilla. It starts with "J'Ouvert," an early morning street parade (beginning at 4 A.M. but get there at 6 A.M. and you'll still have a great time). Flatbed trucks carry top local bands, dancers, and walls of speakers blaring songs newly created for the season. Throngs follow their favorite act in a conga line from The Valley to Sandy Ground. Cocktail trucks greet you every few steps. This creates a trance-like state that holds on to you for the entire day of debauchery. With choruses like "The Wetta de Betta" and "Enjoy U-self," band leaders encourage the crowd's avid participation. No one disappoints: hands wave, people spray water; the whole snake-like procession sways and jumps to the music. Sex steams even at the early morning hour; good thing Anguilla has more churches than bars.

Once at the historical Sandy Ground village, the sweaty throngs jump into the crystal clear waters, where boats from ports throughout the region wait to greet them. Hours later, when you have cooled down, been well fed, and have possibly caught up with a nap on the beach, the boat races begin. When the boats sail off, the partying continues with rum drinks, iced beers, and of course BBQ. A couple of hours later, the boats return and the music picks up again and carries on well into the night. For those who haven't had enough, games of dominoes (Anguilla's other great passion) pop up at roadside neighborhood bars and family homes. You can hear the slapping of the pieces as you drive toward bed to rest for a few hours before the next day's events.

Throughout the week, the daily boat races each start at a different village, each showcasing the town's character and charm for visitors. The "home team" has an advantage in knowledge of the reefs and winds, making things even more interesting. They put their top boat into the race, crewed by a well-seasoned team. The daily races give each home harbor an advantage and possible bragging rights.

The races are hotly followed. Some guys follow by sea in motorboats, while others in souped-up cars tear across the island to different vantage points . . . all straining to see if "their" boat is ahead. Don't forget the ladies. My friend Caroline will "cut you up" if you speak badly about her boat, the UFO from Island Harbour. Anguillians take enormous pride in their locally handmade sailboats. There is much playful banter among the spectators, and I suspect that there may even be some "friendly" money changing hands after all the boats have returned to port. Of course, there are postrace get-togethers with more food, live music, and fun with the racers, and maybe even a cocktail (or three). It's then that you'll hear the passionate tellings and retellings of stolen wind, unfair maneuvers, overweighted boats, and poor captaining from the losing teams, matched by loud backslapping and jollification from the winners. When it all dies down, everyone ends up with a smile on his or her face.

The sun is hot and the beaches are full of "belongers" accompanied by the yearly return of Anguillians from afar. This is real life, the real deal! After a year of catering to romancing honeymooners and garishly sunburned Yanks splashing in the water, I got to see some real celebrating. The Anguillians are a beautiful people and their celebration is something to experience. Whether you're here to remember the brutal past, celebrate current success, look to a positive future, or just eat some good vittles and watch a wickedly wonderful boat race, the Anguillian Summerfest is not to be missed.

Getting Your Grill on— Island Style

Grilling is a way of life in the islands. Each island has its own specialties. In St. Martin, for example, you'll find grilled blood sausage; on other islands, you'll find goat or local fish. The Anguillian BBQ is special because of its charcoal. Locally made by burying hardwood scrub wood and burning it slowly for many hours, it gives the meat a clean-grilled taste that leaves little wanting but salt, pepper, and some good dipping sauce. If you are lucky, you'll stumble on to the fiery local hot sauce. Look for it in small, salvaged glass soda water bottles with a xeroxed label featuring a Scotch bonnet pepper. It is piquant and mind altering and will satisfy the inner chili-head in us all. Go to the "Caribbean Condiments" chapter for more ideas on rubs, sauce, and flavoring to make your next BBQ the bomb!

FOR 6 FRIENDS

1 stalk	lemongrass, tough top and bottom portions removed, tender center portion halved, and sliced very thin
2	garlic cloves
2 slices	unpeeled ginger
1	shallot, roughly chopped
1	jalapeno, roughly chopped
½ c.	sugar
¼ c.	fish sauce
3 lbs.	flank or hanger steak

Grilled Flank Steak in Burnt Cane, Lemongrass, and Ginger Marinade

This is one of the dishes that our Anguillian National Culinary Team won with at the Taste of the Caribbean cook-off in Miami. We were awarded the prize for most creative cuisine in the "Iron Chef–like" competition among thirteen island nations. This marinade is great on everything from salmon to pork to chicken and beef. Once made, it will keep indefinitely in the refrigerator, ready to be used on whatever you dream up. Maybe you will win over your family's affection for your own dishes using it.

Great with rice and beans or a veggie stir-fry.

Place lemongrass, garlic, and ginger in food processor, and process until coarsely ground. Add shallot and jalapeño and process until finely ground. Scrape out into a bowl.

Place sugar in heavy-bottomed medium saucepan and turn heat to medium-high. Cook, breaking apart lumps with wooden spoon until sugar melts and turns amber, about 5 minutes. Stir in lemongrass mixture and cook, stirring constantly, for about 1 minute. Add fish sauce and simmer to blend flavors, about 30 seconds. Remove from heat and cool to room temperature.

Massage mixture into meat and marinate at room temperature for 30 minutes. Grill on medium heat to desired temperature; I suggest rare to medium-rare.

Spit-Roasted Chicken with Haitian Mofongo and Mango Chutney

FOR 4 FRIENDS

FOR THE CHICKEN

1	2 lb. chicken, whole
½	lime
1 T	kosher salt
10	garlic cloves, roughly chopped
1	Spanish onion, roughly chopped
1 bunch	tarragon
1	lemon, cut into eighths
1 T	Kitchen D'Orr Aux Poivres Spice Blend
2 T	Paradise Kitchen Jerk Spice Blend (see recipe)
¼ c.	olive oil

salt and pepper to taste

ACCOMPANIMENTS

Soft Mofongo (see recipe)

Green Mango and Banana Chutney (see recipe)

Mango chicken has almost become a cliché in the Caribbean. You can find one version or another on most islands, especially in tourist towns. The flavors do work, and that's the reason it is so popular. I wanted to come up with my own version. I finish the sauce with diced fresh mangoes and accompany the chicken with a spicy chutney that does the cha-cha-cha across your tongue. The mofongo, a mash of green plantains that I often use as an accompaniment, foils the heat and readies your mouth for the next bite. Many ovens now have rotisserie attachments and they do produce a wonderful product. The constant spinning distributes the juice throughout the cooking, helping you create a juicier bird. If you don't have one, however, don't be discouraged. Cook in a 400° oven and baste. It will be almost as good. The sauce, mofongo, and chutney can all be made in advance, so this is a great dish for entertaining.

See side dishes section for the Soft Mofongo recipe and condiments section for the Green Mango and Banana Chutney recipe.

Remove the giblets from your chicken and reserve for another use. (I usually freeze everything but the liver to use for a stock later and cook the liver for a chef's snack!) Rub the bird well with the half lime and kosher salt and rinse with cold water.

Pat dry with paper towel and stuff the cavity of the bird with the garlic, onions, tarragon, and lemon wedges. Rub the skin with olive oil and season with salt and spices.

Place chicken on the spit of your rotisserie and roast until crispy and cooked through, about 45 minutes to 1 hour depending on the size of your chicken. When cooked the juices should run clear when the thigh is pierced with the point of a knife.

Allow to rest at least 15 minutes before carving so the juices don't run out and the bird stays as moist as possible. During this time you can finish your sauce and the accompaniments.

Animal Husbandry 101, a.k.a. Taking Care of the Kids

At just into my mid-40s, I'm happy to say that I'm still a bachelor. My mother may not be thrilled with that fact, but that's another story. The first time I told her I was planning to have a couple of kids running around my backyard, I think she almost fell off her chair with joy. I had to wait for her to catch her breath before finishing the story that they were a couple of goats named Blacky and Dylan. Island life gave me the opportunity to dabble in animal husbandry. Over my 2-year island stay, I added to my duties by building a chicken coop for my nine chickens and even had the governor's wife tether her horse in the yard.

Animal husbandry is one of those life-changing things you have to experience to truly understand. The joys of the daily feeding and the bond you build with each animal, along with the sadness caused by periodic setbacks, give you a deeper appreciation for what we so easily pick up in the supermarket or have delivered to a restaurant. Raising livestock isn't a joke or a game. Many Anguillians have put themselves through college by herding goats and selling them to restaurants, supermarkets, and resorts. At holiday times, fresh local pork and beef are also available. On an island that is said to have more goats than people, shepherding is big business.

In the old days, the village butcher did most of his work on the weekends. Saturday was a big day, when a neighbor would pick an animal and lead it down to his shop. Beforehand, he would put out the word that there would be fresh meat available and all would put their requests in for desired cuts. Nothing was wasted. Every morsel from the first to the last became part of something, whether it was blood pudding or souse or sausage or stew. Many of the pieces were salted and dried on the roof or corned for later use. Meat was traded and given as gifts and was deeply prized, not taken for granted, as is the case today. Some of these cuts are not available in island grocery stores, fresh or frozen. Northerners can check at Latin and ethnic markets.

My animal tending was not nearly so serious. I loved sitting on the porch in the late afternoon when the sun and temperature were going down and watching the baby goats play "king of the mountain" on their mother's back or listening to them baaaaaaah for their breakfast when they first saw me walking around the house in the morning. It makes one feel needed and loved. But

don't get me wrong: these guys aren't pets. Goat stew (called "goat water" on Anguilla) is one of the national dishes, and since these aren't dairy goats, you know where they're headed, and it's not to a creamy chèvre. To remind my friends and myself not to get too attached, I named the last two kids Sweet and Succulent. I fed them mimosa and wild island sage so they were filled with self-basting goodness.

I named my chickens too, which is a bad start if you are planning to have stewed fowl or curried chicken on the menu. I enjoyed their eggs of all sizes and I'd smile at the way they would gather at the fence and await my arrival with papaya scraps, mango pits, and their favorite, corn on the cob. No matter how well I think I clean those cobs, beaks can do it better. Cleve, one

of the lead gardeners at CuisinArt's hydroponic farm, built me my chicken coop. I asked him to build a coop that looked like a typical old-time "island" house. He used leftover corrugated metal and construction castaways to create a charming addition to the backyard, which overlooked St. Martin and St. Barts. I finished it with wooden wine crates for nesting boxes and a secured driftwood sleeping roost. Even the yard birds gathered on that pole, seeming to discuss the day as the sun went down.

To tell the truth, I left the island without slaughtering any of my animals. I left the island without blood on my hands. My animals must have been the most spoiled chickens and goats on the island. I guess I might make a good husband after all.

Duck with Kumquat Rum Sauce

1	large duck (4–5 lbs.)
1 T	Kitchen D'Orr Sweet Seasons Spice Blend (or Chinese 5-spice powder)

salt and freshly ground black pepper to taste

4 branches	rosemary
4 branches	thyme
2	medium oranges
2	medium lemons

boiling water, as needed

¼ c.	sugar
⅓ c.	white wine vinegar
3 c.	brown chicken stock
2 tsp	cornstarch
1 T	bitter orange marmalade
½ c.	dry white wine
½ c.	homemade kumquat rum (or your favorite orange liqueur)

freshly ground white pepper to taste

This is a play on the old French "canard à la orange" using my Kumquat and Star Anise Rum, which can be found on p. 96. I like using some of the drunken kumquats from the bottle to add to the sauce and serve over the sliced duck. If you don't want to go through the whole process of flavoring the rum, use some Grande Marnier and some sliced fresh kumquats. Try serving this with Island Cornmeal Fungi with Okra (see recipe) or Sautéed Pigeon Peas and Greens (see recipe) or both.

Preheat oven to 350°. Liberally season duck inside cavity with salt, black pepper, and spices. Stuff it with the onions, garlic, and fresh herbs.

Place breast side up on a rack in a pan and prick thighs and breast with a fork to allow fat to escape. Place the duck in the oven and pour 1½ cups of water into the pan with it. Roast until juices run clear when the thigh is pricked, about 1½ hours or until thermometer registers 145–150° at the thickest part of the thigh. If the roasting duck begins to darken, cover lightly with foil and return to the oven. When cooked, remove and allow to rest lightly covered in a warm place for at least 8–10 minutes.

During the time when the duck is cooking, remove zest from the oranges and lemons and cut into a fine julienne. Squeeze juice from the oranges and lemons and set aside. Blanch zest in boiling water to cover for 3 minutes; drain and set aside.

In a heavy-bottomed saucepan over moderate heat, melt sugar and cook until it begins to brown lightly. Add vinegar, orange and lemon juices, and stock; reduce over medium heat to a light sauce consistency.

In a small bowl, mix the cornstarch with a little water and stir into stock mixture. Simmer briefly until slightly thickened. Stir in marmalade and keep sauce warm.

While the duck is resting, spoon off fat from pan juices that have collected in the roasting pan. Place the pan on the stove over high heat. Once it is hot, quickly remove it away from the flame and deglaze roasting pan with wine and kumquat rum. Return to the fire and flambé, all the while scraping up the brown bits. Add the sauce to the pan and return to a boil. Strain. Add reserved zest and kumquats from the rum bottle (or freshly sliced kumquats) and simmer until slightly thickened.

Carve duck, place on a warm serving platter, and pour sauce over pieces.

Spit-Roasted Puerto Rican Pork Loin Marinated with Bitter Orange, Chilies, Molasses, and Herbs

We put this succulent pork dish on as a Sunday "Plat du Jour" to give those carnivores something to look forward to after all the wonderful lobster and fish of the week. I didn't tell them that it was really because the fishermen don't go out on Sundays! The recipe is based, loosely, on a Puerto Rican marinade for pork. We serve it with homegrown tomatoes from the garden tossed with red onions, olive oil, fresh herbs, and Spanish sherry vinegar. The oaky acidity of the vinegar balances the background sweetness of the molasses perfectly.

Combine all ingredients for the marinade and mix well. Place the pork loin in the marinade 2–24 hours before cooking. Remove and season with salt, mixed pepper spice, and jerk seasoning. Place loin in a rotisserie and cook until desired temperature.

Note: You can also use this marinade for pork chops and even for ribs. If pork is not your thing, this marinade is great on poultry. I've used it on turkey, chicken, and duck before roasting or grilling. Remember, there is some sugar in the molasses, so whatever you marinate, low and slow is the way to go. If it starts to get too dark, cover with foil, or if grilling, move off direct heat and cover with the grill dome.

MAKES 1 FULL PORK LOIN OR 8 PORK TENDERLOINS

MARINADE

3 pieces	homegrown key limes, sliced
1 piece	homegrown bitter orange, sliced
1 piece	lemon, sliced
1 piece	celery stalk, chopped
1 piece	onion, sliced
½ c.	mixed organic herbs, (lemongrass, lime leaves, thyme, rosemary, garlic chives, scallion, etc.)
½ c.	molasses
¼ c.	soy sauce
¼ c.	Thai fish sauce
2 T	ginger, minced
1 T	garlic, chopped
1 T	chilies, minced
1 T	Paradise Kitchen Jerk Spice Blend (see recipe)
1 T	Kitchen D'Orr Aux Poivres Spice Blend
1 T	Kitchen D'Orr Sweet Seasons Spice Blend
½ c.	olive oil
2 lbs.	pork loin

salt, Aux Poivres Spice Blend, and Paradise Kitchen Jerk Spice Blend to taste

sides and ACCoM-PaNi-mEnts

Side dishes are often afterthoughts, but why? Northerners tend to think of them as co-stars to the lead actor, which far too often is a boring piece of meat. We tend to cook the same old lamb, pork, beef, chicken, and fish dishes, but side dish possibilities are infinite. Just imagine all the different vegetables in the world, and then five or six different dishes made with each! There is no reason why you can't make a new and interesting meal every night. Side dishes provide most of our fiber, vitamins, and minerals, so there should be at least as much, if not more, love put into their preparation. It's to be hoped, when you are cooking, you are preparing meals for those you care about. What better way to say "I love you" than with a plate of well-prepared, nutritious veggies?

Accompaniments are also a way to fuel a family on a budget. In the Caribbean, the rice and peas dish is omnipresent but don't forget the provisions. Yams, green bananas, plantains, sweet potatoes, pumpkin, yucca, casaba, and other roots all make up an interesting palette to paint from. These are filling and inexpensive and they have a good shelf life. They fill the belly and, quoting my friend John, "stick to the ribs." I also love the vegetables my garden guru, Franklyn, grows for me. His fresh black-eyed peas and okra are the best I've ever had. The abundance of organic eggplant he plucks from his vegetable patch has inspired me with its meaty chew in both side dishes and vegetarian main courses.

When shopping I always go directly to the meat counter or the fishmonger to see what is fresh. Once that is done, I head back to the produce aisle to see what is seasonal and fresh and start thinking about those side dishes. I always like to have something crisp and crunchy, like a green vegetable lightly steamed with herbs and citrus, as well as something that will soak up the sauce. Usually these tend to be fattening things like pasta in cheese sauce, buttery mashed potatoes, or fried johnnycakes. But, don't forget that mashed yams with a touch of olive oil are very nutritious; so are many grains. Go for the whole grains whenever possible. White rice is one of my favorites, but change it up every once in a while with some boiled wheat berries, wild rice, and barley to stretch it out and give it more chew. It makes a great salad the next day as well. Mashed potatoes? Leave the skins on and add low-fat sour cream or buttermilk and chives instead of a ton of butter and you'll have a healthier dish. Add a few chives and no one will know the difference. You might try skipping the spuds all together and instead steam some cauliflower until tender and puree it in your blender with a garlic clove and some fat-free sour cream. Cauliflower mousse is creamy, rich, and a great change of pace.

The protein part of the meal is usually the most expensive part, and you usually don't want to experiment with costly ingredients in a recipe you are unsure about. Side dishes, on the other hand, are often made with less expensive ingredients, so throw caution to the wind and get into the kitchen. Remember my mantra, "Recipes are guidelines, so use them for inspiration only." Add what you and your family like and leave out the bits you don't. The main thing is that you have a bit of fun and cook with the heart. Those pots and pans you are banging around will be the sound of love to all those lucky enough to be within earshot.

FOR 6 FRIENDS

½ lb.	cornmeal
½ lb.	pumpkin, grated
1 c.	flour
1 c.	sugar
1 c.	grated coconut
½ c.	raisins
1 T	vanilla extract or seeds from 1 vanilla bean
1 T	fresh ginger, grated
1 pinch	nutmeg, freshly grated
1 tsp	lemon zest
1 T	butter (room temperature)
1 c.	coconut milk
salt and pepper to taste	

Guy Gumbs's Anguillian Conky Dumplings

Guy makes these dumplin's whenever he's feeling nostalgic. They are a favorite during the holidays and other family gatherings. Guy's mother runs one of the wonderful food vans that parks along the side of the road and serves the "real food" of the island. If you want oxtails, souse, goat stew, or conch with dumplings, you must pay her a visit.

My friend Caroline from Island Harbor loves to tell stories of "da ole days." When she does, she always stresses one thing: Anguillians made use of everything. A perfect example of this ingenuity is the conky dumpling. Anguilla is a virtual vineyard of sea grape trees, and the flat round leaves are perfect to wrap these cornmeal dumplings. Secure the bundle with a piece of green fiber from the cornstalks or the pointed bits from the coconut tree. The conky dumpling would then be boiled and eaten, often as a substitute for bread. Sweet potato dumplings were made much the same way. I've been told that "conky" means corn, and during the harvest season Anguillians made these with freshly grated corn, which was a special treat. Still to this day corn season is celebrated in Anguilla with impromptu roadside shacks set up selling grilled local corn. Conky dumplings are something you usually have to be invited to a local home to experience.

In a bowl, combine the cornmeal, pumpkin, flour, raisins, ginger, seasonings, and butter. Stir in the liquid and mix to form a dough. Season with salt and pepper. Roll into sea grape leaves, banana leaves, corn husks, or aluminum foil and secure with string or natural fiber.

Boil in salted water or steam for 40–45 minutes until cooked through and the starchiness of the flour is cooked out. Serve immediately.

Island Cornmeal Fungi with Okra

FOR 4–6 FRIENDS

Most worldly gourmands see the word "fungi" and they think of Italian mushroom dishes. Well, in the Caribbean, fungi is all about cornmeal, or what the Italians would call polenta.

Fungi, or funchi, is a filling cornmeal mixture usually cooked with okra and other tidbits to create an inexpensive family meal and served with boiled or steamed fish. Here I add butter and Parmesan cheese to make it a bit more decadent. Adding the okra at the very end keeps its texture and prevents it from developing a slippery consistency.

1 c.	cornmeal (polenta)
4 c.	water
4 T	butter
4 T	Parmesan cheese
1 lb.	organic okra, thinly sliced

salt and pepper as needed

Boil water, add okra, and season with a little salt. Stir in cornmeal with a wooden spoon. Stir constantly to prevent clumping. Reduce heat and cook until rawness is removed from mixture, about 5–7 minutes. Fungi should be quite dry because the other ingredients will loosen it considerably.

Remove from heat and stir in butter, cheese, garlic, and okra and mix to incorporate. Polenta should now be soft yet spoonable. Adjust seasoning with salt and pepper.

Serve with any island fish recipe.

If you have leftovers they can be cut up and fried crisp the next day.

2 T	olive oil
2	garlic cloves, thinly sliced
1	small onion, finely diced
1 T	ham, finely minced (I like country ham but sometimes use peppered bacon instead)
1 lb.	greens (whatever type is available and freshest: collards, mustard, bok choy, beet or turnip, callaloo, purslane, etc.), washed well, drained, and roughly chopped
1 can	pigeon peas (or like amount of your favorite cooked bean), rinsed and drained
1 tsp	lemon zest
1 tsp	fresh thyme leaves
1 T	butter
1 T	red wine vinegar
salt and pepper to taste

Sautéed Pigeon Peas and Greens

Stewed greens in the soul kitchen of the American South are a real staple. Collards, mustard greens, kale, turnip greens, and others are all cooked down with a ham hock. Wild greens like dandelions and pig weed were foraged and used when nothing else was available. In the islands similar dishes were also developed to feed the family. Even in southern Indiana, where I grew up, there were stewed greens on the farm table on Sunday afternoons for "supper." We all wanted to drink the "pot liquor," which was the rich, salty juice that would be at the bottom of the pot. A few drops of vinegar from Gramma's crystal cruets would be added and we'd drink it out of little cups. I've updated the recipe, making it a sauté instead of a stew.

Heat a large sauté pan over high heat. Add the olive oil, then the garlic, onion, and ham. Cook until lightly brown, being careful not to burn.

Quickly add the greens and ¼ cup of water to the pan and continue cooking over high heat while stirring. Once greens begin to wilt, add the peas or beans and the lemon zest and thyme.

Reduce heat to medium-high and cook 3–4 minutes. Remove from heat and add the butter and vinegar and stir until the butter melts and coats the greens. Season to taste and serve immediately.

Note: If allowed to sit for too long, the greens will discolor.

FOR 4 FRIENDS

4	beets, pre-cooked until tender and sliced into ¼" slices
2 T	extra-virgin olive oil
5 sprigs	thyme
2 sprigs	fresh rosemary
1 pt.	freshly squeezed orange juice
2 tsp	honey
1	lemon, juiced
2 tsp	sherry vinegar
salt and pepper to taste	

Athenia's Boiled Beets with Orange and Herbs

The orange highlights the beet's natural sweetness while cutting out some of the earthiness some folks aren't crazy about. This is a good way to get everyone in the family to eat beets.

Note on cooking beets: I like to rub the beets lightly with oil and wrap them individually in foil. Bake them in a 350° oven for an hour or so until they are tender when poked with a skewer. Cool in their wrappers. They should peel easily and be silky and velvety to the bite.

Place the beets, olive oil, and herbs in a saucepan over medium-high heat and cook until herbs become fragrant. Add the remaining ingredients and cook until the juices reduce to a glaze. Season to taste with salt and pepper.

Serve warm or at room temperature.

Decorate with orange slices and fresh herbs.

2 T	olive oil (more as needed if not using non-stick)
1	garlic clove, thinly sliced
1 T	ginger, minced
2	medium eggplants, cut into finger-size pieces
1 T	green curry paste
1 T	coconut vinegar
1½	bell peppers, roughly chopped
1	Spanish onion, sliced
½ c.	fresh coconut meat, diced
1 c.	cherry tomatoes, halved
2	scallions, cut thinly on a bias
½ c.	assorted herbs (basil, mint, cilantro, garlic chives, etc.)

salt and pepper to taste

OPTIONAL INGREDIENTS

other ratatouille vegetables

coconut milk

lemon zest

corn kernels

fresh or dried chilies

Warm Eggplant Stew with Coconut Vinegar and Curry

I keep this kind of dish around all the time. It is great to throw on the vegetarian assortment we do nightly in my Bloomington, Indiana, restaurant. It also makes a quick special because it goes with so many different things . . . meat, fish, poultry, pasta, couscous . . . well, you get the picture. Serve it hot, cold, or room temperature. Remember, if you are serving it cold, season it a bit more since chilling mutes the flavors. Check below for other additions you can make depending on what's in season and what's in the fridge. If you are sautéing or roasting meat or fish you can make this in the same pan to save time and energy. It also brings the flavors of the two components together.

Soak eggplant slices in salt water (½ cup salt to 2 cups water) for 15 minutes.

Heat the olive oil, garlic, and ginger in a 10-inch non-stick pan over medium heat and slowly bring out the flavor of the garlic. Cook it until aromatic but not browned and add eggplant. Add the curry paste and increase the heat, cooking until the eggplant colors and becomes tender, about 3 minutes. Add a splash of water if the garlic begins to darken. This will steam the eggplant and make it tender as well.

Remove from heat, toss in the remaining ingredients, and season to taste.

"Provisions" are the starchy vegetables beloved in the Caribbean—foods such as the common sweet potato, boiling potato (known as "Irish potato" in the region), yams, dashine, green banana, casaba, breadfruit, and pumpkin. These ingredients are often boiled and served along with many stews and pressure-cooked or boiled dishes like fish water or goat stew. These are also used in recipes as "fillers," a way to get a few extra portions out of an expensive piece of meat or fish. Provisions are what "keep you going" and get you through the day. They are inexpensive and can make "a bit o' pig tail" into a meal. Caribbean cooking is really all about provisions. They are the staff of life and feed the belly of the industrious peoples of the islands. Next time you visit your local bodega or Caribbean market, make friends with those strange knotty vegetables in the produce section.

Provisional Wisdom

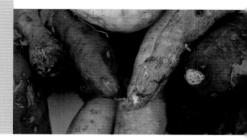

Soft Mofongo

One of the questions I was asked most when guests were looking at our menu was, "What's mofongo?" and my stock answer always was, "Island mashed potatoes made out of plantain bananas." If Puerto Rico had a national dish, this might be it, but they add a lot of crispy pork skin "chicherones" in theirs. I wanted to cut out a little of the fat, so I've replaced that with lean ham and a bit of butter. Mofongo is great to "sop" up sauces, so serve it with roasts and poultry that have light sauces. I love it alongside my roasted chicken with mango chutney, for example.

Heat a medium sauce pot and add the olive oil. Add the garlic and the ham; cook until garlic starts to toast and the ham renders.

Add the plantains and cook for 20 minutes (stir often to prevent the plantain from burning).

Add the stock and continue to cook for 10 minutes until plantains are tender. Add more liquid if needed. Continue cooking until the liquid evaporates and plantains are soft. Mash with a potato masher and add the butter.

Season to taste.

FOR 6–8 FRIENDS

¼ c.	olive oil
6–8	garlic cloves, sliced
¼ c.	ham, diced (with fat)
4–5	whole plantains, ripe, peeled, and sliced 1" thick
1 c.	chicken stock
¼ lb.	butter
salt and pepper to taste	

½	breadfruit, cooked, peeled, and sliced into ¼" slices (see Breadfruit Salad recipe)
¼ c.	olive oil
3	garlic cloves, thinly sliced
1 tsp	crushed black pepper
1 tsp	garlic salt
½	lime

Crisped Breadfruit
with Roasted Garlic Butter

Anyone who likes fried potatoes will love this breadfruit dish. It is a great accompaniment to any breakfast, lunch, or dinner. If you are unable to find breadfruit, you can use starchy provisions such as root vegetables, potatoes of any variety, taro root, or cassava or try green plantains. The fresh lime juice and garlic salt jazz up any fried dish. Try adding a few chilies if you are a "hot head" as I am.

Heat oil in a large sauté pan over high heat. Add breadfruit slices in a single layer, browning slightly on both sides. Turn off heat and remove breadfruit slices from pan and drain on paper towels. Arrange on a serving platter and season with garlic salt.

Remove excess olive oil from the pan. Melt butter over medium heat, add in garlic slices, and cook until crisp and light brown, being careful not to burn. Pour garlic butter over the breadfruit.

Finish with a squeeze of fresh lime.

6 c.	water
4 T	butter
8 oz.	cornmeal, quick-cooking style
1 c.	cooked corn
16	young okra, stemmed and sliced thin on a bias

salt and pepper to taste

grated Parmesan cheese

1	vine-ripe tomato
1	red or orange bell pepper
¼ c.	herbs (parsley, cilantro, basil, etc.)

Coo-Coo

This is another cornmeal dish much like polenta or "island fungi." The dish is best made an hour or so ahead so it can set. Polenta mixed with any type of leftovers can be poured into a loaf pan and then refrigerated for the same effect. The loaf that forms when chilled may be sliced, fried crisp, and served as an accompaniment to any meal. I even like it with eggs for a wonderful breakfast. "Coo-coo" means something very different on some Spanish islands, so be careful where you say it.

Bring a pot of water to a boil. Add 2 tablespoons butter and stir until melted. Stir in the cornmeal and continue stirring mixture over low heat for about 10 minutes. Stir in the corn and add the okra. Season to taste with salt and pepper.

Lightly butter a serving dish with the remaining 2 tablespoons of butter. Pour mixture into serving platter. Sprinkle with cheese, tomato, sweet bell peppers, and herbs.

FOR 6 FRIENDS

4 T	oil
1 T	brown sugar
¼ lb.	salt beef, cut into cubes (see note, p. 128)
8 oz.	white rice
4 oz.	fresh pigeon peas
4 oz.	coconut milk
salt and pepper to taste	

The Anguillian National Culinary Team's Rice and Peace (Pigeon Peas and Rice)

My buddies George from Cap, Dale from Tasty's, and Christopher were all on the Anguillian National Culinary Team with me in 2005. We had "Rice and Peace" embroidered on our chef's jackets to inspire good will and to fight hunger.

Nothing says Caribbean cuisine like pigeon peas and rice. It is the staff of life in the islands, both a workingman's mainstay and a dish for celebration. For everyday fare, rice may far outweigh the peas, whereas in a more festive setting you'll see freshly harvested peas in abundance. For Caribbean man it is a dish that, if cooked correctly, can finally make him hear wedding bells! In any case it should be a star in your culinary lineup whether you're Caribbean or not. Try it with brown rice for an even healthier twist.

In a stew pot, heat the oil. Stir in the brown sugar until it has almost caramelized. Add the beef with a little water and simmer, partially covered, until the meat is half cooked. Add the remaining ingredients. Simmer for 20 minutes. Cover and set aside for 15 minutes before serving.

Note: Canned peas may substituted if fresh are not available.

¼ c.	oil
2	onions, finely chopped
3	garlic cloves, minced
2	chile peppers, seeded and minced
1 lb.	ground chuck
2 tsp	tomato paste
2	tomatoes, seeded and chopped
1 T	Kitchen D'Orr New Regime Spice Blend (or Chinese 5-spice powder)
½ c.	chopped fresh herbs (chives, dill, basil, cilantro, or a combination)
salt and pepper to taste	
1	large unripe papaya, peeled, seeded, and halved (or 4 christophenes)
6 oz.	Parmesan cheese, grated

Stuffed Green Papaya (or Christophene)

This is an unusual version of what northerners would think of doing with bell peppers. The finished product is a wonderful composition of textures and flavors. The papaya is tender and succulent and the filling is spicy and warming. You can substitute christophene (chayote squash) for green papaya or the more readily available zucchini or sweet peppers.

FOR THE FILLING

Heat oil in a large skillet. Sauté the onions, garlic, and chili peppers for approximately 10 minutes over medium-low heat until tender. Add beef and cook for 10 minutes, or until no more pink shows. Stir in the tomato paste along with tomatoes. Add the spices and herbs and stir well. Season with salt and pepper to taste. This may be prepared in advance and refrigerated until ready to use.

Preheat oven to 400°.

While the oven is heating, poach papaya halves in boiling water for 15 minutes. If using christophene, steam until tender, cut in half, and scoop out the middle pit or seed. Drain well on paper towel. Grease a medium casserole or baking dish and arrange papaya or christophene halves in it. Fill with stuffing mixture and top with the cheese. Bake for 30–35 minutes. Serve piping hot.

Chef's note: Nice accompanied by a light tomato sauce and green salad as a main dish. The papaya may be cut into quarters and served as an appetizer.

Roasted Breadfruit

Breadfruit was brought to the Caribbean islands by Captain Bligh of *Mutiny on the Bounty* fame. The plants were distributed throughout the islands soon afterward. Breadfruit was used as cheap food for the slaves but now is a favorite starchy vegetable used in many recipes and something many folks miss most when away from their homeland. This one is the simplest and truest preparation if you want the real favor of this tree-borne staff of life.

Roast the breadfruit whole over charcoal (the best method), or in a 500° oven. Turn the fruit as it begins to char. The roasting takes about an hour. When steam starts to escape from the stem end, the breadfruit is done.

Remove the breadfruit from the fire and cut a circle at the stem end. Scoop out the heart and discard it. Scoop out the meat, or cut off the charred outer skin, cut the meat into slices, and serve it hot, drizzled with olive oil and lime juice and seasoned with salt and pepper.

FOR 4–6 FRIENDS

1 breadfruit

olive oil, fresh lime, salt, and pepper as needed

Coconut Basmati Rice

1 c.   basmati rice

2 c.   water

1   mini-wini or Thai bird pepper (or your favorite chili)

1   kaffir lime leaf

¾ c.   coconut milk

salt and pepper to taste

toasted and shredded coconut or coconut chips as needed for garnish

Basmati rice has been cultivated at the foot of the Himalayas mountain range where the Yamuna and Ganges rivers feed the fields with seasonal flooding. The rice is non-glutinous, long grain, and scented and when literally translated from Hindi it means "pearl of scents" because of its distinctive aroma. It is perfect for coconut rice because it enhances the mellow perfume of the coconut milk without overwhelming it. A timesaving tip: the plain rice can be cooked ahead of time and chilled, then reheated with the coconut milk to serve. Brown basmati rice is a wholesome change of pace.

In a small sauce pot, boil water. Add rice, chili, and lime leaf, then salt the water to taste. Add just enough salt so you can taste it. You can always add more later, but you can't take it out. Reduce to a simmer and cook until liquid is absorbed and rice is cooked, about 12–15 minutes. Add coconut milk and cook until the rice is enveloped in its richness. Remove the chili and lime leaf and season to taste. Place in a serving dish and at the last minute top with the coconut chips.

Roasted Tomatoes with Garlic and Fresh Herbs

These are great to have around for breakfast, lunch, or dinner. Make a big batch and keep them in the fridge. The roasting intensifies the sweet/acidic flavors of the tomato. Great cold in salads and sandwiches, as a topping for canapés and appetizers, or warm as an accompaniment to meats, fish, poultry, or vegetarian dishes.

Pre-heat broiler to medium high. Line a cookie sheet with aluminum foil. Place the tomatoes in a large mixing bowl and toss with remaining ingredients. Pour out onto the cookie sheet and spread out evenly. Season with salt and pepper to taste. Roast until the tomatoes shrivel, the edges start to turn brown, and most of the liquid around the tomatoes has reduced a bit. The tomatoes should have a nice caramelized look to them. Cool to room temperature on the tray and place in a storage container. Drizzle with a little additional olive oil and refrigerate until needed. Serve hot, cold, or at room temperature as desired.

FOR 4–6 FRIENDS AS A SIDE DISH

6	large plum tomatoes cut into quarters
2 T	olive oil (plus more for drizzling)
3	garlic cloves, minced
½ c.	fresh herbs (I like basil, parsley, cilantro, and scallions)
1 T	Kitchen D'Orr Mediterranean Spice Blend or *herbes de Provence*
2 tsp	Kitchen D'Orr Greek Garlic Spice Blend or garlic salt
2 tsp	cane sugar

Juice of 1 lemon plus 1 tsp of the zest

salt and pepper to taste

CaRIB-BEaN CoNDi-MeNTs

Making Every Day Extraordinary

If you don't use any other recipes in this book, you've gotta use these. They will bring the exotic flavors of the Caribbean to your table with such ease that it may inspire you to flip back and try a few of the other recipes in the book. Chutneys, salsas, marinades, and seasonings can be incorporated into your everyday cooking to add that Creole accent to any of your recipes.

At home, I'm like you. A simple piece of grilled or sautéed fish is about all I have the energy or the time to prepare. If you top that same dish with some pepper relish, you've got a winner. Toss some chutney in your couscous, some banana catsup onto your cod before you broil it, or a piece of seasoned compound butter on your steak or salmon, and you've made it a memorable meal. As Emeril says, "Bam!!!! Kick it up a notch!" God, I wish I could have come up with that!

Condiments in all cultures make cooking tasty, easy, and fun. Thai fish sauce, French mustard, English horseradish, Japanese wasabi, and American cheese whiz are all culinary icons in their homelands and abroad. The Caribbean condiments that follow celebrate my joy in discovering the multi-ethnic background of the islands. Chili sauces, Indian chutneys, compound butters, spice rubs, vinaigrettes, and sauces have changed my way of cooking, and I hope they enliven yours.

I encourage everyone to be creative. In my classes, and in this book, I preach that recipes are only guidelines and must never seem restrictive, else cooking becomes a chore. Use recipes as chefs use recipes: for inspiration. The more fun you have in the kitchen, the more time you'll spend in the kitchen and the better cook you'll become. Cooking is not brain surgery; with basic sanitation, you'll *probably* never kill anyone. So what if it isn't perfect, I'm sure it is perfectly good. If it turns out a little too salty or spicy, toss it with some plain pasta or white rice and it'll be fine. No one will know the difference and you'll have learned a new trick.

2	bananas, ripe, peeled and cut into 1" sections
2	large papayas, ripe, peeled, seeded, and cut into 1" cubes
2	Spanish onions, diced large
5	garlic cloves, roughly chopped
1	yellow pepper, roughly chopped
2 T	ginger, peeled and roughly chopped
½ c.	sugar
1 c.	white vinegar
4	seasoning peppers, chopped
1	hot chili, chopped
1½ tsp	salt
1	lemon, zest and juice
salt and white pepper to taste	

Papaya Banana Catsup

Banana catsup is a specialty of St. Kitts, where they try to sell it to you as soon as you get off the boat. I didn't buy any, but I stole the idea. I had 3 papaya trees and 5 banana trees, so this is what I came up with. I love making this type of stuff in big batches so I can share it with family and friends. Keep an eye on your produce section; sometimes they have amazing deals on over-ripe fruits and vegetables. Take advantage and make this exotic, special sauce.

Put all ingredients in a pot.

Boil for 10 minutes until tender.

Cool slightly and place in a blender. Pulse to combine and blend until smooth and catsupy.

Season to taste with salt and pepper.

3	red peppers
3	yellow peppers
3	red onions
3	Holland red hot peppers or your favorite chili to taste
3	jalapeños
3	large garlic cloves, thinly sliced
2 c.	cider vinegar
1 c.	super-fine sugar
2 T	cracked black peppercorns
salt to taste	

Pickled Pepper Relish

This will help out more than a hamburger . . . great on all types of burgers, sausages, hot dogs, and sandwiches. It can also be pureed in a blender for a simple dipping sauce for fried foods. To freshen this up just before serving, stir in some roughly chopped cilantro, basil, or mint when cold. It is great spooned over grilled chicken, pork, or salmon.

If you have the energy to can this up, buy some small Ball jars and knock yourself out. Makes a memorable holiday gift.

Cut sweet peppers and onions into chunks. Slice the hot peppers thinly. Combine with remaining ingredients and bring to a boil.

Cook until peppers and onions are tender and strain, reserving liquid. Reduce the liquids until syrupy. Combine the two and cool. May be finished with roughly chopped cilantro when cold.

Mango, Papaya, and Passion Chili Sauce

This sauce is "very Paris Hilton." Sweet and HOT and full of passion. You'll find tons of uses for it. Great to use to spice up anything from BBQ to vinaigrettes and soups. Make a big batch and give it to friends.

Combine the mango, papaya, peppers, chilies, ginger, garlic, curry, vinegar, and honey in a large, heavy-bottomed, stainless steel saucepan and bring to a boil.

Reduce to a simmer, stirring often to prevent sticking and burning, until fruit is cooked, about 15–20 minutes.

Puree in a blender or food processor until smooth. Fold in passion fruit pulp and diced bell peppers while sauce is still hot. Thin as needed with water or additional vinegar to taste.

Season with salt and cracked black pepper as desired.

MAKES ABOUT 3 QUARTS, DEPENDING ON SIZE OF FRUIT

4	mangoes, peeled and pitted
4	papayas, peeled and seeded
1 c.	peppers and chilies to taste (seasoning peppers, chilies, etc.)
¼ c.	ginger, minced
¼ c.	garlic, minced
2 T	curry powder
1 qt.	white vinegar
1 c.	honey
4	fresh passion fruit (or a bottle of passion fruit nectar)
2	red bell peppers, finely diced
salt and pepper to taste	

Green Mango and Banana Chutney

I learned this recipe in Trinidad and have used it as an accompaniment for all sorts of roasts. I also like it on sandwiches and in chicken or tuna salad.

Sauté onions and garlic in the oil until soft. Add vinegar, orange juice, and mango and bring to a boil. Simmer 10 minutes, stirring occasionally. Add remaining ingredients and return to a simmer. Cook until thick and "chutney-like." Remove from heat and cool to room temperature. Adjust seasoning with salt and pepper and place in storage containers and refrigerate.

Store for up to 3 weeks.

MAKES 3 CUPS

2	green mangoes, peeled and diced
1	banana, ripe, peeled and roughly chopped
1 T	vegetable oil
2	garlic cloves
½	medium onion
½ c.	cider vinegar
½ c.	orange juice
2 tsp	minced ginger
¼ c.	dark raisins
¼ c.	dark brown sugar
½	jalapeño, finely minced
1 tsp	Kitchen D'Orr New Regime Spice Blend
salt and pepper to taste	

1 T	garlic powder
1 T	Kitchen D'Orr Greek Garlic Spice Blend
1 T	Kitchen D'Orr Mediterranean Spice Blend
1 T	Kitchen D'Orr New Regime Spice Blend
1 T	Paradise Kitchen Jerk Spice Blend (see recipe)
½ tsp	salt
½ tsp	pepper

Dry Adobo

This is a dry spice blend that is used throughout the Caribbean in many dishes. You can use it as an everyday seasoning for all your dishes to give them that something special. *When in doubt, adobo out!* There is also a wet adobo recipe that is great to have on hand as well, but this dry version is one to have on the countertop, ready at your beck and call.

Combine all ingredients and store in an airtight container in a cool, dry place. Use as directed in recipes.

¼ c.	garlic, minced
¼ c.	cilantro
¼ c.	parsley
¼ c.	basil
¼ c.	scallions, minced
1 T	ginger
1	serrano chili
½ c.	olive oil
2 T	salt

Wet Adobo

This is a condiment that is used daily in Puerto Rico and throughout the Spanish islands. I use it in paella and as a marinade on a large variety of meats before grilling. It is also great spooned into beans, stews, and soups for the last 15–20 minutes of cooking. Always keep some around. Freeze in an ice cube tray so you can pop some in a dish at a moment's notice! This is a candidate for herb gardeners' holiday gift giving.

Combine all ingredients in a blender or food processor and blend until a paste forms. Store in an airtight container topped off with a little olive oil in the refrigerator. Use as directed in recipes. This will keep a week or 2 in the fridge.

Annatto Oil

Annatto is another typical ingredient giving the tropical aroma, flavor, and color to many Spanish Caribbean dishes. It is tightly tied to the history and culture of the place. We use this colorful oil not only as a flavoring but also as a decorative detail on many of our plates. I like to keep it in a squeeze bottle and get all Jackson Pollock on your ass.

Combine the oil and seeds in a small saucepan. Gently cook over medium heat for 5 minutes, stirring occasionally. The oil will have a strong red-orange color. Cool to room temperature, strain oil, and store in the refrigerator.

1 c.	olive oil
3	garlic cloves, minced
2 strips	lemon peel
10	cracked black peppercorns
½ c.	annatto seeds, cracked with the back of a knife
salt to taste	

Don't Let Your Man-Go Hot Sauce

This orange sauce is a wonder on BBQ, in coleslaw recipes, and in sauces, dressings, ceviches, and other marinated dishes. Remember Scotch bonnets are like "a date with Lucifer," so handle with extreme caution. It's best to wear gloves when cutting and cleaning them. The smallest drop of this high-octane juice on your hands can result in incredible pain should you inadvertently touch your face or your eyes, not to mention other places! Enjoy this Scotch bonnet sauce at your own risk.

Heat the oil in a stainless steel saucepan and sauté the onions until they are translucent but not brown. Add the mango or papaya, carrots, christophene, allspice berries, peppercorns, thyme, and ginger. Sauté the mixture 5 minutes, stirring constantly. Add the sugar and Scotch bonnet peppers. When the sugar becomes syrupy add the vinegar and cook until the carrots are very soft, about 5–10 more minutes.

Puree the mixture in a blender and strain it. Thin as needed with added vinegar. Store it in a tightly closed bottle in the refrigerator. Makes enough to bottle and give to friends and family.

MAKES ABOUT 4 CUPS

1 T	vegetable oil
2	onions, diced
1	mango or papaya, ripe, skinned, seeded, and diced to ¼" cubes
3	carrots, finely diced
1	christophene squash, peeled and diced
10	cracked allspice berries
10	cracked whole black peppercorns
4 sprigs	fresh thyme
¼	ginger root, peeled and finely diced
½ c.	sugar
8	Scotch bonnet peppers
1 c.	cane or cider vinegar

Boat Ride

A trip to Anguilla wouldn't be the same without a day trip to St. Martin, and vice versa. I see St. Martin as Manhattan, and Anguilla, the Hamptons. St. Martin, or St. Maarten depending on your location, is a small, mountainous island divided by the French and Dutch. Their influences, as well as that of the docking cruise liners, have made St. Martin into a busy tourist center full of restaurants, shops, casinos, and nightclubs.

Get up early and take the ferry from Blowing Point in Anguilla to Marigot, the capital of St. Martin's French side. From the boat, head straight to the spice market alongside the pier. (Check with your concierge before you go to make sure the market is open on your day of travel.) You'll have to fight your way through souvenir stalls set up for the cruise ship set, but just behind them there are folks selling some great kitchen finds. Stop when you see colorful arrangements of Caribbean fruits and provisions, Haitian sea salt, cassava flour, vanilla beans, and spices of all types. You can take dried spices and bottles of flavored rum and hot sauce back to the States, so indulge yourself. If you know a little French or Creole, you can get some great recipes, too.

After the market, return to the ferry terminal and rent a car for the day. Look for a guy named "Cash" for a good deal. Head to Grand Case for some Caribbean snacks enriched by French tastes. One of my favorite food stalls is "Talk of the Town Too," where I order boudin noir seasoned deeply with clove and onions, stuffed crab and christophene, and eggplant stuffed with conch and pork, then broiled crispy brown. All are great with local hot sauce and a cold beer.

From there feel free to explore the island, stopping at galleries, rum shops, zoos, and museums on both the Dutch and French sides. Go to Orient Beach on the French side and get oriented on the human anatomy; it is topless. *Mais oui!*

Throw some dice at the casinos, if you must, or see one of the exotic shows on the Dutch side. There are many things available in St. Martin that you won't find on Anguilla, serenity not being one of them. By the end of the day, I always look forward to settling back on to the ferry and heading back home to paradise.

Jerk Rub—Wet Style

½ c.	fresh thyme leaves
2 bunches (about 15)	green onions, finely chopped
¼ c.	ginger root, finely diced
3	Scotch bonnet peppers, stemmed and finely chopped
¼ c.	peanut oil
5	garlic cloves, chopped
3	freshly ground bay leaves
2 tsp	freshly ground allspice
1 tsp	freshly grated nutmeg
1 T	freshly ground pepper
1 T	freshly ground coriander
1 tsp	freshly ground cinnamon
2 tsp	salt
	juice of 1 lime

Jamaicans all grow "country peppers" in small backyard plots. The plants grow tall and wiry and can live for several years, generating numerous batches of jerk marinade. Also known as Scotch bonnets because of their shape, they come in several varieties and colors from yellow to red. All have a similar full-bodied flavor with fruity, apricot overtones and an intense heat. Habanero peppers are a good substitute if true Scotchy b's aren't available.

All the various wet jerk rubs, dry jerk rubs, and marinades have the same core ingredients: scallions, thyme, Jamaican pimento (allspice), ginger, Scotch bonnet peppers, black pepper, nutmeg, and cinnamon. Jamaican pimento (allspice) is essential; it is more pungent than allspice berries found elsewhere. The scallions used in Jamaica more closely resemble baby red onions than the green ones we find in our American produce sections. The thyme is the English variety that grows in the hot sun of the Caribbean. Its leaves are very small, pungently oily, and intensely flavored. You may need to increase the amount if using a tender, quick-growing variety. These are the critical herbal flavors in jerk seasonings, so when tasting make sure they all sing. Use the "country peppers" to your own taste. Jamaicans bring a whole new meaning to "some like it hot" . . . maybe it was chilies that made Marilyn's lips pucker!

Combine all the ingredients in a food processor and blend into a thick, chunky paste. The mixture will keep in a tightly sealed container in the refrigerator for several months.

Many Jamaicans grind their spices by hand with a mortar and pestle. The whole spices tend to retain more aromatic oils in them and therefore more of a natural pungency. To save time, you can pulverize the spices in a spice grinder or coffee mill and then add them to the other ingredients.

Note: If you want to decrease the intense flavor of the peppers, remove the seeds and the interior white membrane, which contain the real heat of the chilies.

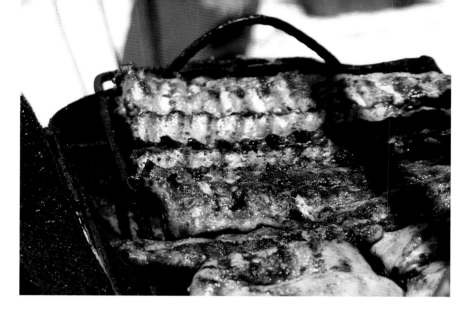

½ c.	kosher salt
¼ c.	raw sugar
3 T	fresh lime zest
3 T	dried chives or scallions
2 T	dried thyme leaves
1 T	ground habaneros (or cayenne pepper) or more to taste
1 T	freshly ground white pepper
1 T	freshly ground black pepper
1 T	ground coriander
1 T	smoked paprika
1 T	ground allspice
1 T	garlic powder
1 T	onion powder
1 tsp	ground cinnamon
1 tsp	ground nutmeg

Paradise Kitchen Jerk Spice Blend

For a quick hit of island flavor, you can sprinkle this on any type of meat or poultry before grilling, sautéing, or roasting. I also use it in vinaigrettes and sauces, soups, and stews as well as on ceviches, fried foods, and roasted nuts. I even use it on my eggs in the morning and popcorn at night. It isn't the traditional way of "jerking," but it is a fast way to take your taste buds on a vacation. Make up a batch and keep it on your counter, or go to www. farm-bloomington.com and we'll ship you some paradise in a bottle.

Mix all the ingredients together or blend in a spice grinder. Adjust to your taste. It should have a nice balance of salt, spice, acid, sweet, and heat.

4	juice oranges, plus 1½ T roughly chopped zest
2	lemons, plus ½ T roughly chopped zest
⅓ c.	honey
1	Granny Smith apple, cored and roughly chopped
2–3 turns	fresh white pepper
1 pinch	salt

Bitter Orange Coulis

Versatile is what this sauce is. Breaded coconut shrimp love it, as do roasted game birds like duck. I even use it with cakes and berries for dessert. It is wonderful for serving with those huge stemmed strawberries you find from time to time in the market. Keep small containers in the freezer for a quick solution to your entertaining dilemmas.

First remove zest from citrus fruits with a grater plane. Juice the citrus fruits by cutting them in half and placing a fork in the center of the "flesh" side, squeezing, and turning the fruit over a bowl, catching all the juice and pith. Discard seeds and pour the rest into a medium sauté pan. (*Note:* To extract the maximum from citrus fruits, place them in the microwave for 30 seconds before squeezing, or at least have them at room temperature.)

Place juice and pith with the zest, honey, apple, salt, and pepper and bring to a boil. Reduce heat and simmer until it is reduced by a third and all the ingredients are tender.

Cool to room temperature and puree with a hand blender or stationary blender until very smooth. Pass through a fine strainer and season to taste. Chill well.

Thickness of sauce may be changed by further reduction or by thinning with added juice.

Stores 5–7 days in refrigerator.

Green Curry Paste

Curry pastes are used throughout Asia in their fiery cooking. I developed this one with Christopher to use in our Caribbean cookery when we tired of the more traditional dusty, dried yellow curry powder. I love having this stuff around for a quick fix of flavor.

~~~~~~

Mix all the ingredients and puree in food processor until it's a smooth paste.

MAKES ABOUT 2 CUPS

15	green hot chilies
3 T	shallots, chopped
1 T	garlic chives
1 tsp	galangal or fresh ginger
1 T	lemongrass
½ tsp	kaffir lime rind
1 tsp	coriander root
5	peppercorns
1 T	coriander seeds, toasted
1 tsp	cumin seeds, toasted
1 tsp	salt
1 tsp	Asian shrimp paste

Orange and Fennel Compote

Incredible with grilled and roasted pork and other sausages, meats, and fowl. Great on sandwiches and with cold meats and fish. Try cutting mayo out of your diet and replacing it with something more flavorful like chutney or this compote.

~~~~~~

Combine all ingredients in a heavy-bottomed sauce pan and bring to a boil. Reduce heat to medium-high and reduce until all liquids evaporate and compote is shiny. Cool and adjust seasoning with salt, pepper, and Tabasco. Store in fridge up to 2 weeks.

MAKES ABOUT 3½ CUPS

2 c.	fresh orange juice
4 c.	fennel, cut in ¼–½" rough dice
4 c.	onion, cut in ¼–½" rough dice
3 T	ginger, chopped medium-fine
1 c.	honey
1 tsp	fennel seeds
1 T	Kitchen D'Orr New Regime Spice Blend
½ T	Kitchen D'Orr Aux Poivres Spice Blend
1½ tsp	salt
½ c.	sherry vinegar
¼ c.	black raisins
¼ c.	white raisins
2 T	orange zest, cut into ½" julienne
	juice of 1 lemon
	salt, pepper, Tabasco to taste

½ c. tomatoes, ripe, peeled, seeded, and roughly chopped

juice of 2 lemons

1 tsp garlic, chopped

2 T sherry vinegar

4 T top-quality extra-virgin olive oil

1 tsp sea salt

1½ T capers

1 tsp lemon zest

salt and pepper to taste

Tomato and Caper Vinaigrette

This vinaigrette is great with all fish and chicken that has been grilled, poached, or roasted. It can be used on all sorts of salads and grilled veggie dishes and is divine on pasta.

Note: Additional chopped herbs such as tarragon, basil, or chives may be added to taste just before serving. If added too far in advance, they will discolor.

In a blender, combine the tomato, lemon juice, garlic, vinegar, olive oil, and sea salt and puree until combined but still slightly chunky. Pour into a storage container and add the capers and lemon zest. Season to taste with salt and pepper.

2 fresh passion fruit, seeds and pulp scooped out

¼ c. rice wine vinegar

¼ c. lime juice

½ c. olive oil

2 T Thai fish sauce

1 T fresh ginger, minced

1 large garlic clove, minced

salt and pepper to taste

minced chilies (optional)

Passion Fruit Vinaigrette

This can be a sauce or vinaigrette. Try it over grilled salmon or other fatty fish and you'll have a revelation. I found this fruit in my parents' local grocery store in rural southern Indiana, so your grocer should be able to get it for you.

Whisk together and season to taste.

Sofrito de Carlos

Use as a marinade or to finish all types of Latino dishes.

Note: If you can't find culantro, then double the cilantro and add a bunch of parsley.

Puree all the herbs and vegetables together in a blender or food processor and slowly add the olive oil. Season to taste with salt and pepper.

Store in small containers in the freezer.

MAKES 2–2½ QUARTS

2 bunches	culantro
1 bunch	cilantro
1	small Spanish onion
1	red onion
½ lb.	ají dulce (flavor peppers) or your favorite fresh chili pepper to taste
1 head	garlic, peeled and roughly chopped
1"	fresh ginger, roughly chopped
2	Italian frying peppers
1	red pepper
1	green pepper
1 qt.	olive oil
salt and pepper to taste	

Tofu Rouille

The forefather of this recipe comes from sunny, coastal Provence. My recipe cuts the fat but keeps the saffron, garlic, and spices. Refrigerate leftover rouille to use with grilled meats and fish and on sandwiches, baked potatoes, steamed broccoli, and cauliflower. The sauce is great with crudités or thinned with a touch of vinegar and used as a salad dressing.

Cook the potato in boiling water until tender, drain, and place in a bowl. Lightly mash the potato with a fork and allow the steam to escape.

In a small saucepan, bring ¼ cup water to a boil. Add the saffron, remove the pan from the heat, and steep the saffron for 8–10 minutes.

Combine the potato, saffron liquid, garlic, chili powder, tofu, and oil in a blender or food processor and puree until the mixture is smooth. Season with the Tabasco, salt, and pepper to taste.

MAKES 2½ CUPS

1	potato, peeled and roughly diced
1 tsp	saffron threads
2	garlic cloves, peeled and roughly chopped
1½ tsp	chili powder
¾ lb.	firm tofu, drained and lightly pressed to remove excess water
¼ c.	extra-virgin olive oil
10 drops	Tabasco
salt and freshly ground pepper to taste	

Green Pea and Wasabi Puree

MAKES 1 CUP

1 c.	peas (fresh or frozen), blanched and quickly chilled in ice water
¼ c.	water
1 T	white soy
1 tsp	wasabi powder (available in Asian or ethnic section of your supermarket)
½	serrano pepper (or to taste; you may use jalapeño if serrano isn't available)
1 T	fresh ginger, chopped
1 tsp	salt (or to taste)

The sinus-opening power of wasabi is slightly tamed by the sweet peas in this dip/sauce that will find a home on your lineup of party recipes. You can use it as a dip for veggies and other hors d'oeuvres, but it can also give a Japanese accent to grilled chicken or poached salmon. It will keep in the refrigerator for 3–5 days.

Note: White soy is a nice pantry item that has become available recently. It has a mild soy flavor but is much lighter in color, so it won't darken your recipes. Once you start using it, you won't be able to live without it. If you can't find it, try using a touch of Asian fish sauce.

Great on all types of grilled, poached, or sautéed poultry, fish, or meat. Keeps up to 5 days in the refrigerator.

Combine all ingredients in a blender and puree until smooth. Taste and adjust seasoning as needed.

You can store the sauce in a squeeze bottle for easy use.

Homemade Chili Vinegar

MAKES 1 CUP

1 c.	white vinegar
10–15	bird peppers
¼ c.	cane sugar
2 tsp	salt
1 piece	star anise
10	black peppercorns
2–3 branches	fresh thyme
1	bay leaf

Using this vinegar is a great way to add a punch to any dish. Try it in sauces, vinaigrettes, marinades, or wet rubs. I like to keep it on the table for drizzling on just about everything. If you are afraid of heat, you can use a few sweet banana pepper rings in place of the Thai bird peppers. I also make chili vinegar with other peppers from the garden like serranos, jalapeños, and even the chili from hell . . . the Scotch bonnet. So, go and blow your chili-head off with a bottle of your new favorite brew.

Bring vinegar to a boil and add the remaining ingredients. Stir to incorporate and quickly remove from the stove. Cool to room temperature, pour into a sterilized jar and store in the fridge.

Spice Blends

Throughout my life I have enjoyed travel and the culinary treats that come with it. I've woven many of the flavor memories into my cooking. Over the past 25 years I've come up with a great number of spice blends that bring out the best natural qualities of the products we use in the kitchen.

Spices add intrigue to your cooking. Most are from faraway places with names as exotic as the spices themselves. I love the complex flavors they give to my dishes, but if you aren't very adventurous or are in too much of a hurry to make the spice blends, simply use what you like and have. You won't break my heart. The blends used throughout this book will bring uniqueness to your cooking, but missing a spice shouldn't keep you from trying a recipe.

The following spice blends can be used as an inspiration to create your own blend. You will find the combinations rich and lingering. They are different from most flavors you come across in the standard pantry. If you can't find an ingredient, simply leave it out and move along. It will still taste good. If you have an old can of some sort of spice, add a little of it to your blend and see if it works.

Blends add flavor without calories and in most cases cut down on salt. You can make up these blends and keep them in an airtight container out of direct sunlight, and they will keep about 1–2 months at peak freshness. I like to use a coffee grinder for the blending, but once it is used for spices, you'll never want to use it for coffee again, unless you want your coffee to taste like chai.

These spices are not prejudiced; they like all foods and you can use them on just about everything. They are not recipe or menu specific. Try amazing your family and friends by cooking the same grilled chicken or fish every day for a week and having it taste fresh and new each night just by using a different one of these spice blends. The simplest way to use them is to brush a little olive oil on the meat or vegetable, generously apply the blend, then cook. Once cooking is complete, dress with a drizzle of a little more olive oil, a squeeze of citrus, and a sprinkle of sea salt. Serve over greens and you have a healthy meal. Done and done!

If you want to try the spice blends without any fuss, go to my website at www.farm-bloomington.com and we'll ship them out to you.

Kitchen D'Orr New Regime Spice Blend

This blend was inspired by garam masala, a warming spice common in India, Bangladesh, and Pakistan. I also included some spices that my friends from North Africa use in their couscous and other dishes. This is my 24/7 spice and can be used all day long. Try it in your hot cereal with raisins and milk for breakfast and on your strawberries flambé at dinner. It accents both the sweet and savory in all it touches. It tastes great on meat, fish, vegetables—everything. You'll make all your cooking more interesting with a touch of New Regime.

T	coriander seed
2 pieces	star anise
1 T	fennel seed
2 tsp	mustard seeds
1 tsp	cumin seeds
1 tsp	ginger powder
1 stick	cinnamon (½")
1 tsp	black peppercorns
1 tsp	white peppercorns
3	dried bay leaves
½ tsp	whole mace

Grind in a spice grinder. Store in an airtight container in a cool, dark place.

Kitchen D'Orr Aux Poivres Spice Blend

Think classic French steak au poivre on steroids and you have Aux Poivres Spice Blend. Instead of just 1 peppercorn the blend has 5, plus fennel and coriander. It makes a great pepper crust on tuna and salmon but can be used on roasts and directly in dishes as a seasoning as well. I find myself using it on all my meat cooking, even on my bacon for breakfast. It is a coarser blend than most, so it should be added a bit earlier in the recipe than standard ground pepper. If you can't find all the various peppercorns in your area, just use the ones you can. You can replace it with a good-quality homemade cracked black pepper, butcher's style.

2 T	cracked black pepper
2 T	cracked white pepper
2 T	Chinese Szechuan pepper
3 T	fennel seeds
4 T	coriander seeds
2 T	guinea pepper
1 tsp	crushed red pepper flakes

Coarsely crack all the peppercorns and spices separately and combine the red pepper flakes. Store in an airtight container in a cool, dry place.

Kitchen D'Orr Sweet Seasons Spice Blend

You will think of apple or pumpkin pie when you first smell this, but it is much more complex. Yes, it is good in lots of desserts, but it is also good on pork, duck, and game and any of the autumn veggies like squash, sweet potatoes, and beets. This is great to highlight the natural sweetness of your ingredients. I also use it as a dry rub on BBQ, in my granola mix, and even mixed with a bit of sugar on my cinnamon toast. You can use a pumpkin pie spice in its place.

1 tsp	ginger powder
1 stick	cinnamon (½")
½ tsp	annatto seed
½ tsp	pomegranate powder
2 tsp	fennel seeds
2 tsp	coriander seeds
2 pieces	star anise
2 pieces	cloves
1 piece	mace
¼ tsp	freshly ground nutmeg
2	bay leaves

Grind to fine in a spice blender. Store in an airtight container in a cool, dark place.

Kitchen D'Orr Mediterranean Spice Blend

This is my version of *herbes de Provence* with a few additions. You can use other herbs of Provence blends in its place or come up with your own multi-herb mix. It is a fun way to use up all those half-empty containers of herbs. When using this blend, rub it between your fingers and sprinkle it into or onto your dishes. This will release the essential oils in the herbs and awake the flavors and aromas. It is great on all types of veggies, fish, and light meats. You'll love it in dips, sauces, and vinaigrettes, and it is great in pasta dishes and marinades as well. Try it in your next tomato sauce.

2 T	dried basil
2 T	dried rosemary
2 T	dried oregano
2 T	dried savory
2 T	dried tarragon
2 T	dried thyme
4 T	dried chervil
1 T	dried lavender flowers
2 T	dried minced shallots
1 T	dried minced garlic

With a mortar and pestle, break up the rosemary and any other larger herbs and mix together with the remainder of the ingredients. Store in airtight containers in a cool, dark place.

Kitchen D'Orr Mellow Yellow Spice Blend

Mellow Yellow gives you the taste of western Asia without the full-throttle flavor of a traditional curry. It flavors and colors like curry but allows the natural flavors of your ingredients to come through. Try it on lighter meats like poultry, pork, or veal as well as on seafood and veggies. It is also great in dips, sauces, and vinaigrettes. Try it in West Indian dishes as well. Curry is a good substitute.

1 tsp	mustard seeds
1 tsp	cardamom seeds
1 tsp	fennel seeds
1 tsp	ground ginger
1 T	turmeric
1 tsp	coriander seeds
1 tsp	white pepper
1 tsp	dried orange peel
2	bird peppers, dried, or small hot chilies (or to taste)

Place ingredients in a spice grinder and blend the mixture until it forms a fine, consistent powder. Store in an airtight container in a cool, dry place.

Kitchen D'Orr Greek Garlic Spice Blend

I love this on all types of fish and roasted vegetable dishes. You can crust a pork roast or chicken with it. It is great in guacamole, ranch dressing, and all your dips and spreads. It's super in soups and salads, too. It is a simple way to create depth in flavor. I don't know why I'm so nuts about these flavors; I guess it's Greek to me! When using this blend, rub it between your fingers and sprinkle into or on your dishes. This will release the essential oils in the herbs and awake the flavors and aromas. A simple addition of salt, pepper, and fresh or powdered garlic can be used in its place.

1 T	dried Greek oregano
1 T	dried basil
1 tsp	ground fenugreek
1 tsp	cracked black pepper, butcher's style
½ tsp	crushed red pepper flakes
1 T	garlic powder
1 T	granulated garlic
3 T	kosher salt

Combine and store in an airtight container.

BuSH tEaS

Bush teas are usually drunk in the morning hours to cleanse the system and get one ready for the day. Generally they are made up of pleasant-tasting herbs like mint, lemongrass, lemon basil, thyme, tarragon, soursop, and lime leaves and often sweetened with honey and flavored with a bit of lime juice.

When you come down with a fever or some other ailment, the bush prescription might change with the addition of spices, fresh garlic cloves, worry vine, neem leaves, and other bitter and strong flavors, sometimes even chilies. If "the bitter bush don't cure ya, it'll at least make you forget how bad you feel" for a while. Or, as the saying goes: "No pain, no gain!"?

Bush teas are usually made in simple combinations. The Jamaican girls shake their heads at some of my concoctions. Athenia says that her granny said never put more than three bush in a pot or "you makin' poison, not a cure." She also teases me that the bush tea I make with ten herbs and spices as an after-dinner tea at our fine-dining restaurant "tastes so good you might not mind not waking up in the mornin.'"

Da Bush Doctor's in da House

John Edwards, the island bush doctor, has come up with a variety of "cures" for just about anything and everything. He times his picking of herbs with the phases of the moon so as to harvest them "when they are full" of their curative properties. I have yet to try any of his medicinal concoctions, but you can't argue with one of his best cures: "drink plenty o' water, da more the better, washes ya right out." That and a bit of herb tea and you're good to go.

User's guide to Caribbean bush teas:

- Garlic is thought to be antiseptic, a purifier of the blood.

- Worry vine fights depression.

- Neem lowers blood sugar.

- Mint contains menthol, which facilitates digestion and is an antiseptic. Mint is used by the Chinese to calm upset stomachs and combat spasms. Mint infusions are said to cure hiccups and to alleviate migraine headaches. It is thought to be an antiviral, antiparasitic, and sweat-inducing cold remedy. It also can be used as a decongestant and to soothe sore muscles, morning sickness, and menstrual cramps.

- Black-and-white peppercorns are used to stimulate taste buds and are thought to be a great digestive. They are antioxidants and also used as an antibacterial. The outer layers of the peppercorn, especially the black peppercorn, are said to break down fats and the accumulation of fat in the body, especially in the liver.

- Lime is a coolant. Lime leaves are used as a natural cleanser, deodorizer, stimulant, astringent, and antiamoebic. Their essential oil is said to be an antidepressant and is good for anxiety. Lime is stimulating, uplifting. It relieves fatigue and improves mental clarity. It is thought to be an antihistamine, anticarcinogen, and antispasmodic and to have antitumor characteristics.

- Ginger helps with nausea and seasickness. It also improves appetite, relieves stomach cramps, improves blood circulation, and is used to help alleviate joint pain and arthritis. It is an expectorant and is used in Asia for colds and influenza.

- Tarragon has been used since the Middle Ages as an antidote for many things, including snakebites. It has been used to promote appetite, relieve stomach cramps, and combat fatigue and is a folkloric remedy for toothaches. It is said to promote the production of bile, which speeds the process of eliminating waste from the body. Also used for de-worming.

- Soursop leaves are used to calm and induce sleep. Said to be better than "weed" to calm you down. Island folk also use it for bladder problems, diarrhea, cough, catarrh, dysentery, and indigestion. Great for insomnia, flu, and fever.

- Lemongrass tea is drunk for antimicrobial properties as well as antifungal uses. Can be rubbed on the skin as an insect repellent.

- Dried hibiscus flowers (also called sorrel) are used as an antioxidant and anticarcinogen.

- Sage helps ward off indigestion and is thought to improve your appetite. Used for teething and oral inflammation, sore throats, and upset stomachs.

- Basils of all types are used for nausea and vomiting as well as an antispasmodic aid for proper digestion.

Bush Teas

Bush teas are the traditional herb teas of the island. They have true medicinal values as well as folkloric qualities to make you feel better. "Bush" can be defined as anything that is green, so it is pretty wide open. You'll find soursop, lime leaves, and stingy thyme in some of the recipes. Don't let your local grocer's inability to supply them get you down. Try dried bush if fresh isn't available. Check your Asian markets for kaffir lime leaves. Sometimes reading about something unattainable can coerce you into doing something new and fun. Take a field trip. Do some local research in your area; there are many natural "bush herbs" you can grow or forage.

Bush tea method: Pick the tea you would like to make and gather the ingredients. Place them in a teapot and pour 2 cups of boiling water over them. Allow to sit for 4–6 minutes before enjoying.

Sour Sorrel

2 T	dried sorrel (hibiscus)
1 T	fresh ginger
1 T	fresh lemongrass
1 T	honey
2 slices	lime
1	lemon or lime leaf, if available (if not, a strip of citrus peel)

Jamaican Ginger

2 T	fresh sage leaves
1 T	fresh ginger, roughly chopped
2 slices	apple
1 T	honey
2 slices	lime
1	lemon or lime leaf, if available (if not, a strip of citrus peel)

Hydro-PepperMint

2 T	fresh mint
2 T	fresh basil
2	peppercorns, lightly crushed
1 T	honey
2 slices	lime
1	lemon or lime leaf, if available (if not, a strip of citrus peel)

West Indian Spice

3	cardamom pods, lightly crushed
3	allspice berries, lightly crushed
2	fresh allspice leaves or bay leaves
1	cinnamon stick, broken
3	cloves, lightly crushed
1 T	honey
2 slices	lime
1	lemon or lime leaf, if available (if not, a strip of citrus peel)

Island Time

2 T	fresh stingy thyme (also called Mexican oregano)
3 branches	fresh English thyme
2 slices	lime
1 T	honey
1	lemon or lime leaf, if available (if not, a strip of citrus peel)

SuNnY sWeeTS

Flans are fine but liquor is quicker. That is the way I used to think about Caribbean sweets: skip desserts and head for the aged rum to finish a meal. But I learned a lot during my island stay and now I feel I've been anointed by a sunny finger from above to the gospel of sunny sweets. There are so many great fruits in the markets and to be foraged in the bush. The rich pantry of confectionary ingredients like exotic spices, coconut milk and meat, raw sugar, *dulce de leche,* honeys, and syrups is at your disposal, not to mention the recipe file steeped in tradition and history waiting to be used and updated. (Most of these items can be found at the local grocery.) Only a deal with the devil could keep me out of the Caribbean pastry kitchen these days.

That said, I've never fancied myself as a real dessert guy. My palate passionately lies in the savory kitchen with its salty fats and infernal flavors of chilies and spices. When I sit with the pastry chefs, I always ask them to make me desserts that people who don't eat dessert will want to eat. My Caribbean desserts aren't overly sweet; they are light on the tongue and combine many flavors, textures, and temperatures. As with all my cooking, I try to achieve something I call "a voyage on a plate": a dish that changes with each bite so each bite tastes a bit different. I also love chilled fruit soups, giggling wine jellies, and light, refreshing ices and have included a few of these as well. Even after a multi-course meal, these types of desserts are welcoming and don't evoke regret for the extra calories. When a team of pastry chefs can create a dessert that is crunchy, silky, warm, and icy all on the same plate, that is my idea of a perfect dessert. At home we don't have the luxury of a brigade of helpers or a special temperature-controlled kitchen to concoct our confections; therefore, the recipes that follow achieve the desired effect without all the complicated techniques used in a professional kitchen.

There are those times, though, when nothing will do but a slab of bittersweet chocolate ganache or that multi-layered torte of buttercream, nuts, and meringue. So I've included a few recipes that really go over the top for those days that your sweet tooth rules. Sadly, dessert has become a pariah. Modern thinking makes ordering pastries a social no-no. But if you balance your menu and follow rich meals with light desserts and follow a simple grilled fish with a chocolate soufflé, you'll be just fine. The key is that when you decide to prepare a dessert, go all the way. Use the best ingredients and make it good so those extra calories are well worth it.

Scaling Down: A Note on Baking

Many of my desserts use weighted ingredients. Pastry is more of a science than the savory kitchen. Digital scales are available at modest prices these days, and everyone who likes to spend time cooking should have one. They are easy and will allow you to cut some time out of your baking. Just put the mixing bowl on the scale, adjust, and go.

FOR 6 FRIENDS

1	large cantaloupe or honeydew melon, chilled
1 c.	orange juice
½ c.	white wine
1 T	honey
2½	limes, zest and juice
1 pinch	salt

OPTIONAL GARNISHES

sorbet

fresh berries

splash of champagne

fresh mint

all of the above!!!!!

Melon and Lime Soup with Sorbet, Berries, and Mint

A light, fresh dessert is often welcomed after a long day in the sun. This one fills the bill. You can use whichever melon and berries are ripest at the market.

Blend the melon in a blender until very smooth, add the remaining ingredients, and pulse to incorporate.

Serve in ice-cold chilled soup bowls with your favorite garnishes listed below.

FOR THE FILLING

4	large mangoes, peeled and cut into slices
½ c.	brown sugar
1 T	cornstarch
1 c.	orange juice
1	lime, juice and zest
1 tsp	Kitchen D'Orr Sweet Seasons Spice Blend (or nutmeg and cinnamon)
1 pinch	salt
1 pinch	freshly ground black pepper

FOR THE TOPPING

1 c.	flour
½ c.	oatmeal
½ c.	shredded coconut
1½ tsp	baking powder
4 T	butter
1 c.	milk
¼ c.	grated Mexican raw sugar (see p. xxiv and p. 130 on raw sugar)

optional (not really!): whipped cream, crème anglaise, ice cream, or all of them!! It's your birthday!!!

Caribbean Birthday Cobbler

My Grampa Orr (a.k.a. Iron Orr) didn't like fancy cakes for his birthday. Give him pie and he was happy! I guess I'm cut from the same cloth; give me some rustic pie or cobbler and my birthday is complete. It helps being an August baby, with plenty of fresh berries and stone fruit at the ready. Besides, who wants to be in the kitchen all day in the summer? Cobblers are simple to make and satisfying to eat both warm from the oven or as leftovers. This is a recipe that Christopher came up with for my 42nd birthday, using the Caribbean as the inspiration.

Place all the ingredients for the filling in a bowl and mix together to combine. Taste and adjust if necessary. Transfer ingredients to a baking dish and set aside.

Mix all the topping ingredients except the course raw sugar together and spoon on top of the mango filling to create an evenly thick crust. Sprinkle with raw sugar.

Bake at 375° for 45 minutes to 1 hour, until bubbling and nicely browned and crunchy on top.

Note: Can be baked in a large dish or as individual servings.

Paul and Darlene's Key Lime Cheesecake

Paul and Darlene are some guests who became friends on the island and have a great love for food and wine. Paul is an oral surgeon who lets off steam in the kitchen on the weekends, perfecting things like this cake. Darlene gets to take the results to the office on Mondays. Theirs is a light and airy version that works great with tropical fruit toppings such as passion fruit, mango, or crushed pineapple. If key limes are out of season or otherwise not available, try using regular limes or lemons in their place. The slow cooling stabilizes the cake, usually with perfect results and without cracking. I also bake these in small individual pans for single servings, but make sure you adjust the cooking time.

Preheat oven to 350°.

Mix the cracker crumbs, melted butter, sugar, and spices together. Press into bottom of 9-inch cheesecake pan and bake crust at 350° for 30 minutes or until lightly browned.

While crust is baking, cream together cheese, sour cream, ¾ cup of the sugar, vanilla, lime products, and egg yolks until smooth. In a separate bowl, whip egg whites and remaining sugar into soft peaks. Mix ⅓ of the whites into the cheese mixture to lighten it, then carefully fold in the remaining whites for volume.

Pour mixture into the crust-lined pan and bake in water bath for 1 hour at 300°. Turn off oven and do not open. Allow the cake to rest for 1 hour in the oven. Open the door for 30 minutes before removing the cake. Chill overnight.

Serve with your favorite fruit topping.

Note: If more color is desired, broil chilled cake until light brown and return to the refrigerator.

FOR 8–10 FRIENDS

CHEESE MIXTURE

16 oz.	cream cheese (room temperature)
1 pt.	sour cream (room temperature)
seeds from 1 fresh vanilla bean (or 2 T vanilla extract)	
2 T	key lime juice plus zest of 2 limes
5	eggs, separated
1 c.	sugar

CRUST

1½ c.	graham cracker crumbs
2 T	melted butter
1 T	sugar
1 tsp	Kitchen D'Orr Sweet Seasons Spice Blend (or Chinese 5-spice powder)

Hot Chocolate Soufflé

This is a best seller wherever I work. I learned how to make soufflé at La Grenouille, the famous restaurant on 52nd Street in Manhattan. I hope Charles, the owner, doesn't mind, but I have had soufflés on my menus ever since. This recipe is a quick and easy variety of soufflé and is actually quite stable, so those old rules about tiptoeing by the oven are not applicable. If you are lucky enough to go to La Grenouille, tell Charles I sent you.

Note: Old kitchen proverb—failure to plan is planning to fail. These need to go right from the oven to the table, so make sure you have everything ready before you put them in the oven. Sauces, garnishes, under-liner plates, and any beverages you are planning to serve should all be laid out ahead of time.

7 oz.	dark chocolate
5 oz.	unsalted butter, softened
6	egg yolks
5 oz.	white sugar, divided
7	egg whites

Butter 8 ramekin dishes, then evenly dust with remaining sugar.

Melt the chocolate in a mixing bowl over a water bath. Incorporate egg yolks and the butter into the chocolate and whisk until creamy. In another bowl, make a meringue by beating the egg whites and progressively adding 4 oz. of sugar until very stiff. Fold the meringue into the chocolate.

Fill each ramekin dish with soufflé mixture, up to ¼ inch from the rim. Bake the soufflés at 370° for approximately 18–20 minutes. Serve right away.

Can be served with fruit, chocolate sauce, or vanilla ice cream.

6 oz.	passion fruit puree with seeds
1 T	cornstarch, dissolved in
1 T	cold water
5 oz.	unsalted butter, softened
6	egg yolks
4 oz.	white sugar
7	egg whites

extra butter and sugar for coating ramekins

Quick Passion Fruit Soufflés

Soufflés are always a show-stopping dessert. This recipe with passion fruit couldn't be easier. I like the way the seeds crunch, but if you want to take them out, simply strain the mixture. The aroma of passion fruit is amazing and, for me, it smells like the Caribbean. If you can't find fresh fruit, frozen passion fruit puree can be found in some specialty shops or on the internet.

Butter 6–8 ramekin dishes, then evenly dust with white sugar, making sure all surfaces are covered. Set aside until needed.

Bring the puree to a boil in a saucepan and add the cornstarch previously dissolved in cold water. Cook for 2 minutes, stirring until it thickens. Chill and stir in the butter and egg yolks. Set aside, covered, at room temperature until needed (this can be done up to 30 minutes before cooking).

Just before baking: in a separate bowl, whisk the egg whites with sugar until firm peaks form.

Mix ⅓ of the whites into the passion fruit mixture. Then carefully fold in the remainder.

Fill each ramekin dish ¾ full with the soufflé mixture.

Bake the soufflés in a water bath made by using a cookie tray with ½ inch of water in a pre-heated 375° oven for approximately 15–18 minutes.

Must be served immediately.

Can be served accompanied by passion fruit rum sauce and vanilla ice cream.

10 oz.	top-quality dark chocolate, melted
2 tsp	instant espresso powder mixed with 1 tsp water
6 oz.	butter (room temperature)
5	eggs
3	egg yolks
3 oz.	flour
¼ tsp	salt

several turns of white pepper

6 oz.	sugar
6 scoops	vanilla ice cream, melted

powdered sugar as needed

grated chocolate

6	dark roasted coffee beans, crushed

non-stick spray, as needed

optional accompaniments: ice cream and melted ice cream (see note below)

Chocolate Volcano Cake with Espresso and Melted Vanilla Ice Cream

This is another of those famous "Jean-Georges molten chocolate cakes" loved by everyone. The problem is, once you put it on your menu, the guests won't let you take it off. Anguilla being surrounded by volcanic islands made the name a no-brainer. This is one of those recipes that must be run to the table as soon as it comes out of the oven, so plan ahead.

Preheat oven to 375°.

In a mixing bowl, whisk together melted dark chocolate, espresso concentrate, and butter. In a separate bowl, whisk the whole eggs and egg yolks together. Slowly add the melted chocolate to the egg mixture.

In a separate bowl, mix the flour, salt, white pepper, and sugar and fold in the egg and chocolate mixture.

Spray the inside of 6 ramekin dishes (or small cake rings) with non-stick spray and coat them with sugar. Place on a cookie tray and fill with batter.

Bake for 12–15 minutes.

To serve: Pour equal amounts of the melted ice cream into 6 soup plates. Unmold the cakes and place them in the center. Dust with powdered sugar, grated chocolate, and crushed coffee beans.

Note: The English call it "custard sauce," the French crème anglaise. In any language, it is the easiest dessert sauce recipe in the world! Take some of your best-quality rich vanilla ice cream out an hour before serving the dessert and the sauce is done. It's great with any dessert and even just poured over berries! You can add your favorite liqueur for a fun version. Chocolate sauce? Strawberry sauce? Pistachio sauce? You get the idea.

We are all dragged—some of us kicking and screaming—into the future, but there are certain times of the year when our yearning for the past becomes stronger. We hark back to the simpler times of our childhood, often forgetting just how difficult those times were, if not for us then for our folks. Holidays are a perfect example of this. Each year we pull out those boxes of decorations, cookie cutters, heirloom recipes, and family game boards. It isn't until New Year's Day, while putting everything away and swearing we will never do it again, that we realize all the work that goes into our celebrating. Luckily we forget this by the next time the holidays roll around and we do it all over again.

Ho, Ho, Ho and a Bottle of Rum

Caribbean Holidays

Caribbean fetes are no different. Weeks before the holidays roll around you start making your sorrel drink, rum punches, ginger beer, and cookies and sweets for the kids. Local cattle, hogs, and sheep are fattened. Anguillians may even stop calling their favorite goats by their "pet names," putting a bit of distance between themselves and the inevitable.

The house is decorated on the outside with colored lights and jelly jars of flowers brighten every interior corner. Family and friends arrive, sharing their homemade sweets and savories, and are invited in for a drink. Punches and soft drinks are favored by the women, but the men drift off to the corner for a "strong" drink and salty conversation about business, sports, women, and the sea. One hopes a katydid (green cricket) will fly through an open door or window, bringing good luck to a happy home.

The women decorate the dinner table, put the food out, and call everyone in for the meal. The menus often consist of five pots: one of rice, one of beans, one of meat and gravy, one of provisions, and one of greens. The contents differ slightly from island to island. In Anguilla, the dish of choice is a bountiful pot of fresh peas and rice (not rice and peas). Anguillians also love conky dumplings, cornmeal- or coconut-based dumplings wrapped in sea grape leaves or, these days, in foil. Fish would be on the table somewhere. The mood is light, and everyone feels full and happy.

When dinner dishes are cleared, desserts are laid out in the middle of the table: coconut pies and cakes, custards, rum-soaked fruit, puddings, and trifles with cake soaked in ginger wine. Don't forget that bowl of honey with tangerine segments carefully placed by Granny. Life is sweet; Granny makes it sweeter.

Caribbean holidays, like gatherings throughout the world, reunite us and leave us promising to stay in better touch throughout the year. But as with the holiday boxes that are packed back away under the stairs or in the attic, we often put our family and friendships on a back shelf. Make this the year you don't need a reason to get together; our humanity is as fragile as brittle shiny decorations.

Warm "Gateau" of Coconut with Crème Fraîche, Pineapple, and Anguillian Pyrat Rum

This warm cake takes just 8–10 minutes to cook and it is a wonderful finish for a meal. It is full of contradictions in that it is rich yet light, crisp yet tender, and both warm and cool. It is a wonderful twist on a Caribbean classic that will remind you of something between your gramma's macaroon and the finest of soufflés. It is what modern Anguillian cooking is all about. If you want more information on Pyrat rums, visit them at www.pyratrum.com. They're one of my favorites.

FOR 4 FRIENDS

FOR THE RUM SAUCE

1	pineapple, peeled, cored, and roughly chopped
½ c.	sugar
¼ c.	water
juice of 1 lime	
1 pinch	salt
1 pinch	black pepper
6 T	Pistol Pyrat rum (or other rich, dark rum)

FOR THE COCONUT CAKES

4	buttered and floured ring molds (well-washed tuna cans with both top and bottom removed also work well)
¾ stick	butter (room temperature)
5	egg yolks
⅓ c.	powdered sugar
2 T	pastry cream (or custard pudding)
1 T	Coco Lopez
1 c.	(packed) shredded coconut (unsweetened)
1 tsp	cornstarch
1 tsp	freshly grated lime zest
1 pinch	salt
1 pinch	Kitchen D'Orr Sweet Seasons Spice Blend (or Chinese 5-spice powder)
3 turns	white pepper
2 T	Pistol Pyrat rum (or other rich, dark rum)

FOR THE MERINGUE

2	egg whites
2 T	sugar

FOR THE PLATING

1 recipe	Rum Sauce (see recipe, left)
4 sprigs	mint and/or pineapple leaves
4 scoops	crème fraîche, coconut sorbet, or vanilla ice cream
3 T	toasted coconut curls

~~~~~~

FOR THE RUM SAUCE

Place all ingredients in a heavy-bottomed saucepan and bring to a boil. Cook until tender and puree into a semi-smooth sauce. Cool to room temperature and add the rum. Adjust seasoning as needed. Chill until ready for plating.

FOR THE CAKES

In a small bowl, fold together the butter, egg yolks, sugar, coconut, pastry cream, Coco Lopez, salt, pepper, spice blend, lime zest, and cornstarch. Mix well until combined. Add the rum, and combine.

Whisk egg whites and sugar to firm peaks and carefully fold into the coconut mixture, making it as light and airy as possible

Taste and adjust flavorings as needed.

Fill prepared cake rings with the mixture and bake on non-stick or buttered parchment paper–covered sheet pans until just set and browned on top. Do not over-bake. You want them lightly browned and crunchy on the exterior but still soft inside. They should *just* hold when rings are removed. Dust tops with a little powdered sugar.

Place cakes on plates and run a knife around the rings to loosen them from the molds. Carefully remove the rings.

Spoon the chilled Rum Sauce around the cakes and decorate with coconut curls, mint, and a scoop of crème fraîche and sorbet or ice cream.

Note: The bottom half of a pineapple is generally the sweetest part. To evenly ripen them and disperse the sugars, stand them on their green tops 1–2 days before cutting to encourage even sweetness.

FOR THE PINEAPPLE

| 1 | pineapple, ripe, core, top, bottom, and skin removed and cut in half vertically |
| 4 | fresh vanilla beans, split in half |

FOR THE BASTING SAUCE

1 c.	good dark rum
½ c.	dark brown sugar
½ lb.	butter
2 tsp	Kitchen D'Orr Sweet Seasons Spice Blend (or Chinese 5-spice powder)
1 pinch	salt
a couple turns of fresh pepper	

FOR THE PLATING

coconut sorbet or vanilla ice cream

mint leaves

Anguillian Grilled Vanilla-Studded Caribbean Pineapple, Basted with Local Rum

Blow your friends and family away by doing this on the BBQ on the next Fourth of July. This can be done either on the grill or the stove top. It is easy and dramatic, everything a dessert should be. You can use powdered vanilla in the basting sauce and forego the vanilla spiking to cut preparation time.

Skewer the pineapple with the vanilla beans using a barding needle or a chopstick to insert the vanilla into the pineapple.

Combine the remaining ingredients and warm over a slow fire until butter melts. Set aside.

Build a fire, turn on a gas grill, or pre-heat oven to 350° and wait for a nice even heat. A grill pan may also be used on the stove top.

Place the pineapple at a warm part of the grill away from direct heat and cook slowly, brushing often with the rum syrup. Turn as needed until evenly browned, caramelized, and tender when stuck with a chef's fork. This should take 25–30 minutes depending on the heat. Baste throughout the cooking but reserve about ⅓ of the sauce to finish the plate.

Slice the pineapple into half moons and top with coconut sorbet or vanilla ice cream. Spoon over a little of the remaining sauce. Serve while warm.

Note: If grilling, you can start the pineapple while finishing the cooking of other items and it will be done just in time for dessert. If the pineapple is under-ripe you may need to cover it lightly with foil during cooking so it will steam slightly and become more tender.

Honey and Pepper Mango Upside-Down Cake

This is a play on a pineapple upside-down cake, but one on flavor steroids. You'll love the way this dances in your mouth. Flavors meet and go their own way. Try it with papaya, peaches, apples, or pears (or even pineapple). If you don't have individual non-stick sauté pans, use a larger 8-inch pan and cut it into smaller portions once you turn the cake out and let it sit for a few minutes.

Serve with vanilla ice cream or mango sorbet.

Heat the small pans and add the honey and butter and melt. Add the mangoes, rounded side down so they caramelize. Cook over medium-high heat until nicely colored. Remove from heat and season with a touch of salt, pepper, and lime juice.

Cool to room temperature. Top with approximately ½-cup prepared Frangipane mixture and smooth with icing spatula.

Bake 15–20 minutes on sheet pan until Frangipane has firmed and browned. With a spatula, carefully go around each pan to loosen and turn cake out of molds while hot. If sugars harden and stick, reheat pans carefully over a burner.

Serve warm.

FOR 4 FRIENDS

2	mangoes, peeled, cut in half, and fanned
4 T	honey
4 tsp	butter
	sea salt
	cracked black pepper
	lime juice
	Frangipane mixture with Pyrat rum (see recipe below)

EQUIPMENT

small individual Teflon sauté pans

icing spatula

½ sheet pan

Frangipane (Almond Cream)

Using a food processor, combine all ingredients until a smooth, creamy paste is formed.

½ c.	ground almond meal
¼ c.	granulated sugar
1	egg
3 T	butter, softened
¾ tsp	vanilla extract
1 T	all-purpose flour
2 T	Pyrat rum or other rich dark rum

FOR THE COCONUT MIXTURE

3	eggs
7 oz.	sugar
zest of 6 limes	
7 oz.	cream
1 T	vanilla extract
1 tsp	cinnamon powder
½ tsp	nutmeg
7 oz.	coconut powder (you can pulse unsweetened coconut flakes in a food processor until powder-like)

FOR THE SUGAR DOUGH

¾ stick	butter (room temperature)
1	egg yolk
½ c.	water
1½ c.	all-purpose flour
3½ T	granulated sugar
¼ tsp	salt

Warm Coconut Lime Tarts

This recipe is based on a classic Caribbean coconut pie, but we've lightened it quite a bit. It is best served right out of the oven but is nice at room temperature as well. Try serving the tart with lime or mango sorbet for contrasting flavors, temperatures, and textures. I like these served as fancy individual tarts, but sometimes slices from a large tart are more homey and comforting.

FOR THE TART SHELLS (SUGAR DOUGH)

Mix the egg yolk and water with the butter and sift in the dry ingredients; stir to combine. Wrap in plastic and refrigerate at least 1 hour before rolling. Roll out dough and line 1 9-inch tart ring or 8 individual tart molds with prepared dough. Return to refrigerator until needed. May be done a day ahead.

FOR THE TARTS

In a medium bowl, mix together the eggs, sugar, and lime zest. Add the cream, vanilla, cinnamon, nutmeg, and coconut powder. Mix well and pour into prepared tart pan(s). Bake in a 350° oven for 15 minutes or until golden brown, reduce heat to 325°, and bake until crust is brown and coconut mixture is set, about an additional 15 minutes.

Caribbean Cashew Brittle with Chili Flakes and Ginger

This is an unusual recipe that uses sweet, heat, and ginger to make an unforgettable candy. It was inspired by a candy I had from Thailand but uses the most West Indian of ingredients. Use your favorite nuts for this. Store in an airtight container.

~~~~~~

Coat a baking sheet with oil; set aside.

In a 3-quart, heavy-bottomed saucepan over high heat, cook sugar and corn syrup until mixture reaches a medium caramel color. Brush down the sides of the pan with a pastry brush twice dipped in warm water to prevent the sugar from crystallizing. Add baking soda, nuts, chilies, ginger, and sea salt, then stir with a wooden spoon to coat completely with caramel. Stir in butter to combine.

Remove pan from heat and quickly pour mixture onto prepared baking sheet.

Working quickly, spread mixture thinly with the back of a wooden spoon.

Let brittle cool completely (about 30 minutes), then break into pieces.

Store in a tightly covered container.

2 c.	granulated sugar
1 c.	corn syrup
1 tsp	baking soda
2 c.	roasted cashews (or peanuts, pumpkin seeds, mixed nuts, etc.)
1 tsp	red pepper flakes
2 T	minced ginger
2 tsp	Kitchen D'Orr Sweet Seasons Spice Blend (or Chinese 5-spice powder)
2 tsp	sea salt
2 T	butter

9 oz.	top-quality 70 percent cacao dark chocolate
5 oz.	white chocolate
7 T	butter
½ c.	sugar
3	eggs
4	egg yolks
1	pre-baked tart shell—your favorite tart dough or use my Chocolate Short Dough (see recipe below)

MAKES 2 TART SHELLS

4 c.	all-purpose flour
½ tsp	salt
¼ c.	cocoa powder
1 c.	sugar
¾ lb.	butter
¼ lb.	bittersweet chocolate, melted
½ c.	cream

FOR 6–8 FRIENDS

5 c.	extra-strong brewed coffee (preferably a Jamaican Blue Mountain variety)
1 c.	sugar
4 T	Kahlúa liqueur
1 c.	water

Double Chocolate Tart with Blue Mountain Coffee Granité

For me, a marriage of chocolate and coffee is one made in heaven. Use Blue Mountain coffee and your honeymoon will be on the beaches of Jamaica. Only the best-quality chocolate should be used, so splurge a bit. It will cost less than a trip to the Caribbean.

Melt chocolates and butter over water in a double boiler or in a microwave. Be careful not to overheat and scorch the chocolate. Set aside.

In a mixing bowl, combine eggs, yolks, and sugar. Whip until thick and pale yellow, about 10 minutes. Fold ⅓ of egg mixture into chocolate. Gently fold the lightened chocolate mixture back into the remaining yolks. Scoop into pre-baked shell. Bake in a pre-heated 325° oven until lightly set, about 7 minutes. Remove and cool to room temperature.

Serving suggestions: serve at room temperature with Blue Mountain Coffee Granité (see recipe below) and whipped cream.

Chocolate Short Dough

Heat the cream and pour it over the chocolate, then cool to room temperature. Sift together dry ingredients. Cream the butter, fold in the sifted dry mix, and stir to combine. Add the chocolate cream to the dough and stir to incorporate. Refrigerate at least 2 hours. Roll and use as needed.

Blue Mountain Coffee Granité

This is great with the tart above but also works well in a coupe glass layered with vanilla ice cream or just on its own with whipped cream. You need to plan ahead, as it takes 24 hours to make, but it can be made up to a week ahead of time. Once frozen, cover tightly so it doesn't pick up any extra freezer flavors.

Mix the hot coffee and sugar together until sugar dissolves. Add remaining items and pour into a glass baking dish and freeze. Stir every 30–60 minutes until the mixture starts to set. Allow to freeze solid. Use a fork to shave the ice into uniform crystals.

Note: If the granité doesn't freeze hard enough to shave, add a touch of water.

6 c.	fresh papaya puree, left a little chunky
1½ c.	honey
¼ c.	lime juice
¼ c.	vodka
1 pinch	salt
2¾ c.	water

Papaya Granité

Papayas in the Caribbean are like zucchini in the midwestern zucchini season. You need to come up with 101 ways to use them up or leave them on a neighbor's doorstep. This granité works well as one of those uses. Get it in the freezer when the papayas are ripe and it is ready for you whenever you want it. Great with berries and other fresh fruit or in a coupe glass layered with vanilla ice cream or whipped cream. You can also use ripe mango or melon in place of the papaya if you want to experiment. Great for a brunch or breakfast fruit salad as well.

Mix together all of the ingredients, pour into a glass baking dish, and freeze. Stir every 30–60 minutes until it sets. Allow to freeze solid. Use a fork to break up the ice and serve.

Jamaican Red Banana Fritters

This is another of Athenia's recipes from her island. She prefers to make them with extra-ripe red bananas, but any banana will do. They make a great dessert with caramel dipping sauce or served with hot chocolate for Sunday brunch. They are addictive, so watch out.

Mash the 2 extra-ripe bananas until they form a chunky puree. Mix with the flour, sugar, baking powder, vanilla, rum, milk, and seasoning until a nice batter forms. Dice the remaining banana into ¼-inch dice and fold in.

Chill until needed, at least 15–20 minutes.

Fry in 350° oil until crisp. Drain on paper towels to remove excess oil and sprinkle with powdered sugar and additional spices.

Serve with melted vanilla ice cream for dipping.

FOR 12 FRIENDS

2	bananas, extra-ripe
1	banana, ripe
1 c.	flour
¼ c.	brown sugar
½ tsp	baking powder
½ tsp	vanilla extract
1 T	banana rum
½ c.	milk
¼ tsp	crushed black pepper
¼ tsp	Kitchen D'Orr Sweet Seasons Spice Blend (or freshly grated nutmeg)
¼ tsp	salt

oil for frying

powdered sugar for garnish

melted vanilla ice cream with rum for dipping (optional)

ReCiPEs for the BodY

We need to feed our bodies in many ways. Obviously we do this through the mouth at least three times a day, but there are other ways: through laughter and conversation with family and friends, education, and art and music, to name a few. We also can do this through the skin with touch, antioxidants, and nutrition. Try some of these recipes with someone special. Put on some soft music, turn down the lights, and get out the aromatherapy candles for an escape to your own little paradise right at home.

Lavender and Rosemary Massage Oil

MAKES 1 CUP

1 c.	organic vegetable oil
¼ c.	organic lavender flowers (dried)
1 sprig	fresh rosemary
2 T	water

Lavender and rosemary are both calming herbs. This is a great oil for massages before bed. I like to massage my temples with it after a hard day in the kitchen.

Simmer the water and lavender over low heat until water completely evaporates.

Add oil and rosemary and heat to a medium-hot temperature and remove from flame.

Cool to room temperature and strain.

Store in a decorative bottle.

Kumquat and Sea Salt Foot Scrub

MAKES 2 CUPS

¼ lb.	sea salt
¼ lb.	kosher salt
¼ lb.	table salt
¼ c.	extra-virgin olive oil
1 c.	washed kumquats

I use this straight out of the fridge when giving friends a foot rub. Removes rough patches and dead skin cells.

Place in a food processor and blend until smooth.

Store in Ball jars in a cool, dry place.

3	large globe tomatoes
5	basil leaves
2 T	olive oil

The Human Bruschetta [Tomato and Basil Body Scrub]

I had this mixture spread over me the first time I went to the CuisinArt spa and I actually got hungry during my treatment! Get out a big towel, mix it up, and have a loved one spread it on. Relax for 15–20 minutes, and you will be glowing and hungry after you rinse. Tomatoes contain antioxidants as well as natural sun block, so it is a great treatment when you are planning to spend your days in the sun. Remember, never refrigerate your tomatoes whether you are wearing them or eating them. They are best at room temperature.

Puree in a food processor or blender. Have your partner lie down on a towel and evenly massage the mixture all over the body. Allow the skin to enjoy for 15–20 minutes. Shower.

Switch places and repeat.

MAKES 2 FACIALS

1	large European cucumber (cut 4 thin slices for your eye pads; grate the rest with a carrot grater)
½ bunch	fresh mint, finely chopped
2 T	drained thick yogurt

Cool Cucumber Facial Mask

Do this for a friend and take turns. Read one another poetry or a good book while the other is relaxing. Great rainy day fun! Leaves the skin refreshed and vibrant.

Lightly squeeze the grated cucumber. Mix in mint and yogurt. Have your partner lie back on a towel. Apply the cucumber discs to the closed, relaxed eyes, and then half of the mixture to the face. Relax for a half hour and switch.

Note: Don't put any mask too close to the eyes to prevent it from leaking behind the cucumber disks.

Papaya, Coconut, and Strawberry Facial Mask

At CuisinArt we grew our own papayas, cucumbers, and coconuts for this wonderful mask. The kitchen prepares it when the fruits are plentiful and sends it over to the spa. Papaya contains a strong enzyme called papain, which dissolves oil and dead skin cells; it is one of the best non-abrasive masks that you can use. The coconut and strawberries also help exfoliate those dead skin cells.

Puree all ingredients in a blender and process until smooth, apply to face, and relax with your head on a towel for 15 minutes.

If there is any stinging sensation, rinse your face immediately. (This reaction will alert you to the fact that you have a sensitivity to one of the ingredients.)

MAKES 2 FACIALS

2	large strawberries
¼ c.	grated fresh coconut
2 T	papaya pulp
1	egg white
½	English cucumber

the PeRFECT SToRm

How to Prepare
for a Hurricane

In this time of global warming, we must all be ready for an emergency.

The following is adapted from CuisinArt's hurricane manual from a few years ago which was designed specifically for an island resort. But you can adapt it for whatever location or type of storm emergency you may want to be prepared for.

Living in paradise has its drawbacks, and one of them is the hurricane. Given the destruction of Katrina and the chaos left in her wake in New Orleans and surrounding areas, I feel compelled to help you ready yourself for a storm or natural disaster that might come your way. The main thing is to be prepared and have safe shelter. After the last big storm in Anguilla, most of the charming old wood homes have been replaced with stronger, less romantic, poured concrete structures. You only need to be hit once to learn the lessons that a hurricane has to teach. I've weathered many a storm in Anguilla but never a hurricane, and that is PERFECTLY all right with me.

Storm Crisis Planning Steps

- Convene a family meeting.

- Track storm on computer.

- Put change of clothing in sealed plastic bags for each family member.

- Personal documents, jewelry, and other valuables should be placed in safe deposit boxes.

- Gather medication, if necessary.

- Gather baby and children's supplies.

- Gather toiletries (including toilet paper).

- Inspect all fire protection equipment, such as fire extinguishers.

- Prepare computer data backups for the entire system. Store computer covered in plastic in a strong, dry, elevated place.

- Secure important documents in plastic and store.

- Ready portable radio to be monitored for weather updates.

- Check hurricane supplies (see list below).

- Remove all screen doors and store.

- Identify and purchase necessary food supplies. You will need items that don't need cooking and have a shelf life of 2 weeks. Confirm if present supply is adequate.

- Gas all vehicles.

- Fill buckets and containers with fresh water for bathing and washing dishes.

- Clear yard of all items that can be blown about.

- Store all patio furniture.

- Close all awnings and umbrellas.

- Close storm windows.

- All department heads to establish a list of employees willing to work during the hurricane.

- Make sure you have petty cash set aside in a secure place.

- Videotape entire property and take photos of the same.

- Inspect and clean roof drains if necessary.

- Contact family members off-island and tell them of plans.

Just before She Hits

- Distribute duct tape to start taping all windows not covered by hurricane shutters.

- Turn off electric main breakers.

- Unplug all electrical equipment from outlets if possible.

- Close off all water supplies.

- Remove gutters from cisterns.

- Shut off gas to minimize fire loss.

- Protect or shut off other possible flame sources.

- Close gas supply at tank.

- Get yourself and your family to a safe, secure location.

The Calm (Hopefully) after the Storm

- Call family meeting for headcount and debriefing.

- Treat any personal injuries.

- A general follow-up session of videotaping and picture taking should be done for insurance purposes.

- Conduct brief assessment of damage and priority for cleanup and salvage. Cover broken windows and damaged roof immediately. Separate damaged from undamaged goods immediately, but beware of accumulating too much combustible debris inside building.

- Assess impact of hurricane in terms of support systems, including electrical supply, water, food, etc.

- Determine communications availability and contact relatives.

- Structural damage should be especially photographed and videotaped for insurance purposes.

Hurricane Supplies Inventory Sheet

The list below should be gathered far ahead of any storm warning and placed in a separate location from items ordinarily used day to day. This will prevent panic during the pre-storm period.

ITEMS	QUANTITY NEEDED	CURRENT STOCK	NEEDED STOCK
Flashlights	One for each family member		
Batteries	Refills for all battery-operated equipment		
First Aid Kits	1 fully stocked		
Rope 3/8"	1		
Boots	1 pair per family member		
Shovels/Spades	1		
Mops	2		
Buckets	2		
Raincoats	1 per family member		
Work Gloves	4 pairs		
Tarpaulins	1		
Plastic Sheeting	2 large rolls		
Camera and Film	2 cameras and 2 rolls of 36 exposures per camera		
Vide recorder and Tapes	1 recorder and 6 tapes		
Garbage Bags	4 boxes (large, heavy duty)		
Bottled Water	4 cases		
Duct Tape	4 rolls		
Matches	4 large boxes, in waterproof bags		
Candles	20		
Hammers	1		
Radios	1 battery-operated radio		
Safety Helmets	1–2		
Plywood	As needed to cover windows		
Chain Saw (Gas)	1		
Water Disinfectant	2 bottles		
Bug Spray	4 cans		
Jumper Cables	1 set		
Tire Repair Kits	1 kit		
Tow Ropes	1		
Crowbars	1		
Nails, Assorted Sizes	Several boxes of assorted sizes		
Lumber	As needed		
Wheelbarrows	1		

Hurricane and Tropical Storm Description

Tropical storms and hurricanes are tropical cyclonic storms accompanied by violent winds, heavy rains, and high seas.

Advisory: A message released by a hurricane center updating information on a storm or hurricane. Tropical Storm and Hurricane Advisories are normally issued at 6-hour intervals, e.g., 0500, 1100, and 1700 hours. The eye position, intensity, forecasted movement of the storm, and immediate flash bulletins are also issued and are especially important as a storm or hurricane approaches closer to your location.

Tropical Disturbance: Moving areas of thunderstorms or other disturbance air masses that maintain identity for 24 hours or more. This is a common occurrence in the tropics.

Tropical Depression: Closed circulation of air mass at the surface. Winds can go as high as 38 M.P.H.

Tropical Storm: A depression becomes a tropical storm when sustained winds reach 39–73 M.P.H. The storm now has a distinct rotation of winds around a point of low pressure.

Hurricane Watch: This is issued when there is a possibility that a hurricane may threaten the area. This alert is normally issued 36 hours before estimated landfall.

Hurricane Warning: This is normally issued 24 hours before estimated landfall. Hurricane warnings identify coastal areas where winds of at least 74 M.P.H. are expected to occur. A warning may also describe areas where dangerously high water or waves are forecasted. If the hurricane is erratic, the warning may be issued only a few hours before actual landfall.

Hurricane: A Hurricane is a counterclockwise rotating tropical storm with winds in excess of 74 M.P.H. There are five categories of hurricanes:

> **Category 1:** Winds of 74–95 M.P.H.
>
> **Category 2:** Winds of 96–110 M.P.H.
>
> **Category 3:** Winds of 111–130 M.P.H.
>
> **Category 4:** Winds of 131–155 M.P.H.
>
> **Category 5:** Winds of 155 M.P.H. and greater.
>
> In a hurricane there are two major forces that cause damage, the most serious being the storm surge, which is the waves of water that are caused by heavy winds sweeping into tide and causing high tide to move far beyond its normal boundaries. The other force would be the high velocity of wind and rain.

Yellow Alert: A tropical depression/tropical storm or hurricane is forming within the tropics or the Atlantic basin, which includes the Atlantic Ocean, Caribbean Sea, and the Gulf of Mexico.

Orange Alert: A hurricane or tropical storm is within an estimated 36-hour threat before landfall.

Red Warning: A hurricane or tropical storm is posing an estimated 24-hour threat before landfall. All precautions should be taken immediately. If the path of the hurricane is erratic or unusual, the warning may be given only a few hours before the hurricane strikes.

from OnE iSLaND to aNOTHeR

Daniel Orr's Article from the *Anguillian*

As printed in the *Anguillian,* Anguilla's national newspaper, March 20, 2006.

I always told my guests that Manhattan and Anguilla are pretty much the same. After they laugh, I explain that they are both 16 miles by 3 miles in size; the difference is that Anguilla has 11 thousand inhabitants and New York City has 11 million. Manhattan is an island between America and Europe; it is fast paced like America, but steeped in the classic arts and culture like Europe. It is extremely modern, free, and forward-thinking; an amazing place to live. Anguilla has been exciting, rewarding, and educational, altering my life in ways Manhattan never could have. The one thing that is constant is change. We've all heard that before! And now it is time for me to change hemispheres and return to my other island.

I'll miss my goats and chickens and all the fruits from the trees I planted . . . things you can't grow on a rooftop in Manhattan. Bananas, papayas, noni, limes, avocados, and the fruits from my old bitter orange tree too. Wow, those oranges make wonderful gin and tonics! I'll miss the smell of grilling chicken and ribs sizzling over hot local charcoal as I drive down the road. I won't forget the souse at the Blue Food Van just past Ace. I'll miss the sound and the rhythmic thump of the bands playing deep into the night during Summerfest and the fun of Fun Day. I'll miss seeing the kids dressed in their weekday school uniforms and watching the cricket and soccer matches on the weekends. I'll also miss the view of St. Martin, St. Barts, and Saba and watching the sun rise, set, and hide behind rain showers. I'll miss the heat and I'll miss the windy chill that follows a heavy evening spring storm. I'll miss it all, Anguilla.

The last two years have been life changing. Living in another culture has taught me to be more patient and understanding as well as to listen, not just to hear. I've grown to love my staff and feel like they are more family than folks who work for me. It will be hard to leave them behind. My time outside of work has been stimulating, too . . . fishing for whelks, urchins, potfish, and conch with "Nature Boy" up at Island Harbour, climbing the rope down and skin-diving at Little Bay, long afternoons with Carol and her famous Mango Daiquiris at Elodia's and just limin' as the Caribbean sun slowly sets and offers her honey hues to Anguilla's late afternoon beauty. Evening open-window rides around the island listening to laugher and dominoes slamming down. Let's not forget the Juvet parades and late nights at Johnno's and

Pumphouse. Maybe I'll still get to Red Dragon before I go!

At work I've had the opportunity to "play" with some of the best products available to any chef: how super to buy local spiny lobsters and crayfish in old burlap bags from Roy and Ronny. Cleve delivered to me some of the freshest fish I've ever worked with, and Joseph always arrived with a smile when he dropped off his catch of the day. I've loved the Caribbean fruits and vegetables I got from Fruity Web and the People's Market, as well as the stuff my staff brought in from their own gardens or those of friends and neighbors. The local soursops, ginips, and mangoes are amazing, as well as coco plums and sea grapes and other things a farm boy from southern Indiana had never seen: oxtails, goat stew, roasted "shellfish" with sea water and lime, conch and dumplings, bull's foot, pig's snout, callaloo, rice and peas, roti, and sea lice to name a few. I now have a whole new vocabulary for my kitchen to take back with me! Franklyn Brooks taught me about Caribbean gardening and Dr. Resh showed me the magic of hydroponics. But it really all goes back to my wonderful kitchen team and dining room staff, whom I'd love to thank individually but don't have the space, and I wouldn't want to miss a single one! Everyone else, from landscaping to laundry, from the beach guys to the bar people, have been wonderful as well.

Many on the island have opened their hearts to me, especially everyone who was involved in the Anguillian National Culinary Team. There was so much wonderful support in Miami. Was I impressed! I can't forget my neighbors on Old Ta, including the governor and his wife, who have been simply charming. All the people in the island's many restaurants and in the hospitality industry have not only been extremely professional but kind and generous. Nat from the *Anguillian* has been a gem, running my weekly articles and recipes. I almost feel Anguillian! After two years of driving the Chef's Mobile, my white paneled and blue-topped jeep, I can't go a mile down the road without someone honking, waving, or shouting "Hey Cheffy." Sometimes all three.

But alas, the U.S. and the little island of Manhattan are my home and I must return, but I return changed. I return with a map of Anguilla tattooed on my soul. Memories of moon-filled nights and Moonsplash, powdery sands and curry powder, coconuts and coco plums, days in the sun and the sounds of crickets at dusk. I will return for more of that sand between my toes as soon as I can. Who knows, maybe even for Carnival every August Monday! Anyone have a spare room???

Thanks for the memories Anguilla . . .

Daniel Orr

Index

ackee, in Anieta's Ackee and Saltfish, 12

Alligator Daiquiri, 93

Anguill-Asian Pomelo Salad, 50

Anguilla
fishing in, 1, 134, 142–143
gardening in, 44–47
visiting St. Martin from, 204
See also culture, Caribbean

Anguillian Conch Chowder (a.k.a. Island Viagra), 38

Anguillian Grilled Vanilla-Studded Caribbean Pineapple, Basted with Local Rum, 234

Anguillian Jerked Fisherman's Steak, 136

Anguillian Jerked Fresh Ham, 171

Anguillian Jerked Quail, 103

Anguillian National Culinary Team, 192, 254

The Anguillian National Culinary Team's Rice and Peace (Pigeon Peas and Rice), 192

Anguillian Paella, Sofrito de Carlos, Local Crayfish, Spiny Lobster, and Island Hen, 150

Anguillian Roasted Tomato Bloody Mary, 87, 105

Anieta's Ackee and Saltfish: Jamaica's National Breakfast Dish, 12

animal husbandry, 163, 178–179

annatto, xix

in Annatto Oil, 203

appetizers, 101
Anguillian Jerked Quail, 103
Callaloo and Black-Eyed Peas Fritters, 117
Crab Fritters with Lemon Zest and Parmesan, 114
Grilled Tiger Shrimp with Papaya Banana Catsup, 108
Irie Conch Salad, 110
Island Tuna Crudo, Coconut Water, and Scotch Bonnets, 111
Johnnycakes with Sour Cream and Corn, 116
Marinated Island Conch with Citrus and Coconut Milk, 109
Mushroom and Sweet Pepper Skewers with Purslane Salad, 106
Pepper and Chili Carpaccio with Wild Herbs and Bloody Mary Granité, 105
Quick Caribbean Blood Pudding, 119
Saltfish Salad, 123
Sashimi Salad of Island Snapper with Fresh Herbs and Scotch Bonnets, 112
"Sea Cat" in Ginger Miso Sauce, 116
Shrimp Quesadilla with Cilantro and Scallions, 113

See also tapas

apples
in Beet Sangria, 64
in Feel the Burn (vegetable juice), 64

Athenia's Anguill-Asian Slaw, 54, 117

Athenia's Jamaican Carrot Juice, 92

avocados, in Alligator Daiquiri, 93

Baby Shrimp Ernise, 55

bananas, xix–xx, 1
in Banana Black Peppercorn Rum, 98
in Banana Waffles with Passion Fruit Rum Syrup and Mango Butter, 16
in Ginger Rat (cocktail), 91
in Green Mango and Banana Chutney, 201
in Grilled Tiger Shrimp with Papaya Banana Catsup, 108
in Jamaican Red Banana Fritters, 241
in Kitchen D'Orr Banana Bran Muffins, 5
Papaya Banana Catsup, 200
in Pressure Cooker Goat Stew, 126
in Sun, Sea, and Soy (smoothie), 22
in West Indian Pumpkin and Banana Bisque, 26

Banx, Bankie, 53, 146

basil, 218
in The Human Bruschetta, 244

bath and body recipes, 242–245
Cool Cucumber Facial Mask, 244

The Human Bruschetta, 244
Kumquat and Sea Salt Foot Scrub,
    243
Lavender and Rosemary Massage
    Oil, 243
Papaya, Coconut, and Strawberry
    Facial Mask, 245
BBQ
    charcoal for, 163, 176
    popularity of, 163–164
    sauces for, 176
Be Irie Cocktail, 92
beans
    in The Anguillian National Culinary
        Team's Rice and Peace, 192
    in Black Bean Soup, 35
    in Caribbean Cassoulet, 127
    in Sautéed Pigeon Peas and Greens,
        186
    See also black-eyed peas; lentils
beans, green
    in Greek Island Pasta Salad, 58
    in Grilled Tuna Niçoise with Paradise
        Kitchen Vinaigrette, 49
beans, kidney
    in Boiled Salt Beef and Beans, 128
beans, red
    in Red Bean Butter with Garlic Pita
        Crisps, 69
beef
    in The Anguillian National Culinary
        Team's Rice and Peace, 192
    Boiled Salt Beef and Beans, 128
    filet mignon, 166
    Grilled Flank Steak, 176
    ground chuck, 194
    Jerked Steak and Eggs with Lime
        and Chili Pepper Hollandaise,
        13–14
    liver, 119
    Pepper and Chili Carpaccio with
        Wild Herbs and Bloody Mary
        Granité, 105
    Quick Caribbean Blood Pudding, 119
    salt, xxi, 128, 192
    Spicy Caribbean Tripe Stew, 129

steak, 13–14, 176
    in Stuffed Green Papaya, 194
    tenderloin, 105
    tripe, 129
beets
    in Athenia's Boiled Beets with
        Orange and Herbs, 187
    Balsamic Emulsion, 141
    in Beet Sangria, 64
    in Vision Finder (vegetable juice), 63
beverages
    Alligator Daiquiri, 93
    Anguillian Roasted Tomato Bloody
        Mary, 87
    Athenia's Jamaican Carrot Juice, 92
    Banana Black Peppercorn Rum, 98
    Be Irie Cocktail, 92
    Beet Sangria, 64
    The Big Bamboo, 84
    Bush Dr. in da House (vegetable
        juice), 63
    The Bush Garden (cocktail), 79
    bush teas, 217, 219
    Caribbean Passion Fruit Punch, 86
    Citrus Trio Master Recipe, 21, 63
    cocktails, 79–93
    Coconut Martini, 80
    Cucumber Cooler, 64
    Da Pom Pom, 90
    Duneshine, 146
    Feel the Burn (vegetable juice), 64
    for fetes, 231
    Frozen Mojito, 86
    Ginger and Honey Rum, 98
    Ginger Beer, 90
    Ginger Rat, 91
    homemade flavored rums, 95–99
    Hydro-PepperMint Bush Tea, 219
    Island Rum Punch, 82
    Island Time Bush Tea, 219
    Jamaican Ginger Bush Tea, 219
    John's St. Kitts Cooler, 93
    Jungle Juice, 63
    Kumquat and Star Anise Rum, 96
    Lavender Lemonade, 65
    Lemongrass Rum, 99

Oh Be Joyful, 85
Old Time Cuba Libre, 84
Orange Spice Rum, 99
Passionate Bubbles, 84
Petal's Welcome Potion, 65
Pineapple and Cucumber Limeade,
    88
Pineapple and Vanilla Rum, 96
Pineapple Wine, 89
Pucker and Kiss, 85
Salt Pond, 92
shakes and smoothies, 20–22
Sour Sorrel Bush Tea, 219
The 3 Cs (Caribbean Coconut
    Cooler), 79
Tropical Pineapple Mango Frappé, 83
vegetable juices, 62–65
Vision Finder (vegetable juice), 63
West Indian Spice Bush Tea, 219
Bitter Orange Coulis, 208
Black Bean Soup, 35
black-eyed peas
    in Callaloo and Black-Eyed Peas
        Fritters, 117
    in Caribbean Cassoulet, 127
Blanquette de la Mer au Curry (Shark
    or Monkfish Stew with Curry), 137
Bloody Mary Granité, 87
    uses of, 29, 105
Blue Mountain Coffee Granité, 238
Boiled Salt Beef and Beans, 128
bok choy
    in Potfish (Island Bouillabaisse) with
        Tomatoes, Fennel, Saffron, Chilies,
        and Lime, 154
    in Snapper in Chili and Ginger Broth
        with Island Vegetables (a.k.a.
        Island Fish Water), 144
    in Tamarind-Glazed Grouper Fillet,
        Baby Bok Choy, Crispy Shallots,
        and Beet Emulsion, 140
breadfruit, xx
    Breadfruit Homefries with
        Mushrooms and Garlic, 18
    Breadfruit Salad, 56
    Crisped Breadfruit with Roasted

Garlic Butter, 190
    Roasted Breadfruit, 195
breads, quick
    Banana Waffles with Passion Fruit
        Rum Syrup and Mango Butter, 16
    Johnnycakes with Sour Cream and
        Corn, 116
    Kitchen D'Orr Banana Bran Muffins, 5
    Tropical Muffins, 4
breakfast, 1
    Anieta's Ackee and Saltfish, 12
    Banana Waffles with Passion Fruit
        Rum Syrup and Mango Butter, 16
    Breadfruit Homefries with
        Mushrooms and Garlic, 18
    Caribbean "Pain Perdu" with West
        Indian Spiced Caramel Syrup, 19
    Chef D's Famous French Bread
        French Toast Casserole, 8
    Coconut and Sesame Cereal, 3
    Island Cornmeal Breakfast Porridge, 8
    Jerked Steak and Eggs with Lime
        and Chili Pepper Hollandaise,
        13–14
    Johnnycakes with Sour Cream and
        Corn, 116
    Kitchen D'Orr Banana Bran Muffins, 5
    Lobster Benedict with Key Lime
        Hollandaise and Shaved Nori, 7
    Paradise Kitchen "Homies," 14
    Saltfish and Yam Cakes, 11
    shakes and smoothies for, 20–22
    Surreal Tropical Cereal Parfait, 4
    Tropical Muffins, 4
Brooks, Franklyn "Doc," 44–46, 74
Bush Dr. in da House (vegetable juice),
    63
The Bush Garden (cocktail), 79
bush teas, 217, 219
    in Georgia on My Mind (smoothie), 22
    Hydro-PepperMint, 219
    Island Time, 219
    Jamaican Ginger, 219
    Sour Sorrel, 219
    West Indian Spice, 219
butter

compound butters, 159–160
    Mango Butter, 16
    Red Bean Butter with Garlic Pita
        Crisps, 69
    substitutes for, 69

cabbage, in Athenia's Anguill-Asian
    Slaw, 54
callaloo, xx,
    in Bush Dr. in da House (vegetable
        juice), 63
    in Callaloo and Black-Eyed Peas
        Fritters, 117
    in Callaloo and Crab Stew, 36
    in Island Vegetable Pistou with
        Spiny Lobster and Herbs, 33
    in Jerk-Rubbed Filet Mignon with
        Steamed Kale and Calaloo, 166
candy
    Caribbean Cashew Brittle with Chili
        Flakes and Ginger, 237
Caribbean Birthday Cobbler, 224
Caribbean Cashew Brittle with Chili
    Flakes and Ginger, 237
Caribbean Cassoulet, 127
Caribbean Chicken Soup with Pigeon
    Peas and Coconut Dumplings, 31
Caribbean "Pain Perdu" with West
    Indian Spiced Caramel Syrup, 19
Caribbean Passion Fruit Punch, 86
Caribbean Sugarcane Vinaigrette, 52
Carnival, 173
carpaccio, 105
carrots
    in Athenia's Jamaican Carrot Juice, 92
    in Beet Sangria, 64
    in Breadfruit Salad, 56
    in Bush Dr. in da House (vegetable
        juice), 63
    in Chilled Curried Carrot Soup with
        Orange, 27
    in Don't Let Your Man-Go Hot Sauce,
        203
    Feel the Burn (vegetable juice), 64
    in Grape and Grain Salad, 41
    in Jungle Juice, 63

in Potfish (Island Bouillabaisse) with
        Tomatoes, Fennel, Saffron, Chilies,
        and Lime, 154
    in Snapper in Chili and Ginger Broth
        with Island Vegetables (a.k.a.
        Island Fish Water), 144
    in Vision Finder (vegetable juice), 63
Carty, Dale, 110
celery
    in Petal's Welcome Potion, 65
    in Vision Finder (vegetable juice), 63
champagne
    in Passionate Bubbles (cocktail), 84
    in Pucker and Kiss (cocktail), 85
cheese
    in Shrimp Quesadilla with Cilantro
        and Scallions, 113
cheese, Cheddar
    in Shrimp Quesadilla with Cilantro
        and Scallions, 113
cheese, cream
    in Paul and Darlene's Key Lime
        Cheesecake, 225
cheese, feta
    in Greek Island Pasta Salad, 58
cheese, Monterey Jack
    in Cornmeal and Okra Rellanos with
        Sauce Creole, 74
    in Shrimp Quesadilla with Cilantro
        and Scallions, 113
cheese, Parmesan
    in Stuffed Green Papaya, 194
Chef D's Famous French Bread French
    Toast Casserole, 8
chicken
    in Anguillian Paella, Sofrito de
        Carlos, Local Crayfish, Spiny
        Lobster, and Island Hen, 150
    in Caribbean Chicken Soup with
        Pigeon Peas and Coconut
        Dumplings, 31
    in Good Vibration Chicken Salad, 57
    Paradise Kitchen Grilled Chicken
        with Chilies, Garlic, and Lime, 165
    raising and eating, 179
    Spit-Roasted Chicken with Haitian

Mofongo and Mango Chutney, 177
Chili Vinegar, 130, 172
Chilled Curried Carrot Soup with
    Orange, 27
chocolate
    in Chocolate Short Dough, 238
    in Chocolate Volcano Cake with
        Espresso and Melted Vanilla Ice
        Cream, 230
    in Double Chocolate Tart with Blue
        Mountain Coffee Granité, 238
    in Hot Chocolate Soufflé, 227
christophene (chayote squash), xx
    in Don't Let Your Man-Go Hot Sauce,
        203
    in Stuffed Green Papaya, 194
cilantro
    in Shrimp Quesadilla with Cilantro
        and Scallions, 113
    in Sofrito de Carlos, 211
Citrus Trio Master Recipe, 21, 63
coconut, xxi
    in Coconut and Sesame Cereal, 3, 4
    in Coconut Rum, 80, 92
    in Fresh Coconut Dumplings, 125
    gathering and eating, 143
    in Guy Gumbs's Anguillian Conky
        Dumplings, 184
    in Papaya, Coconut, and Strawberry
        Facial Mask, 245
    in Warm Coconut and Lime Tarts,
        236
    in Warm Eggplant Stew with
        Coconut Vinegar and Curry, 188
    in Warm "Gateau" of Coconut with
        Crème Fraîche, Pineapple, and
        Anguillian Pyrat Rum, 232–233
coconut milk, xxi
    in Callaloo and Crab Stew, 36
    in Coconut Basmati Rice, 196
    in Coconut Martini, 80
    in Crab Fritters with Lemon Zest
        and Parmesan, 114
    in Guy's Coconut Dumplings with
        Cornmeal, 31
    making, 81

in Pressure Cooker Goat Stew, 126
    in West Indian Slam'n Yam Salad, 60
Coconut Rum
    in Be Irie Cocktail, 92
    in Coconut Martini, 80
coconut water
    in Be Irie Cocktail, 92
    in Island Tuna Crudo, 111
    in The 3 Cs (cocktail), 79
coffee
    in Chocolate Volcano Cake with
        Espresso and Melted Vanilla Ice
        Cream, 230
    in Double Chocolate Tart with Blue
        Mountain Coffee Granité, 238
collard greens, in Caribbean Cassoulet,
    127
compound butters, 159–160
conch, xxi
    in Anguillian Conch Chowder, 38
    gathering, 143
    in Marinated Island Conch with
        Citrus and Coconut Milk, 109
condiments
    Annatto Oil, 203
    Bitter Orange Coulis, 208
    creativity in, 199
    Don't Let Your Man-Go Hot Sauce,
        203
    Dry Adobo, 202
    Green Curry Paste, 209
    Green Mango and Banana Chutney,
        201
    Green Pea and Wasabi Puree, 212
    Homemade Chili Vinegar, 212
    Jerk Rub--Wet Style, 206
    Mango, Papaya, and Passion Chili
        Sauce, 201
    Orange and Fennel Compote, 209
    Papaya Banana Catsup, 200
    Paradise Kitchen Jerk Spice Blend,
        207
    Passion Fruit Vinaigrette, 210
    Pickled Pepper Relish, 200
    Sofrito de Carlos, 211
    spice blends, 213–215

Tofu Rouille, 211
    Tomato and Caper Vinaigrette, 210
    Wet Adobo, 202
Coo-coo, 191
Cool Cucumber Facial Mask, 244
corn
    dumplings made from, 184
    in Iced Golden Summer Bisque with
        Organic Herbs, 34
    in Johnnycakes with Sour Cream
        and Corn, 116
cornmeal
    in Coo-coo, 191
    in Cornmeal and Okra Rellanos with
        Sauce Creole, 74
    in Guy Gumbs's Anguillian Conky
        Dumplings, 184
    in Guy's Coconut Dumplings with
        Cornmeal, 31
    in Island Cornmeal Breakfast
        Porridge, 8
    in Island Cornmeal Fungi with Okra,
        185
crabmeat, xxi
    in Crab Fritters with Lemon Zest
        and Parmesan, 114
    Paradise Kitchen Caribbean Crab
        Burgers, 135
crayfish
    in Anguillian Paella, Sofrito de
        Carlos, Local Crayfish, Spiny
        Lobster, and Island Hen, 150
    grilled, 157
    See also seafood
crème anglaise, 224, 230
Crisped Breadfruit with Roasted Garlic
    Butter, 190
cucumbers
    with Anguillian Jerked Fisherman's
        Steak, 136
    in Bush Dr. in da House (vegetable
        juice), 63
    in Cool Cucumber Facial Mask, 244
    in Cucumber Cooler (vegetable
        juice), 64
    in Green Gazpacho, 28

in Papaya, Coconut, and Strawberry
	Facial Mask, 245
in Petal's Welcome Potion, 65
in Pineapple and Cucumber
	Limeade, 88
CuisinArt Resort and Spa
	bath and body recipes from,
		244–245
	gardens at, 44–46, 74
	hurricane manual from, 247–251
culantro, in Sofrito de Carlos, 211
culture, Caribbean
	boat races, 173–174
	community life, 1
	cooking in, xxvii, 163–164, 167, 176
	handshakes, 110
	holidays and celebrations in,
		146–147, 173–174, 231
Curaçao, blue, in Salt Pond (cocktail), 92
Curry Vinaigrette, 139

Da Bush Doctor's in da House (herbal
	cures), 218
Da Pom Pom (cocktail), 90
Daniel Orr, Real Food, 65
Daniel's Spicy Nuts, 77
desserts, 221
	Anguillian Grilled Vanilla-Studded
		Caribbean Pineapple, Basted with
		Local Rum, 234
	Caribbean Birthday Cobbler, 224
	Caribbean Cashew Brittle with Chili
		Flakes and Ginger, 237
	Chocolate Volcano Cake with
		Espresso and Melted Vanilla Ice
		Cream, 230
	Double Chocolate Tart with Blue
		Mountain Coffee Granité, 238
	for fetes, 231
	Honey and Pepper Mango Upside-
		Down Cake, 235
	Hot Chocolate Soufflé, 227
	Jamaican Red Banana Fritters, 241
	Melon and Lime Soup with Sorbet,
		Berries, and Mint, 222
	Papaya Granité, 240

Paul and Darlene's Key Lime
	Cheesecake, 225
Quick Passion Fruit Soufflés, 228
Warm Coconut and Lime Tarts, 236
Warm "Gateau" of Coconut with
	Crème Fraîche, Pineapple, and
	Anguillian Pyrat Rum, 232–233
dips
	Red Bean Butter with Garlic Pita
		Crisps, 69
	Sauce Creole, 71
	Sweet Pea Guacamole, 67
	Yogurt Dip with Tamarind Ginger, 76
"Doc" Resh's Butter Lettuce with
	Oven-Roasted Tomatoes and Four
	Basils, 51
Don't Let Your Man-Go Hot Sauce, 203
	uses of, 119, 172
Double Chocolate Tart with Blue
	Mountain Coffee Granité, 238
duck
	in Caribbean Cassoulet, 127
	Duck with Kumquat Rum Sauce, 180

Edwards, John, 218
eggplant, in Warm Eggplant Stew with
	Coconut Vinegar and Curry, 188
eggs
	in Grilled Tuna Niçoise with Paradise
		Kitchen Vinaigrette, 49
	in Hearts of Palm with New
		Potatoes and Herbs, 52
	in Hot Chocolate Soufflé, 227
	in Jerked Steak and Eggs with Lime
		and Chili Pepper Hollandaise,
		13–14
	in Lobster Benedict with Key Lime
		Hollandaise and Shaved Nori, 7
	in Quick Passion Fruit Soufflés, 228

Feel the Burn (vegetable juice), 64
fennel
	in Chilled Curried Carrot Soup with
		Orange, 27
	in Orange and Fennel Compote, 209
fingerbowls, 150

fish, 1
	for Anguillian Jerked Fisherman's
		Steak, 136
	in Anguillian Paella, Sofrito de
		Carlos, Local Crayfish, Spiny
		Lobster, and Island Hen, 150
	in Blanquette de la Mer au Curry
		(Shark or Monkfish Stew with
		Curry), 137
	combining side dishes with, 183
	freshness of Anguillian, 134
	Grilled Potfish "en Papillotte," 153
	Grilled Trunkfish, 152
	a Niçoise with Paradise Kitchen
		Vinaigrette, 49
	limited access to, 133
	Pan-Roasted Mahimahi with Thai
		Green Papaya Slaw and Roasted
		Peanuts, 138
	in Paradise Kitchen Caribbean Crab
		Burgers, 135
	in Potfish (Island Bouillabaisse) with
		Tomatoes, Fennel, Saffron, Chilies,
		and Lime, 154
	in Rosemary's Jamaican Sea Shells
		and Bow Ties, 59
	in Sashimi Salad of Island Snapper
		with Fresh Herbs and Scotch
		Bonnets, 112
	shark or monkfish, 137
	shopping for, 134
	in Snapper in Chili and Ginger Broth
		with Island Vegetables (a.k.a.
		Island Fish Water), 144
	in Tamarind-Glazed Grouper Fillet,
		Baby Bok Choy, Crispy Shallots,
		and Beet Emulsion, 140
	Whole Blue Runner Roasted in
		Banana Leaves, 148
	See also saltfish
fishing, pleasures of, 1, 142–143
Frangipane (Almond Cream), 235
French toast
	Caribbean "Pain Perdu" with West
		Indian Spiced Caramel Syrup, 19
	Chef D's Famous French Bread

French Toast Casserole, 8
Fresh Coconut Dumplings, 125
Frozen Mojito, 86
fruit
    ackee, 12
    in Baby Shrimp Ernise, 55
    in Bitter Orange Coulis, 208
    in Duck with Kumquat Rum Sauce,
        180
    in Melon and Lime Soup with
        Sorbet, Berries, and Mint, 222
    in My Big Fat Greek Summer Salad,
        43
    pomelos, 50
    in shakes and smoothies, 20–22
    in soups, 26–27
    soursop, 85
    in Surreal Tropical Cereal Parfait, 4
    and vegetable juices, 62–65
    See also specific fruits
fruit, dried
    in Coconut and Sesame Cereal, 3
    in Tropical Muffins, 4
fruit juices
    in Athenia's Boiled Beets with
        Orange and Herbs, 187
    in Da Pom Pom (cocktail), 90
    in Ginger Rat (cocktail), 91
    in Marinated Island Conch with
        Citrus and Coconut Milk, 109
    in Salt Pond (cocktail), 92
full moons, Caribbean, 146–147
fungi, island definition of, 185

gardening, 44–47
    "bush gardens," 167
    at CuisinArt Resort and Spa, 74
    hydroponic, 51
garlic, medicinal qualities of, 218
Georgia on My Mind (smoothie), 22
gin, in Old Time Cuba Libre, 84
ginger
    in Bush Dr. in da House (vegetable
        juice), 63
    in Don't Let Your Man-Go Hot Sauce,
        203

in Feel the Burn (vegetable juice), 64
in Ginger and Honey Rum, 84, 98
in Ginger Base Syrup, 93
in Ginger Beer, 90
in Ginger Rat (cocktail), 91
in John's St. Kitts Cooler, 93
in Mango, Papaya, and Passion Chili
    Sauce, 201
medicinal qualities of, 218
in Orange and Fennel Compote, 209
in Petal's Welcome Potion, 65
in Pineapple Wine, 89
in Sofrito de Carlos, 211
storing in rum, 99
goat meat, in Pressure Cooker Goat
    Stew, 126
goat water, as national dish, 163, 179
goats, raising and eating, 178–179
Good Vibration Chicken Salad, 57
grains
    in Grape and Grain Salad, 41
    in Rasta Rap, 53
grapes, in Grape and Grain Salad, 41
Greek Island Pasta Salad, 58
Green Curry Paste, 209
Green Gazpacho, 28
Green Mango and Banana Chutney, 201
Green Papaya Slaw, 139
Green Pea and Wasabi Puree, 212
greens
    in Caribbean Cassoulet, 127
    in Pepper and Chili Carpaccio with
        Wild Herbs and Bloody Mary
        Granité, 105
    in Sautéed Pigeon Peas and Greens,
        186
Grilled Flank Steak in Burnt Cane,
    Lemongrass, and Ginger
    Marinade, 176
Grilled Potfish "en Papillotte," 153
Grilled Tiger Shrimp with Papaya
    Banana Catsup, 108
Grilled Trunkfish, 152
Grilled Tuna Niçoise with Paradise
    Kitchen Vinaigrette, 49
Grilled West Indian Leg of Lamb, 170

Gumbs, Guy, 31
Guy Gumbs's Anguillian Conky
    Dumplings, 184
Guy's Coconut Dumplings with
    Cornmeal, 31

handshakes, Caribbean, 110
healthy cooking and eating, xvi,
    183–184, 221
Hearts of Palm with New Potatoes and
    Herbs, 52, 114
herbs
    in Anguillian Paella, Sofrito de
        Carlos, Local Crayfish, Spiny
        Lobster, and Island Hen, 150
    in The Bush Garden (cocktail), 79
    in "bush gardens," 167
    in bush teas, 217
    in "Doc" Resh's Butter Lettuce with
        Oven-Roasted Tomatoes and Four
        Basils, 51
    in Grape and Grain Salad, 41
    in Green Gazpacho, 28
    in Hearts of Palm with New
        Potatoes and Herbs, 52
    in Kitchen D'Orr Mediterranean
        Spice Blend, 214
    in Lavender and Rosemary Massage
        Oil, 243
    lemongrass, 99
    in Marinated Island Conch with
        Citrus and Coconut Milk, 109
    medicinal qualities of, 217–219
    in My Big Fat Greek Summer Salad,
        43
    in Paradise Kitchen Caribbean Crab
        Burgers, 135
    in Petal's Welcome Potion, 65
    purslane, 106
    in Roasted Tomatoes with Garlic
        and Fresh Herbs, 197
    in Sofrito de Carlos, 211
    in Stuffed Green-Lipped Mussels
        with Pine Nuts, Tomatoes and
        Garlic, 68
    in Wet Adobo, 202

hibiscus (sorrel), medicinal qualities of, 218–219

Hollandaise Sauce, 13
    Key Lime, 7
Homemade Chili Vinegar, 212
Honey and Pepper Mango Upside-Down Cake, 235
Hot Chocolate Soufflé, 227
The Human Bruschetta (Tomato and Basil Body Scrub), 244
hummus
    in Rasta Rap, 53
    Red Bean Butter substituting for, 69
Hydro-PepperMint Bush Tea, 219

Iced Golden Summer Bisque with Organic Herbs, 34
Irie Conch Salad, 110
Island Cornmeal Breakfast Porridge, 8
Island Cornmeal Fungi with Okra, 185
    accompaniments for, 129, 180
Island Rum Punch, 82
Island Time Bush Tea, 219
Island Tuna Crudo, Coconut Water, and Scotch Bonnets, 111
Island Vegetable Pistou with Spiny Lobster and Herbs, 33

Jamaican Chili and Lime Jerk Butter, 160
Jamaican Ginger Bush Tea, 219
Jamaican Red Banana Fritters, 241
jerk blends, 103, 206, 207
Jerk-Rubbed Filet Mignon with Steamed Kale and Calaloo, 166
Jerked Island Ribs, 172
Jerked Steak and Eggs with Lime and Chili Pepper Hollandaise, 13–14
Johnnycakes with Sour Cream and Corn, 116
John's St. Kitts Cooler, 93
Jungle Juice, 63

kale
    in Jerk-Rubbed Filet Mignon with Steamed Kale and Calaloo, 166
    in Kale Salad, 119

Key Lime Hollandaise, 7
Kitchen D'Orr Aux Poivres Spice Blend, 214
Kitchen D'Orr Banana Bran Muffins, 5
Kitchen D'Orr Greek Garlic Spice Blend, 215
Kitchen D'Orr Mediterranean Spice Blend, 214
Kitchen D'Orr Mellow Yellow Spice Blend, 215
Kitchen D'Orr New Regime Spice Blend, 213
Kitchen D'Orr Sweet Seasons Spice Blend, 214
kumquats
    in Kumquat and Sea Salt Foot Scrub, 243
    in Kumquat and Star Anise Rum, 96, 180

lamb
    Grilled West Indian Leg of Lamb, 170
    Spice-Crusted Rack of Lamb, 168
Lavender and Rosemary Massage Oil, 243
Lavender Lemonade, 65
lemongrass
    in Grilled Flank Steak, 176
    in Lemongrass Rum, 99
    medicinal qualities of, 218
lemons
    in Anguillian Roasted Tomato Bloody Mary, 87
    in Citrus Trio Master Recipe, 21, 63
    in Lavender Lemonade, 65
lentils
    in Grape and Grain Salad, 41
    in Rastafarian West Indian Yellow Lentil Bisque, 30
    in Yellow Lentil Spread, 76
lettuce
    in "Doc" Resh's Butter Lettuce with Oven-Roasted Tomatoes and Four Basils, 51
    in Hearts of Palm with New Potatoes and Herbs, 52

lime juice
    in Anguillian Jerked Fresh Ham, 171
    in Be Irie Cocktail, 92
    in Citrus Trio Master Recipe, 21, 63
    in Frozen Mojito, 86
    in Island Rum Punch, 82
    in Pineapple and Cucumber Limeade, 88
limes
    in Ginger Beer, 90
    in Grilled West Indian Leg of Lamb, 170
    medicinal qualities of, 218
    in Melon and Lime Soup with Sorbet, Berries, and Mint, 222
    in Paul and Darlene's Key Lime Cheesecake, 225
    in Stewed Garlic Pork with Lime and Chilies, 130
    in Warm Coconut and Lime Tarts, 236
liqueur, amaretto
    in Athenia's Jamaican Carrot Juice, 92
liqueur, orange-flavored
    in Duck with Kumquat Rum Sauce, 180
    in The 3 Cs, 79
liqueur, sour apple
    in Pucker and Kiss (cocktail), 85
liver, in Quick Caribbean Blood Pudding, 119
lobster, xxv–xxvi
    as alternative seafood: in Grilled Trunkfish, 152; in Potfish (Island Bouillabaisse) with Tomatoes, Fennel, Saffron, Chilies, and Lime, 154; in Shrimp Quesadilla with Cilantro and Scallions, 119
    in Anguillian Paella, Sofrito de Carlos, Local Crayfish, Spiny Lobster, and Island Hen, 150
    Caribbean vs. Maine, 157
    as garnish, 28, 35
    gathering, 142–143
    grilled, 157
    in Island Vegetable Pistou with Spiny Lobster and Herbs, 33

in Lobster Benedict with Key Lime
Hollandaise and Shaved Nori, 7
marinade for, 158
in Red Hot Gazpacho with Lobster
Meat and Frozen Bloody Mary Ice,
29
in Rosemary's Jamaican Sea Shells
and Bow Ties, 59
See also seafood

mangoes, xxii
in Athenia's Anguill-Asian Slaw, 54
in Caribbean Birthday Cobbler, 224
in Don't Let Your Man-Go Hot Sauce,
203
in Green Mango and Banana
Chutney, 201
in Honey and Pepper Mango
Upside-Down Cake, 235
in Mango, Papaya, and Passion Chili
Sauce, 201
Mango Butter, 16
Mango Chutney, uses of, 177
in Spit-Roasted Chicken with
Haitian Mofongo and Mango
Chutney, 177
in Tropical Pineapple Mango
Frappé, 83
marinades
for Anguillian Jerked Quail, 103
for Grilled Flank Steak, 176
herbs and spices in jerks and, 206
for Island Tuna Crudo, 111
for Marinated Island Conch with
Citrus and Coconut Milk, 109
for Paradise Kitchen Grilled Chicken
with Chilies, Garlic, and Lime, 165
Paradise Kitchen Wet Marinade for
Lobsters and Seafood, 158
for Pressure Cooker Goat Stew, 126
for Rosemary's Jamaican Sea Shells
and Bow Ties, 59
for Sashimi Salad of Island Snapper
with Fresh Herbs and Scotch
Bonnets, 112
Sofrito de Carlos as, 211

for Spit-Roasted Puerto Rican
Pork Loin Marinated with Bitter
Orange, Chilies, Molasses, and
Herbs, 181
for Stewed Garlic Pork with Lime
and Chilies, 130
Wet Adobo as, 202
Marinated Island Conch with Citrus
and Coconut Milk, 109
Marinated Mixed Olives, 73
massage oils, 243
mayonnaise, substitutes for
Orange and Fennel Compote, 209
Red Bean Butter, 69
meat
combining side dishes with, 183
cooking methods, 163, 176
unusual, 121
See also specific meats
melons
in Beet Sangria, 64
in Melon and Lime Soup with
Sorbet, Berries, and Mint, 222
in My Big Fat Greek Summer Salad,
43
in Petal's Welcome Potion, 65
in Scoopy Dew (smoothie), 21
Midnight Picnics, 147
mint
in The Bush Garden (cocktail), 79
in Cool Cucumber Facial Mask, 244
in Cucumber Cooler (vegetable
juice), 64
in Frozen Mojito, 86
in Good Vibration Chicken Salad, 57
medicinal qualities of, 218
in Melon and Lime Soup with
Sorbet, Berries, and Mint, 222
Miso/Tahini Dressing and Dipping
Sauce, 53
mofongo
Soft Mofongo, 189
in Spit-Roasted Chicken with
Haitian Mofongo and Mango
Chutney, 177
Moonlight Nights, 146–147

muffins
Kitchen D'Orr Banana Bran Muffins, 5
Tropical Muffins, 4
mushrooms
in Breadfruit Homefries with
Mushrooms and Garlic, 18
in Mushroom and Sweet Pepper
Skewers with Purslane Salad, 106
mussels
in Anguillian Paella, Sofrito de
Carlos, Local Crayfish, Spiny
Lobster, and Island Hen, 150
in Stuffed Green-Lipped Mussels
with Pine Nuts, Tomatoes and
Garlic, 68
My Big Fat Greek Summer Salad, 43

neem, medicinal qualities of, 218
nuts
in Caribbean Cashew Brittle with
Chili Flakes and Ginger, 237
Daniel's Spicy Nuts, 77
in Frangipane (Almond Cream), 235

octopus (sea cat), xxiv
in "Sea Cat" in Ginger Miso Sauce, 116
Oh Be Joyful (cocktail), 85
okra, xxii, 74
in Coo-coo, 191
in Cornmeal and Okra Rellanos with
Sauce Creole, 74
in Island Cornmeal Fungi with Okra,
185
in Potfish (Island Bouillabaisse) with
Tomatoes, Fennel, Saffron, Chilies,
and Lime, 154
in Snapper in Chili and Ginger Broth
with Island Vegetables (a.k.a.
Island Fish Water), 144
Old Time Cuba Libre, 84
olives
in Greek Island Pasta Salad, 58
in Marinated Mixed Olives, 73
orange juice
in Caribbean Birthday Cobbler, 224
in Citrus Trio Master Recipe, 21, 63

in Melon and Lime Soup with Sorbet, Berries, and Mint, 222
in Orange and Fennel Compote, 209
oranges
in Athenia's Boiled Beets with Orange and Herbs, 187
in Orange Spice Rum, 99
organic gardening, at CuisinArt Resort and Spa, 46

Pan-Roasted Mahimahi with Thai Green Papaya Slaw and Roasted Peanuts, 138
panko, in Stuffed Green-Lipped Mussels with Pine Nuts, Tomatoes and Garlic, 68
papayas, xxiii
in Breadfruit Salad, 56
in Don't Let Your Man-Go Hot Sauce, 203
in Green Papaya Slaw, 139
in Jungle Juice, 63
in Mango, Papaya, and Passion Chili Sauce, 201
in Papaya, Coconut, and Strawberry Facial Mask, 245
in Papaya Banana Catsup, 200
in Papaya Granité, 240
in Stuffed Green Papaya, 194
Paradise Kitchen Caribbean Crab Burgers, 135
Paradise Kitchen Grilled Chicken with Chilies, Garlic, and Lime, 165
Paradise Kitchen "Homies," 14
Paradise Kitchen Jerk Spice Blend, 207
as ingredient, 14, 26, 29, 69, 117, 166, 168, 171, 172, 177, 181, 202
Paradise Kitchen Vinaigrette, 49
Paradise Kitchen Wet Marinade for Lobsters and Seafood, 158
passion fruit, xxiii
in Caribbean Passion Fruit Punch, 86
in Mango, Papaya, and Passion Chili Sauce, 201
in Passion Fruit Vinaigrette, 210
in Quick Passion Fruit Soufflés, 228

Passionate Bubbles (cocktail), 84
pasta
in Greek Island Pasta Salad, 58
in Rosemary's Jamaican Sea Shells and Bow Ties, 59
pastry
Chocolate Short Dough, 238
Double Chocolate Tart with Blue Mountain Coffee Granité, 238
Paul and Darlene's Key Lime Cheesecake, 225
Warm Coconut and Lime Tarts, 236
Paul and Darlene's Key Lime Cheesecake, 225
peaches, in Georgia on My Mind (smoothie), 22
peas, green
in Green Pea and Wasabi Puree, 212
in Sweet Pea Guacamole, 67
Pepper and Chili Carpaccio with Wild Herbs and Bloody Mary Granité, 105
peppercorns, medicinal qualities of, 218
peppers, Ají Dulce (seasoning peppers), 71
in Mango, Papaya, and Passion Chili Sauce, 201
in Pressure Cooker Goat Stew, 126
in Sofrito de Carlos, 211
peppers, banana
in Pressure Cooker Goat Stew, 126
peppers, bell
in Coo-coo, 191
in Good Vibration Chicken Salad, 57
in Greek Island Pasta Salad, 58
in Irie Conch Salad, 110
in Mango, Papaya, and Passion Chili Sauce, 201
in Mushroom and Sweet Pepper Skewers with Purslane Salad, 106
in Pickled Pepper Relish, 200
in Potfish (Island Bouillabaisse) with Tomatoes, Fennel, Saffron, Chilies, and Lime, 154
in Pressure Cooker Goat Stew, 126
in Saltfish Salad, 123

in Sauce Creole, 71
in Shrimp Quesadilla with Cilantro and Scallions, 113
in Snapper in Chili and Ginger Broth with Island Vegetables (a.k.a. Island Fish Water), 144
in Sofrito de Carlos, 211
in Warm Eggplant Stew with Coconut Vinegar and Curry, 188
in Whole Blue Runner Roasted in Banana Leaves, 148
peppers, bird, 170
in Homemade Chili Vinegar, 212
peppers, chili
in Chili Vinegar, 130
in Green Curry Paste, 209
in Mango, Papaya, and Passion Chili Sauce, 201
in Pickled Pepper Relish, 200
in Sweet Pea Guacamole, 67
peppers, jalapeño
in Mango, Papaya, and Passion Chili Sauce, 201
in Pickled Pepper Relish, 200
peppers, mini-wini
in Coconut Basmati Rice, 196
in Marinated Island Conch with Citrus and Coconut Milk, 109
peppers, Scotch Bonnet chili, 206
in Don't Let Your Man-Go Hot Sauce, 203
in Island Tuna Crudo, 111
in Jerk Rub--Wet Style, 206
in marinade, 165
in Sashimi Salad of Island Snapper with Fresh Herbs and Scotch Bonnets, 112
in Sauce Creole, 71
in Spicy Caribbean Tripe Stew, 129
use of, 71, 206
peppers, serrano
in Green Pea and Wasabi Puree, 212
Pernod, in Tropical Pineapple Mango Frappé, 83
pesticides, natural, 46–47, 72
Petal's Welcome Potion, 65

Pickled Pepper Relish, 200
pigeon peas
    in The Anguillian National Culinary
        Team's Rice and Peace, 192
    in Sautéed Pigeon Peas and Greens,
        186
pine nuts, in Stuffed Green-Lipped
    Mussels with Pine Nuts, Tomatoes
    and Garlic, 68
pineapple
    Anguillian Grilled Vanilla-Studded
        Caribbean Pineapple, Basted with
        Local Rum, 234
    in Athenia's Anguill-Asian Slaw, 54
    in Cucumber Cooler (vegetable
        juice), 64
    in Good Vibration Chicken Salad, 57
    in Jungle Juice, 63
    in Pineapple and Cucumber
        Limeade, 88
    in Pineapple and Vanilla Rum, 96
    in Pineapple Wine, 89
    in Rasta Frappé, 21
    in Tropical Pineapple Mango
        Frappé, 83
    in Warm "Gateau" of Coconut with
        Crème Fraîche, Pineapple, and
        Anguillian Pyrat Rum, 232–233
plantains
    in Soft Mofongo, 189, xxiii
    in Spit-Roasted Chicken with
        Haitian Mofongo and Mango
        Chutney, 177
pomelos, 50
pork
    Anguillian Jerked Fresh Ham, 171
    in Caribbean Cassoulet, 127
    ham, 171, 189
    Jerked Island Ribs, 172
    pig snouts, 127
    pig tails, 127
    Pigs' Trotters, 122
    in Quick Caribbean Blood Pudding,
        119
    sausage, 119, 127
    in Soft Mofongo, 189

Spit-Roasted Puerto Rican Pork Loin
    Marinated with Bitter Orange,
    Chilies, Molasses, and Herbs, 181
Stewed Garlic Pork with Lime and
    Chilies, 130
porridge, 1
    Island Cornmeal Breakfast Porridge, 8
potatoes
    breadfruit's similarity to, 18
    in Grilled Tuna Niçoise with Paradise
        Kitchen Vinaigrette, 49
    in Hearts of Palm with New
        Potatoes and Herbs, 52
    in Paradise Kitchen "Homies," 14
Potfish (Island Bouillabaisse) with
    Tomatoes, Fennel, Saffron, Chilies,
    and Lime, 154
poultry
    Anguillian Jerked Quail, 103
    in Caribbean Cassoulet, 127
    Duck with Kumquat Rum Sauce, 180
    See also chicken
pressure cookers, 121
    for Caribbean Cassoulet, 127
    for Pressure Cooker Goat Stew, 126
    for Stewed Garlic Pork with Lime
        and Chilies, 130
Pucker and Kiss (cocktail), 85
Puerto Rican Cilantro Butter, 160
pumpkin
    in Guy Gumbs's Anguillian Conky
        Dumplings, 184
    in West Indian Pumpkin and Banana
        Bisque, 26
purslane, xxiv
    in Purslane Salad, with Mushroom
        and Sweet Pepper Skewers, 106

Quick Caribbean Blood Pudding, 119
Quick Passion Fruit Soufflés, 228

Rasta Frappé, 21
Rasta Rap (a.k.a. The Spa Wrap and
    Roll), 25, 53
Rastafarian West Indian Yellow Lentil
    Bisque, 30

raw sugar, piloncillo, xxiv, 130
recipes
    experimenting with, 2, 199
    weighted ingredients in, 222
Red Bean Butter with Garlic Pita Crisps,
    69
Red Hot Gazpacho with Lobster Meat
    and Frozen Bloody Mary Ice, 29
Regime Cuisine, for weight control, 65
Resh, Howard, 44, 51
rice
    in The Anguillian National Culinary
        Team's Rice and Peace, 192
    in Anguillian Paella, Sofrito de
        Carlos, Local Crayfish, Spiny
        Lobster, and Island Hen, 150
    in Coconut Basmati Rice, 196
Roasted Breadfruit, 195
Roasted Tomatoes with Garlic and
    Fresh Herbs, 197
    with "Doc" Resh's Butter Lettuce, 51
roe, in Sea Urchin and Scallion Butter,
    159
Rogers, Petal, 62, 65
Rosemary's Jamaican Sea Shells and
    Bow Ties, 59
rum
    in Alligator Daiquiri, 93
    in Anguillian Grilled Vanilla-Studded
        Caribbean Pineapple, Basted with
        Local Rum, 234
    Banana Black Peppercorn Rum, 98
    in Be Irie Cocktail, 92
    in The Big Bamboo (cocktail), 84
    in Caribbean Passion Fruit Punch, 86
    coconut: in Be Irie Cocktail, 92; in
        Coconut Martini, 80
    cooking with, 99
    in Da Pom Pom (cocktail), 90
    in Frangipane (Almond Cream), 235
    in Frozen Mojito, 86
    Ginger and Honey Rum, 98
    in Ginger Beer, 90
    homemade flavored, 95–99
    in Island Rum Punch, 82
    Kumquat and Star Anise Rum, 96

Lemongrass Rum, 99
in Oh Be Joyful (cocktail), 85
in Old Time Cuba Libre, 84
Orange Spice Rum, 99
in Passionate Bubbles (cocktail), 84
Pineapple and Vanilla Rum, 96
in Tropical Pineapple Mango
Frappé, 83
uses of, 99
varieties of, 97
in Warm "Gateau" of Coconut with
Crème Fraîche, Pineapple, and
Anguillian Pyrat Rum, 232–233

saffron, in Tofu Rouille, 211
sage, medicinal qualities of, 218
salad dressings
Beet and Balsamic Emulsion, 141
Caribbean Sugarcane Vinaigrette, 52
Curry Vinaigrette, 139
Miso/Tahini Dressing and Dipping
Sauce, 53
Paradise Kitchen Vinaigrette, 49
Tofu Rouille, 211
Tomato and Caper Vinaigrette, 210
Verjus Vinaigrette, 41
Vinaigrette, 58
salads, 41–43
Anguill-Asian Pomelo Salad, 50
Athenia's Anguill-Asian Slaw, 54
Baby Shrimp Ernise, 55
Breadfruit Salad, 56
"Doc" Resh's Butter Lettuce with
Oven-Roasted Tomatoes and Four
Basils, 51
Good Vibration Chicken Salad, 57
Grape and Grain Salad, 41
Greek Island Pasta Salad, 58
Grilled Tuna Niçoise with Paradise
Kitchen Vinaigrette, 49
Hearts of Palm with New Potatoes
and Herbs, 114
Irie Conch Salad, 110
Kale Salad, 119
My Big Fat Greek Summer Salad, 43
Rosemary's Jamaican Sea Shells and

Bow Ties, 59
Saltfish Salad, 123
Sashimi Salad of Island Snapper
with Fresh Herbs and Scotch
Bonnets, 112
West Indian Slam'n Yam Salad, 60
Salt Codfish Stew, 40
Salt Pond (cocktail), 92
saltfish
in Anieta's Ackee and Saltfish, 12
in Salt Codfish Stew, 40
in Saltfish and Yam Cakes, 11
in Saltfish Beignets with Sauce
Creole, 71
in Saltfish Salad, 123
sandwiches
Rasta Rap, 53
Sashimi Salad of Island Snapper with
Fresh Herbs and Scotch Bonnets,
112
sauces
for Baby Shrimp Ernise, 55
Balsamic Vinegar Pan Sauce, 166
custard/crème anglaise, 224, 230
Don't Let Your Man-Go Hot Sauce,
203
Hollandaise, 13
Key Lime Hollandaise, 7
Miso/Tahini Dressing and Dipping
Sauce, 53
Passion Fruit Vinaigrette, 210
Sauce Creole, 71
Tofu Rouille as, 211
sausage
in Anguillian Paella, Sofrito de
Carlos, Local Crayfish, Spiny
Lobster, and Island Hen, 150
in Caribbean Blood Pudding, 119
in Caribbean Cassoulet, 127
Sautéed Pigeon Peas and Greens, 180,
186
Scoopy Dew (smoothie), 21
"Sea Cat" in Ginger Miso Sauce, 116
sea eggs, xxiv, 159
sea grapes, xxiv
cooking in leaves, 184

sea moss, xxv
in Reef-Freshing (smoothie), 22
sea urchins, xxiv
in Sea Urchin and Scallion Butter,
152, 159
seafood
in Anguillian Conch Chowder, 38
in Anguillian Paella, Sofrito de
Carlos, Local Crayfish, Spiny
Lobster, and Island Hen, 150
in Callaloo and Crab Stew, 36
in Green Gazpacho, 28
in Irie Conch Salad, 110
in Island Vegetable Pistou with
Spiny Lobster and Herbs, 33
limited access to, 133
marinade for, 158
in Potfish (Island Bouillabaisse) with
Tomatoes, Fennel, Saffron, Chilies,
and Lime, 154
in Rosemary's Jamaican Sea Shells
and Bow Ties, 59
shopping for, 49, 133
in Stewed Whelks with Fresh
Coconut Dumplings and
Scallions, 124
seaweed, xxv
seaweed salad, in Athenia's Anguill-
Asian Slaw, 54
sesame, in Coconut and Sesame
Cereal, 3
shakes and smoothies
Georgia on My Mind, 22
Rasta Frappé, 21
Reef-Freshing, 22
Scoopy Dew, 21
Silky Strawberry, 21
Sun, Sea, and Soy, 22
shopping, 49
in Caribbean markets or bodegas,
128
for fish, 134
for fruit, 20
in Latin markets or bodegas, 127
for meat vs. produce, 183
for seafood, 133

at St. Martin market, 204
shrimp
  in Baby Shrimp Ernise, 55
  in Grilled Tiger Shrimp with Papaya
    Banana Catsup, 108
  in Shrimp Quesadilla with Cilantro
    and Scallions, 113
  See also seafood
side dishes
  The Anguillian National Culinary
    Team's Rice and Peace, 192
  Athenia's Boiled Beets with Orange
    and Herbs, 187
  Coconut Basmati Rice, 196
  combining with main course, 183
  Coo-Coo, 191
  creativity in, 183–184
  Crisped Breadfruit with Roasted
    Garlic Butter, 190
  Guy Gumbs's Anguillian Conky
    Dumplings, 184
  Island Cornmeal Fungi with Okra,
    185
  Roasted Breadfruit, 195
  Roasted Tomatoes with Garlic and
    Fresh Herbs, 197
  Sautéed Pigeon Peas and Greens,
    186
  Soft Mofongo, 189
  Stuffed Green Papaya, 194
  Warm Eggplant Stew with Coconut
    Vinegar and Curry, 188
Silky Strawberry (shake), 21
slaws
  Athenia's Anguill-Asian Slaw, 54
  Green Papaya Slaw, 139
  novel ingredients for, 25
snapper
  in Sashimi Salad of Island Snapper
    with Fresh Herbs and Scotch
    Bonnets, 112
  Snapper in Chili and Ginger Broth
    with Island Vegetables (a.k.a.
    Island Fish Water), 144
Sofrito de Carlos, 150, 211
Soft Mofongo, 177, 189

soups/stews
  Anguillian Conch Chowder, 38
  Black Bean Soup, 35
  Blanquette de la Mer au Curry
    (Shark or Monkfish Stew with
    Curry), 137
  Callaloo and Crab Stew, 36
  Caribbean Cassoulet, 127
  Caribbean Chicken Soup with
    Pigeon Peas and Coconut
    Dumplings, 31
  Chilled Curried Carrot Soup with
    Orange, 27
  goat as national dish, 163, 179
  Green Gazpacho, 28
  Iced Golden Summer Bisque with
    Organic Herbs, 34
  Island Vegetable Pistou with Spiny
    Lobster and Herbs, 33
  Melon and Lime Soup with Sorbet,
    Berries, and Mint, 222
  Potfish (Island Bouillabaisse) with
    Tomatoes, Fennel, Saffron, Chilies,
    and Lime, 154
  Pressure Cooker Goat Stew, 126
  Rastafarian West Indian Yellow
    Lentil Bisque, 30
  Red Hot Gazpacho with Lobster Meat
    and Frozen Bloody Mary Ice, 29
  Salt Codfish Stew, 40
  Snapper in Chili and Ginger Broth
    with Island Vegetables (a.k.a.
    Island Fish Water), 144
  Spicy Caribbean Tripe Stew, 129
  Stewed Garlic Pork with Lime and
    Chilies, 130
  Warm Eggplant Stew with Coconut
    Vinegar and Curry, 188
  West Indian Pumpkin and Banana
    Bisque, 26
Sour Sorrel Bush Tea, 219
soursops, xxv
  medicinal qualities of, 218
  in Oh Be Joyful (cocktail), 85
spice blends
  Dry Adobo, 202, 213

Kitchen D'Orr Aux Poivres Spice
  Blend, 214
Kitchen D'Orr Greek Garlic Spice
  Blend, 215
Kitchen D'Orr Mediterranean Spice
  Blend, 214
Kitchen D'Orr Mellow Yellow Spice
  Blend, 215
Kitchen D'Orr New Regime Spice
  Blend, 213
Kitchen D'Orr Sweet Seasons Spice
  Blend, 214
Paradise Kitchen Jerk Spice Blend,
  207
Wet Adobo, 202
Spice-Crusted Rack of Lamb, 168
Spice Syrup, in Island Rum Punch, 82
spices
  in jerks and marinades, 206
  medicinal qualities of, 218
  toasting before use, 105
  See also spice blends
Spicy Caribbean Tripe Stew, 129
spinach, in Bush Dr. in da House
  (vegetable juice), 63
Spit-Roasted Chicken with Haitian
  Mofongo and Mango Chutney, 177
Spit-Roasted Puerto Rican Pork Loin
  Marinated with Bitter Orange,
  Chilies, Molasses, and Herbs, 181
spreads
  Mango Butter, 16
  Red Bean Butter with Garlic Pita
    Crisps, 69
  Sweet Pea Guacamole, 67
  Yellow Lentil Spread, 76
squash, in West Indian Pumpkin and
  Banana Bisque, 26
squid
  in Anguillian Paella, Sofrito de
    Carlos, Local Crayfish, Spiny
    Lobster, and Island Hen, 150
  See also seafood
St. Martin, 204
Stewed Garlic Pork with Lime and
  Chilies, 130

Stewed Whelks with Fresh Coconut
Dumplings and Scallions, 124
stock/broth
improving canned, 31, 33
suggested ingredients for, 34
storm preparations, 247–251
strawberries
in Papaya, Coconut, and Strawberry
Facial Mask, 245
in Silky Strawberry shake, 21
Stuffed Green-Lipped Mussels with
Pine Nuts, Tomatoes and Garlic, 68
Stuffed Green Papaya (or
Christophene), 194
Summerfest, 173–174
Sun, Sea, and Soy (smoothie), 22
Surreal Tropical Cereal Parfait, 4
Sweet Pea Guacamole, 67
sweet potatoes. *See* yams
syrups
Ginger Base Syrup, 93
Spice Syrup, 82
West Indian Spiced Caramel Syrup,
19

tamarind, xxvi
in Tamarind-Glazed Grouper Fillet,
Baby Bok Choy, Crispy Shallots,
and Beet Emulsion, 140
in Yogurt Dip with Tamarind Ginger,
76
tapas, 67–77
Cornmeal and Okra Rellanos with
Sauce Creole, 74
Daniel's Spicy Nuts, 77
Marinated Mixed Olives, 73
Red Bean Butter with Garlic Pita
Crisps, 69
Saltfish Beignets with Sauce Creole,
71
Stuffed Green-Lipped Mussels with
Pine Nuts, Tomatoes and Garlic, 68
Sweet Pea Guacamole, 67
Yellow Lentil Spread, 76
Yogurt Dip with Tamarind Ginger, 76
See also appetizers

tarragon
medicinal qualities of, 218
in Tarragon and Ginger Butter, 159
The 3 Cs (Caribbean Coconut Cooler),
79
tofu
in Silky Strawberry shake, 21
in Sun, Sea, and Soy (smoothie), 22
in Sweet Pea Guacamole, 67
in Tofu Rouille, 211
tomatoes
with Anguillian Jerked Fisherman's
Steak, 136
in Anguillian Roasted Tomato
Bloody Mary, 87
in Coo-coo, 191
in "Doc" Resh's Butter Lettuce with
Oven-Roasted Tomatoes and Four
Basils, 51
in Good Vibration Chicken Salad, 57
in Grilled Tuna Niçoise with Paradise
Kitchen Vinaigrette, 49
in The Human Bruschetta, 244
in Iced Golden Summer Bisque with
Organic Herbs, 34
in My Big Fat Greek Summer Salad,
43
in Potfish (Island Bouillabaisse) with
Tomatoes, Fennel, Saffron, Chilies,
and Lime, 154
in Red Hot Gazpacho with Lobster
Meat and Frozen Bloody Mary Ice,
29
in Roasted Tomatoes with Garlic
and Fresh Herbs, 197
in Salt Codfish Stew, 40
in Snapper in Chili and Ginger Broth
with Island Vegetables (a.k.a.
Island Fish Water), 144
in Spicy Caribbean Tripe Stew, 129
in Stuffed Green-Lipped Mussels
with Pine Nuts, Tomatoes and
Garlic, 68
in Stuffed Green Papaya, 194
in Tomato and Caper Vinaigrette, 210
in Warm Eggplant Stew with

Coconut Vinegar and Curry, 188
tomatoes, sun-dried
in Greek Island Pasta Salad, 58
in Stuffed Green-Lipped Mussels
with Pine Nuts, Tomatoes and
Garlic, 68
Tropical Muffins, 4
Tropical Pineapple Mango Frappé, 83
T&T Shallot and Curry Butter, 160
tuna
in Grilled Tuna Niçoise with Paradise
Kitchen Vinaigrette, 49
in Island Tuna Crudo, 111

vegetable juices, 62–65
vegetables
Athenia's Boiled Beets with Orange
and Herbs, 187
in Iced Golden Summer Bisque with
Organic Herbs, 34
Island Vegetable Pistou with Spiny
Lobster and Herbs, 33
provisions as starchy, 189–190
in Stewed Whelks with Fresh
Coconut Dumplings and
Scallions, 124
variety for side dishes, 183
in Warm Eggplant Stew with
Coconut Vinegar and Curry, 188
See also specific vegetables
Verjus Vinaigrette, 41
village hearth, 1
Vinaigrette, 43
for Greek Island Pasta Salad, 58
vinegars
chili, 130
Homemade Chili Vinegar, 212
Vision Finder (vegetable juice), 63
vodka
in Bloody Mary Granité, 87, 105
in The Bush Garden (cocktail), 79
in Caribbean Passion Fruit Punch,
86
in Salt Pond (cocktail), 92

waffles

Banana Waffles with Passion Fruit
Rum Syrup and Mango Butter, 16
Warm Coconut and Lime Tarts, 236
Warm "Gateau" of Coconut with Crème
Fraîche, Pineapple, and Anguillian
Pyrat Rum, 232–233
weather, Caribbean, 92, 118
storm preparations, 247–251
weight control, 65
West Indian Pumpkin and Banana
Bisque, 26
West Indian Slam'n Yam Salad, 60
West Indian Spice Bush Tea, 219

West Indian Spiced Caramel Syrup,
with Caribbean "Pain Perdu," 19
whelks, xxvii
gathering, 142–143
Stewed Whelks with Fresh Coconut
Dumplings and Scallions, 124
Whole Blue Runner Roasted in Banana
Leaves, 148
worry vine, medicinal qualities of, 218

yams
for dumplings, 184
in Saltfish and Yam Cakes, 11

in West Indian Slam'n Yam Salad, 60
Yellow Lentil Spread, 76
yogurt
in Breadfruit Salad, 56
in Cool Cucumber Facial Mask, 244
labne and, 30
in Scoopy Dew (smoothie), 21
in Yogurt Dip with Tamarind Ginger,
76
yogurt, frozen
in Reef-Freshing (smoothie), 22
in Sun, Sea, and Soy (smoothie), 22

Daniel Orr has been cooking professionally for over 25 years. He has taken his chef knives throughout the Americas, the Caribbean, and Europe. He is chef/owner of FARM, a restaurant in Bloomington, Indiana, that focuses on simple yet sophisticated cuisine. He is author of *Daniel Orr Real Food: Smart and Simple Meals and Menus for Entertaining* and *FARMfood: Green Living with Chef Daniel Orr* (Indiana University Press, 2009). Chef Orr also co-hosts *Earth Eats* on National Public Radio (eartheats.org), creates his signature line of Kitchen D'Orr spices and flavorings, and is an avid gardener and forager.